NEWS AS CULTURE

Anthropology of Media
Series Editors: John Postill and Mark Peterson

The ubiquity of media across the globe has led to an explosion of interest in the ways people around the world use media as part of their everyday lives. This series addresses the need for works that describe and theorize multiple, emerging, and sometimes interconnected, media practices in the contemporary world. Interdisciplinary and inclusive, this series offers a forum for ethnographic methodologies, descriptions of non-Western media practices, explorations of transnational connectivity, and studies that link culture and practices across fields of media production and consumption.

Volume 1
Alarming Reports
Communicating Conflict in the Daily News
Andrew Arno

Volume 2
The New Media Nation
Indigenous Peoples and Global Communication
Valerie Alia

Volume 3
News as Culture
Journalistic Practices and the Remaking of Indian Leadership Traditions
Ursula Rao

Volume 4
Theorising Media and Practice
Edited by Birgit Bräuchler and John Postill

Volume 5
Localizing the Internet
An Anthropological Account
John Postill

Volume 6
The Making of the Pentecostal Melodrama
Religion, Media and Gender in Kinshasa
Katrien Pype

News as Culture

Journalistic Practices and the Remaking of Indian Leadership Traditions

Ursula Rao

Berghahn Books
New York • Oxford

Published in 2010 by

Berghahn Books

www.berghahnbooks.com

©2010, 2013 Ursula Rao

First paperback edition published in 2013

Library of Congress Cataloging-in-Publication Data
Rao, Ursula.
 News as culture : journalistic practices and the remaking of Indian leadership
traditions / Ursula Rao.
   p. cm. -- (Anthropology of media ; v. 3)
 Includes bibliographical references and index.
 ISBN 978-1-84545-669-6 (hbk.)--ISBN 978-0-85745-905-3 (pbk.)
 1. Journalism--Political aspects--India. 2. Press and politics--India. 3.
Journalism--Social aspects--India. 4. Hindi newspapers--India. 5. English
newspapers--India. I. Title.
 PN5377.P6R36 2010
 302.230954--dc22

                                                           2010007969

British Library Cataloguing in Publication Data
A catalogue record for this book is available from the British Library

Printed in the United States on acid-free paper.

ISBN: 978-0-85745-905-3 (paperback)   eISBN: 978-0-85745-926-8 (retail ebook)

Contents

List of Abbreviations   vii

List of Figures and Tables   ix

Acknowledgements   xi

1. Introduction   1

2. Lucknow News   21

3. Local Voices: Empowerment through News-Making   45

4. Political Reporting: Sites of Engagement – Performances
       of Distance   91

5. Infotainment: Re-Writing Politics after Economic
       Liberalisation   143

6. Conclusions   193

References   203

Index   217

List of Abbreviations

AIADMK	Anna's Dravida Munnetra Kazhagam (Federation for the Advancement of the Dravidians)
BHU	Banaras Hindu University
BSP	Bahujan Samaj Party (Majority Society Party)
BJP	Bharatiya Janta Party (Indian People's Party)
CM	Chief Minister
KSRSS	Kashi Sanskriti Raksha Sangharsh Samiti (Organisation for the Defence of the Culture of Kashi)
LDA	Lucknow Development Authorities
MLC	Member of Legislative Council
MLA	Member of Legislative Assembly
OBC	Other Backward Classes
RKP	Rashtriya Kranti Party (National Revolutionist Party)
RSS	Rashtriya Svayam Sevak Sangha (National Voluntary Service Organisation)
SP	Samajvadi Party (Socialist Party)
UP	Uttar Pradesh (State in North India)
V-C	Vice-Chairman
VHP	Vishva Hindu Parishad (World Hindu Association)

List of Figures and Tables

Figures

2.1. Schematic representation of working places given to journalists at the offices of *Dainik Jagaran* (not to scale).   37

2.2. Schematic representation of working places provided at the *Times of India* office for journalists working for the main pages of the newspaper (not to scale).   37

Tables

2.1. Schematic overview of the internal hierarchy of the reporting section at *Dainik Jagaran* and *Hindustan*.   26

2.2. Schematic overview of the internal hierarchy of the reporting section at the *Times of India*.   33

2.3. Schematic overview of the internal hierarchy of the reporting section at the *Hindustan Times*.   34

5.1. Press coverage of the press conference at the Sahara 'India Festival' of 28 January 2000.   157

5.2. Information about the company Sahara, quoted from *Sahara Indian Pariwar*, a coffee table-like book distributed during the press conference.   162

5.3. Summary of the content of reports from the press meeting with Bhagwat, 16 February 2000.   179

Acknowledgements

There are many people who have helped me in the making of this book – too many to thank individually. But let me mention at least a few. I wish to offer special thanks to all the people in Lucknow who made this study possible. I am very grateful to the Lucknow residential editors of *Times of India, Hindustan Times, Hindustan* and *Dainik Jagaran* who were exceptionally generous to me. I was made welcome, allowed to work in their organisations and given free reign to conduct interviews. Throughout my study I found the journalists to be extremely patient and kind in their responses to my requests. My presence created extra work for many yet all possible support and assistance was given.

I feel particularly indebted to Hemand Narayan and Uttam Sengupta. Uttam and his wife were always available for my questions and worries. They became personal friends whose emotional support I cherished a great deal; their kindness carried me through many difficult days. I want to thank Hemand who was a fantastic facilitator. No matter how complicated the task I wanted accomplished, he always found a way. He stayed in contact via email for all the years of writing up my study and always produced an answer to my queries. He provided many insights into the publishing business and I am grateful for his friendship.

In order to protect the anonymity of my informants, I have changed all names in the text. I refer to persons by real name only if they are public personalities, who received media attention. Members of the writing professions are never referred to by their real names.

I also wish to thank the Gupta family, who hosted me during my stay and generously shared their home with me and treated me like their own daughter. I am particularly indebted to Mrs Gupta for her care and attentiveness to my small daughter during the long hours of my absence for work. I also enjoyed the company of many Indian academics who helped me grow intellectually, supported me in making sense of my data and facilitated my work organisationally. I especially want to mention Veena Das and Dipankar Gupta for their support and intellectual input.

My academic development was influenced greatly by Klaus-Peter Köpping. I admire him for his great knowledge, his innovative thinking and thank him for the trust and time he invested in me. I remember with delight the many heated debates we had about theories and developments in the social sciences. In Halle I worked with Burkhart Schnepel who was a fantastic mentor. He always asked the right questions and thus contributed significantly to shaping the final version of this book. There were many others in Halle who helped me refine my argument. I want to thank Richard Rottenburg and Thomas Kirsch for many helpful comments and support as well as Patrick Neveling for listening to all my worries over many coffees. I also want to mention the joint colloquium of the Institute of Anthropology and Max-Planck Institute for Social Anthropology. These regular meetings were extremely inspiring and the comments I received for my draft papers made me think afresh. Furthermore I profited from the lively debate of the EASA Media Anthropology network organised by John Postill. It is an excellent platform and a very supportive intellectual environment. There are many others who commented at conferences or meetings. I want to mention especially Frank Heideman, Per Ståhlberg, John Postill, Nina Glick-Schiller and Steve Reyna. Finally, there are many anonymous reviewers whose comments helped me revise and refine my argument.

I must also thank my new colleagues at the University of New South Wales. Their support during my first year of settling down in Sydney was crucial and enabled me to finish the book whilst acclimatising to my new academic environment. The head of the School of Social Sciences Rogee Pe-Pua was always receptive to my proposals; without her support the book would have not been completed as quickly. I must also thank Ross Buckley for his extremely helpful comments and Andrew Metcalf for his emotional support.

Lastly, this work would not have been possible without the fiscal support of the DFG (Deutsche Forschungsgesellschaft), who financed several tips to India. I also thank the Institute of Anthropology Heidelberg, the Institute of Anthropology Halle and the School of Social of Social Sciences and International Studies (UNSW) in Sydney for technical, material and financial support.

Ursula Rao, 30 July 2009

CHAPTER I

Introduction

I travelled to Lucknow in October 1999 to start my research on press institutions and political journalism. I was nervous about beginning fieldwork in a city I had never visited and in which I had no friends and relatives. My worries were aggravated by accounts I had read about anthropologists 'studying up' (Nader 1999 [1969]).[1] Academics working in elite institutions, like the press, had found it difficult to become a trusted member in these companies. Hence, I expected many obstacles. The experience of my first week seemed to disprove all the warning voices. After only five days in the field, I had met several journalists, all of whom invited me to meet with them. What followed was my unusual first socialisation into the field.

I arranged to visit one of my new 'journalist friends' at his house. He lived in humble lower-middle class accommodation in one of the new neighbourhoods in the expanding Eastern suburbs. Upon arrival I was given tea, introduced to the family, questioned about my background, my family, my home town and my country, admired for my Hindi skills and interrogated about my work at the university and my salary. After an hour of polite small talk I began to ask the head of household about the nature of his press work. My host answered by handing me a thick file with several years of yellowed newspaper cuttings. The texts were written in Hindi and covered matters of religious traditions and the importance of maintaining them as a buffer against the negative impacts of modernity. The author regularly wrote these comments during his free time and sent them to a friend who was an editor of a Hindi newspaper; these comments were published on the editorial page. He presented his activity as instrumental to the publishing process which justified his self-description as journalist: 'They use me to write for their editorial page!' he explained.

My next meeting was with an angry citizen who was appalled by the dire condition of the political culture in the state. He frequently expressed his disgust in letters to the editors of English- and Hindi-language newspapers, which were regularly printed, as he proved by pulling out a file of cuttings. I met a contractor for motor vehicles who as a side business acted as an informant for the major regional Hindi daily *Dainik Jagaran*. He had come by this role as a member of a Muslim cultural organisation from which he reported news. There were political activists turned reporters and local reporters who left their jobs to start a political career.

While I was initially pleased to be surrounded by 'journalists' everywhere, talking to all these people, meeting their families and drinking their tea started to become tiresome and did not really seem to bring me anywhere with regard to observing political reporters doing their job. After a couple of weeks I began to ignore peoples' self-declarations and concentrated on the major publishing houses. I did go back later, when I began to understand the intricate relations between professional journalists and the various layers of urban publics. I extended my research further into state politics and the corporate world. Working out their interconnections became a crucial task that enabled me to go beyond the narrow focus on news room culture and explore the social relevance of making and consuming news.

Journalists are professionals dealing in information. Their position as professionals in a respected institution that manages and disseminates news makes them powerful individuals who come to occupy a position as nodal points in a culture of connectivity. They are sought out by a range of social agents who establish exchange relations, exert pressure or seek patronage to acquire influence over a highly valued process of image production. This activity of networking has consequences for the news discourse, the structure of urban relations and the character of the public sphere. It is these wider social consequences that I wish to highlight with a study that focuses on the social activity of knowledge production through the media. The study engages with three different areas: (1) the engagement of resource poor citizens with local reporters; (2) the exchange relations between politicians and state journalists; (3) and the influence of advertisers on media professionals.

Through the analysis news emerges as a fetishised commodity deployed to intervene in power negotiations. People position themselves in news networks, write press releases or acquire news coverage as a means of self-promotion. News is an instrument which enables citizens to gain an advantage in petty fights. It increases the visibility of political agents and functions to consolidate an emerging consumer society. By taking account of the multiple agencies and ideologies that contribute towards the formation of news as a social force, this study breaks with the standard dichotomy that exists between writers and readers. That distinction obscures the ways in which the activities of journalists, other professionals and urban citizens more generally intersect. I will show how at the conjuncture of various communication networks events are framed collectively and news-making is turned into a profitable business that shapes the social environment in significant ways.

Treating news as a cultural asset, I aim to extend the field of news analysis beyond the text. Journalism studies tend to focus on how information is gathered and selected, and how it can be manipulated, hidden or given a spin. The process of transformation that generates news from information is debated with regard to two different approaches. Social structures, and the way in which they prefigure news through standardisation, are scrutinised. A more open and dynamic approach follows negotiations in between journalists and informants from elite institutions and demonstrates the impact of relations on news discourse. Both approaches concentrate on the way in which information travels and gets transmuted while travelling, from sources to news articles. I will demonstrate that the cultural significance of news exceeds the meaning communicated through content. News as object creates social relations and shapes identity negotiations. It performs these functions thanks to the collective assumptions that celebrate the press as powerful institution and prompt people about the significant impact of publishing.

My context is specific. The investigation is set in the Indian cultural space and located at a particular historical juncture. Fieldwork took place at the turn of the millennium, when the effects of Indian liberalisation politics were already clearly felt. The position of newspapers was influenced by rapid economic growth, the fast spread of media technology and more generally the commercialisation of urban society. Hence, my investigation into the social efficacy of news as fetish contributes towards describing this process of change. I will demonstrate how news-making serves to update a cultural repertoire under conditions of accelerated globalisation. News related activities also help to define possible ways of inhabiting the changing cultural spaces. My study considers Hindi- and English-language news-making and elaborates on a market that oscillates between the re-making and deconstructing of the language division.

The remaining part of the introduction will spell out in greater detail the position of my study in the context of the contemporary social science debate. I begin with a short summary of landmarks in the history of Indian journalism and situate my own research in this narrative. The second section will focus more generally on the theoretical thrust of my argument that contributes towards a paradigmatic shift of studying media engagement as social practice. I sum up current debates in media anthropology and cultural studies and demonstrate their relevance for the formulation of a radical critique of journalism studies. Finally, I introduce my methodology. An investigation into news relations demands an in-depth approach that considers the position of a wide range of urban citizens.

News in India

The book is set against the background of radical economic reforms in the early 1990s that moved the Indian economy from a system of state management to free market practices (Nayar 2001). One consequence was the rapid growth and diversification of the mass media. Electronic media experienced an almost explosive expansion (Butcher 2003; Kohli-Khandekar 2006 [2003]; Sharma 1998). This development had a resonance also in the community of social scientists. There is an impressive number of anthropological studies about the impact of the new electronic media as well as significant scholarship on emerging forms of visual representations (see, for example, Brosius 2005; Butcher 2003; Dell 2005; Juluri 2003; Mankekar 2000 [1999]; Manuel 1993; Mazzarella 2003b; Pinney 1997, 2004). In contrast, much less attention has been paid to the press (Jeffrey 2000; Ninan 2007; Peterson 1996; Ståhlberg 2002). While newspapers no doubt represent an 'old' medium, they have not become old-fashioned. In India newspapers have not been marginalised by electronic media, but have participated in the growth with a steady rise in circulation figures, the number of publications as well as income. Growth has been accompanied by change. I will engage with this change to show how emerging forms of engagement with the press are relevant for the re-making of leadership traditions.

Newspapers came to India as a colonial import. Founded by a British national in 1780, the first Indian newspaper was written in the English language and traded exclusively in gossip about colonial representatives. However, Indians soon adopted mass communication for their own purposes. The first Indian owned newspaper made its debut in 1818, followed by the first vernacular newspaper in 1820. By India's independence in 1947 a total of 120 newspapers had been founded – many of which did not last long. During this time publishing was instrumental to the projects of colonising and proselytising on one hand and the struggle for independence on the other hand. This heritage of publishing, not for money but to advocate social transformation, was carried over into postcolonial India (Kohli-Khandekar 2006 [2003]). The first Prime Minister of independent India, Jawaharlal Nehru, argued that the press should work hand in hand with the political avant-garde to advance the nation-in-the-making. According to Nehru, newspapers had the power to shape society and he saw them as an instrument apt for spreading modernity and reconfiguring social identities pertaining to class, gender, caste, occupation and religion. For at least forty years the ideology of a 'progressive' press provided the blueprint for defining and understanding journalistic tasks. In practice this promoted an excessive closeness between the government and journalism and a generally tame press (Peterson 1996; Raghavan 1994: 142–64).

When Indira Gandhi imposed censorship that lasted for fifteen months, between 1975 and 1977, the publication business was deeply affected. Retrospectively this intervention marks a watershed in Indian publishing. The years following the declaration of the State of Emergency[2] saw the beginning of a steep and continuing rise in circulation figures and a profound transmutation of news ideologies, now turned to commercial interests. The factors advancing these changes were political and social as well as economic. Harassment experienced during the emergency, as well as the new popularity of the Hindu nationalist movement, heightened political awareness and left people craving information. Growing literacy and the increased purchasing power of consumers further boosted circulation figures. Most importantly economic transformation triggered radical revisions in business culture. The 1980s saw the first movement away from a state regulated economy. A dramatic 'u-turn' occurred between 1991 and 1996 when a set of radical economic reforms turned India into a place that wholeheartedly embraced market economy. The reforms led to swift economic growth and rapid globalisation (Nayar 2001). As a corollary the print business experienced sky-rocketing revenue from private advertisements. The quality of newspapers was enhanced through the import of advanced technology for printing and distribution, and new aggressive forms of marketing were adopted. In the emerging neo-liberal environment, money-making began to supersede political propaganda as the *raison d'être* for news-making (Jeffrey 1993, 2000; Kohli-Khandekar 2006 [2003]).

My study begins at this point and will discuss the changed position of news-making in the neo-liberal environment. In this book I will identify and describe two trends that predominate in the current, ongoing phase of transformation. They are continuing commercialisation and regionalisation. Regionalisation is the core project of the vernacular press and is at the heart of its expansion policy. In 1979 for the first time vernacular newspapers overtook the English-language press in circulation figures and have since experienced exponential growth. Improved quality has led to a substantial rise in status. Jeffrey (2000) calls the triumph of the vernacular press a 'newspaper revolution', which is justified considering the enormous social impact of vernacular newspapers. Local newspapers have contributed substantially to the transformation of the political landscape, poignantly summarised by Pande (2006) as: 'English for the Elite and Hindi for the Power Elite'. Recent developments have produced new powerful and influential political elites with strong regional ties whose political projects increasingly challenge national powers. The engagement of journalists with regional leaders has made vernacular newspapers major players in this process (Rajagopal 1998 and 2001). My study moves down the social hierarchy to the news-making activities of local citizens who take advantage of and feed the regionalisation of newspapers and politics. I demonstrate how ambitious personalities and aggrieved citizens mimic political techniques of self-promotion by entertaining media connections and using the press to manipulate social relations. Their press engagement is encouraged by the open-door policy of local news-teams, which offer local news-pages as a publication platform from the people for the people. We encounter a multiplicity of voices that are fed back into the political process of manipulating proximate and distant power relations.

The discussion of commercialisation moves the analytical gaze to the other end of the social spectrum: the powerful position of corporate interests in contemporary Indian society. Associated with the up-market segment of society, the English-language press has profited most from growing advertisement revenue. Hence, they form the spearhead of a new aggressive movement to promote consumerist messages and pioneer the development of 'feel-good' journalism. Reporting politics in this environment demands the careful balancing of political against economic interests. Journalists maintain close ties to the political field and exchange favourable articles about leaders for access to decision-makers. However, there is another force that pulls journalists in the opposite direction. Commercialisation has made newspapers independent from political financing and given them increased freedom in political reporting. The desire to cover politics differently promotes the formulation of new genres of political criticism. Articles that ridicule leaders are placed next to descriptions of political heroes.

Exploring the trajectories of news under the conditions of localisation and commercialising means moving across a wide social spectrum. I will begin with local news-making (chapter three) and then move on to the political (chapter four) and economic elite (chapter five). This passage is accompanied by a shift from a predominant engagement with Hindi-language newspapers to a debate that focuses largely on English-language nationals. The rationale is that the regionalisation of the press is driven mainly by the vernacular press while English-language newspapers lead the process of commercialisation. This division corresponds to Rajagopal's image of a 'split public'. He uses the term to describe the distinct role of vernacular and English-language newspapers in Indian society. Hindi-language newspapers, he argues, give a wide and diverse picture of social processes, the reporting of which is based on authentic involvement with people, their thoughts, ideas, practices and organisations. In contrast, English-language newspapers speak from an elitist point of view, quoting only decision-makers and portraying social and religious movements – such as the Ayodhya conflict[3] – as something that was happening 'out there', in a society far away from elite institutions, like the English-language press itself (Rajagopal 2001: 151–211).

This image of a 'split public' is justified as a macro-perspective, describing a general trend. However it understates the complexity of media practices. The analysis of everyday routines perforates the clear boundary between the idealised images of two publics. While the journalists of both types of newspapers occupy different niches in the news market, they do not hold radically different positions and are not producing two fundamentally distinct products that split the public. All newspapers are competing in one rapidly changing market and competitors are constantly monitored for initiatives that will bring success. The managers of Hindi-medium newspapers do not only envy their English-language competitors for their advantages in securing advertisements but work hard to catch up. They copy marketing strategies and make their product more attractive to advertisers by increasing circulation, printing infomercials and catering more and more to the upper-middle classes. They also profit from an incipient vernacular advertisement industry born of the media expansion. Today vernacular advertisements for 'down market' products add a new dimension to an industry that previously demonstrated a heavy bias towards the English-speaking upper class (Jeffrey 2000: 52, 60–62; Rajagopal 2004). Similarly, the English press has jumped on the bandwagon of regionalisation, and part of their marketing strategy is to move into the regions. Recent years brought a rapid rise in the number of local editions of English nationals, and English-language papers have also begun to expand their section for local news. By these means they are targeting the traditional readers of vernacular newspapers. The rationale is that only by making significant inroads into the vernacular market can they ensure long-term growth.

To reiterate the gist of the argument, news-making practices embrace diverging tendencies. All newspapers enshrine in a different way and to a different degree the contradiction that they are becoming more and more a product of citizens for citizens while also acting as the long arm of corporate interests propagating the views of the super-rich. The internal organisation of the news teams and the design of newspapers show significant differences across the language divide. This has an impact on the position that newspapers occupy in the market, the type of people that reach out to the newspaper and the strategies for appropriation and consumption. Yet there is no absolute bifurcation. Journalists communicate in one field, where they negotiate standards for reporting. Newspapers also compete in the market. In a rapidly changing environment, managers perceive the possibility of making inroads into what was traditionally the domain of their competitor from across the language divide. As a result there is a new 'middle ground' in the making, in which policies merge to create the hybrid style of regionally successful newspapers. I will follow this process, describe the conditions for its emergence and debate its relevance for the reshaping of leadership traditions. My focus on the social relevance of the media is informed by anthropological research methods and research questions. In the following section I will elucidate this dimension of my work and the way in which anthropology as a disciplinary perspective can help to fill a gap in the study of journalism.

Media as Practice

Anthropology has been a latecomer in the study of mass media, gaining popularity only from the 1980s onwards.[4] The beginning of the anthropology of mass media[5] was marked by a major influence from cultural studies and has inherited an interest in reception processes, asking how media products serve the reconstruction of meaning in different (sub-)cultures.[6] Because it enabled a deep involvement with people in a particular locality, fieldwork provided a necessary and highly suitable method for answering this question. Unlike scholars from other disciplines, anthropologists have studied societies outside Europe and

North America and thus have greatly increased knowledge about the cultural embedding of media usage. We learned that American-produced soap operas are interpreted in different ways across the globe (Abu-Ludghod 1995; Das 1995; Liebes and Katz 1988), that going to the movies is culturally embedded (Dickey 1993a, 2001) and that consuming television has a multitude of effects, depending on variables like locality, class, gender and age (Ang 1996; Butcher 2003; Gillespie 1995; Jensen 1986; Lee and Cho 1990; Mankekar 2000 [1999]).

Another central concern in media anthropology has been the question of how people use mass media to re-construct themselves, their identities and relationships. Although media technology has been developed in and spread by the West, today it has been appropriated across the globe. 'There have been too many examples of cross-cutting, non-Western cultural/economic/media expansions to justify the idea of a unidirectional American/European global takeover: Bollywood films, Mexican teleserials, and Japanese ownership of Columbia Pictures are but a few examples' (Askew 2002: 9). To uncover the agency of the media in concrete settings, anthropologists have analysed a broad range of usages of media technology. Studies inform us how cultural (self-)images are produced through photography (Landau and Kaspin 2002; Pinney 1997, 2004); how people are using film and television technology to create and communicate cultural identities (Brosius 2005; Ginsburg 1994, 1996; Rajagopal 2001; Turner 1992); and how the internet has changed social relations, for example, by facilitating the formation of transnational communities (Miller and Slater 2001).

The strength of all these studies has been their ability to understand the media within their particular cultural contexts and to show how they become relevant to people in actual life situations. Anthropology brought its particular agenda, the study of social engagement, to contribute to an understanding of the media. In the light of this development the fear that an engagement with mass media might move anthropologists away from the central concern of their discipline, that is, to study human relations, seems out of place (Dracklé 1999: 262). Studying the media from an anthropological point of view means understanding how media technologies and products are used to make, maintain, change and give meaning to social relations.

The anthropological analysis of engagement with mass media is party to a paradigmatic shift in media studies, with practice theory re-centring the way in which mass media are analysed (Postill and Bäuchler, forthcoming). In a recent article Nick Couldry (2004) argues that the media should occupy the 'epicentre of a new research question'

(p. 116). The new question should break away from an older obsession with media text and look at the broader contexts of social activities that are related to mass media's presence in the world. Couldry's formulation is not without problems. While he promotes practice theory, he appears to favour a particular structuralist version of it, assuming demarcated sets of ordered practices that influence each other in a domino style, with media practices in the poll position. His article confronts the reader with a media-centric understanding of society reminiscent of the approach that views culture as a functioning whole, in which sets of regulated practices play definite roles (Rao, forthcoming).

This criticism aside, his article does open up new horizons for considering the future of media studies as a field for investigating the way in which media related practices inform cultural bearings. On a similar note, Elizabeth Bird has called for the study of 'media *as* culture' (Bird 2003: 2, emphasis in the original). Her reception research avoids fixing media practices in a separate domain. In a media saturated world, she argues, the term 'audience' does not denote any specific group, but is a position adopted routinely by all members of society. The way in which people embody this position has consequences for social relations and cultural perceptions (see also Alasuutari 1999).

I think it is high time that such a broad view is also extended to news production. Traditionally, the sociology of journalism focused on professional elites and the role they are assigned in functioning organisations. This approach is concerned with output – and structures that streamline output – while lacking to analyse other social consequences of production-related activities. I will push beyond this point and demonstrate how media networks influence how people build and experience relations. News-making and news consumption are arenas where modern identities are forged. The way in which access to the press is negotiated and interpreted, as well as the way in which news as information and commodity feeds back into the cycle of meaning production, has consequences for social identities and power relations.

In analysing news as a cultural practice, I am breaking with the typical sociological tradition of studying news-in-the-making. Early studies into post-war societies defined journalists as gate-keepers and located them in a nodal position between informants and publishing house. According to this position, journalists exercise their agency by applying a definite set of selection criteria (news values) to a broad information supply and in doing so arrive at news (White 1950). This position has been deconstructed as being naïve by scholars who reject the notion of news as objective representations, viewing it rather as the product of culturally coded acts of interpretation.

Following the latter line of argument, studies of news organisations have demonstrated how work routines, internal hierarchies and news policies determine news-making. Inspired by Garfinkel's (2002 [1971]) ethnomethodology, sociologists investigated the character of professional cultures, the rules that regulate them and structure outcomes (Tuchman 1978: 188; see also Fishman 1980). Participant observation became a means to understanding the role of journalistic practices in processes of social structuration. Studies reveal the bias of media institutions toward authorised speakers, the organising roles of the beat system[7] and made-for-media events, as well as the implications of time and space constraints on social visibility (Fishman 1980; Gans 1979; Goldenberg 1975; Hess 1984; Marcinkowski 1993; Roshco 1975; Sigal 1973; Schlesinger 1978: Tuchman 1978). In line with this reasoning – although more abstract – are the theories of the German constructivist school. In this tradition news constitutes a second-degree observation that reinterprets shared perceptions in line with the particular priorities of a media system. The paramount aim of the media system is its self-authorisation. The selection and presentation of news recursively reinstates news media as the main source for information (Luhmann 2000 [1996]; Schmidt 1994). While there are substantial differences in the details of these studies, they all follow a paradigm that assumes stability within structure. Professional practices produce predictable images in tune with a particular elitist version of society.

In the Indian context, Per Ståhlberg (2002) has borrowed from this approach. In *Lucknow Daily*, he investigates working practices at *Dainik Jagaran*, the most successful Hindi newspaper in western Uttar Pradesh.[8] He describes the connection between a vernacular medium and global modernity by unravelling a particular local incarnation of a global profession. He concludes that news output in Lucknow is shaped by universal journalistic work structures, such as the beat system, and by the more locally specific character of negotiating with (elite) sources, as well as by Indian social hierarchies of education, caste and gender. Ståhlberg's work moves beyond the structure-functionalist paradigm. Focusing on the act of 'translation' through which a universal standard becomes a local practice allows him to embrace negotiations – of standards and power relations – as important dimensions of press output. Daily work demands the re-appropriation of ideals in an environment that is full of contradictions and conflicts. Hence, his approach overlaps with a more recent tendency in journalism studies to focus on power contests.

In recent years several studies have moved beyond news organisations to investigate the encounter between journalists and other relevant elites. Turning away from the straightjacket of functionalist and structuralist interpretations, these studies interrogate the complex workings of power hierarchies and the exercise of control. Debates on the relationship between sources and journalists demonstrate the negotiated and often contested nature of media coverage (Ericson, Barnek and Chan 1989; Manning 2001). There is evidence of the powerful intervention of proprietors and the relevance of market dynamics (Bourdieu 1998 [1996]; Eckman and Lindlof 2003; Edwards and Cromwell 2005; Murdock 1982; Weber 1995). Outside of news organisations, coverage is swayed by staging made-for-media events in order to compel professional attention (Boorstin 1962; Molotoch and Lester 1974).

While all these studies have increased knowledge of the news-making profession and the social forces which shape news, they remain constrained by their focus on the logic of text production. I wish to move research on news-making out of this niche and relocate it in the 'web of culture' (Bird 2003: 2).[9] In the following pages I analyse news-making as a process of cultural signification formed through the intersecting agency of a range of media related activities. I interpret news not as a predictable product of a well-oiled machine or as a text disconnected from the flow of social life. I rather view the role of news-making in a process of cultural remediation. I will highlight the potentially subversive effects of multiple influences on journalists, the individuality of reporters, and the relative independence of sources. While journalists are at the centre of attention, I consider how their agency is interlinked with those who appropriate, use, create and subvert the daily interpretative work of the press through their intervention. I demonstrate how the making of the tangible commodity – the newspaper – also produces intangible cultural images, social orientations and political techniques. Journalists produce publics not only through texts but also through their embodiment of a particular elite position. Their acts are recognised and interpreted as cultural actions. They are appropriated, copied and rejected in the process of reinventing a way to inhabit a rapidly globalising environment. Journalists shape and circulate evaluative criteria and an interpretative posture for reflecting on social reality. They also propose possible positions for acting upon this reality. They are news-makers, role models and nodal points in networks. Scrutinising these dimensions I unravel the working of a culture in the making in which news texts are objects of exchange.

Fieldwork

This interpretative approach is tied to a particular methodology typical of most anthropological research. At the heart of anthropology lies the writing of concrete ethnography based on a long-term, intensive involvement with people in defined localities. The inspiration is taken from Malinowski's pioneering concept of 'participant observation'. Anthropologists travel across space to find 'a field' in which they arrive as strangers and struggle to become familiar. Long-term involvement serves the production of deep knowledge (Geertz 1999 [1973]). While these descriptions circumscribe an attitude and an aim, they say little about how to conduct fieldwork on something as abstract and idealised as 'news cultures'. Struggling to find answers I was reminded of Gupta and Ferguson (1997), who demanded that anthropologists should engage in 'location-work' by consciously constructing their fields of research and reflecting on both localising strategies and on the implications these bear for their results (see also Coleman and Collins 2006). The authors identified a tendency in anthropology to take the local for granted and – through the anthropological gaze – turn it into an original, natural and authentic place of being.

Working in an untypical environment, there was little I could take for granted and I never overcame the sense that I had no field or that the field was blurry and indistinct. It appeared to be without clear boundaries in a social and a physical sense. Firstly, I learned that news-making creates and depends on relationships. To grasp how they come into being, how they are maintained and their significance, I worked my way through several intersecting sets of connections and layers of narrative approaches. I followed networks that extended into all levels of society. Secondly, the field was unbounded in a physical sense because the journalists' areas of involvement are constantly in flux and depend on agents and events that become the focus of the day. Reporters visit different localities and organisations, and at times they also travel outside the city. They draw on information from the internet. They respond to pressure from head office and debate with colleagues from other cities. Of course, there are routines and daily routes, but reporters keep moving, physically and intellectually, in their efforts to identify sites of excitement.

To develop my approach I benefited from Marcus's (1995) concept of strategically situated ethnography. Marcus argues that there is a need for (and a practice of) multi-sited ethnography in which the setting is not a pre-given place, a locale that is fixed by informants' practices of boundary-making. It is, rather, strategically designed research in which the ethnographer defines the path according to the aims of his study, possibly following people, things, metaphors, stories, biographies or conflicts and thus crossing borders between spaces and social groups.[10] I followed news and people involved in news-making. My strategy was to study networks (not bounded groups), which meant shifting positions and locations. I mingled with journalists, worked in urban neighbourhoods and moved in the political circles of Lucknow. I travelled to the field in Varanasi, Etawa and Kannauj, visited leading press institutions in Kolkota and Delhi, and attended mass media courses at academic institutions in Lucknow, Bhopal and Delhi. I answered as academic, acted as journalist, functioned as teacher and became the pupil. I studied up the social hierarchy as well as down (Rao 2006).

What for me was a 'normal' adoption of the idea of deep involvement in an urban research site was a terrible provocation for journalists. I began my research as a welcomed co-intellectual and was readily absorbed into their flows of work. However, the honeymoon did not last and soon conspicuous differences in our interests, perspectives and professions emerged. Everything about me seemed wrong. I constantly wasted time. I was hanging around too much in an environment where everyone is always busy, or at least has to pretend to be busy. I also went much too deep: I never knew when to stop and continued to ponder over events and texts for days and months after they had passed. I lost 'objectivity' because I dared to get close to informants and take their perspectives as seriously as that of journalists. My work had no date value. Journalists were genuinely shocked about the time frame I anticipated for the completion of my project. Things only became worse when I returned a year later, asking the same questions again – not having published one article on the matter. On top of all this, I was an awful pupil. I wanted to know everything, but never implemented what I had been taught. I continued doing my own thing, recurrently committing the same 'mistakes', when I could have learned high-quality journalism from my informants.

The friction was aggravated by the characteristics of press work. Firstly, journalists are highly competitive. Becoming intimate with some had major consequences for relationships with others, in a field where distrust, manipulation and intrigue are common currencies. It was never easy to get all the different sides to a story. Secondly, work pressures are extreme. Employees have to work hard to complete the daily stints. Many reporters were still young and had to worry about their careers. Some had short-term contracts and could not afford to waste time or compromise on quality for the sake of entertaining an anthropologist. Thirdly, as social observers journalists are used to forming critical opinions. They were looking at me in much the same way that I looked at them: I became a subject to be studied. They scrutinised, analysed, understood, framed and judged me and my actions. I was constructed as an 'Other' through their theorising and writing[11] and hence also became a subject of their pedagogical efforts.

Describing his experience in a similar situation, Hannerz (1998a, 1998b, 2002) coined the term of studying sideways, by which he means research among co-professionals. For Hannerz journalists are co-professionals because they are like him active 'in a transnational contact zone, and engaged there in managing meaning across distances, although perhaps with different interests, under other constraints' (Hannerz 1998b: 109). My sense of working among co-professionals arose from two experiences. Firstly, I related to people who like me traded in knowledge and were responsible for forming images of social life through texts. For all the differences between knowledge production in the press and that in academia, it was undeniable that we occupied positions in neighbouring professions and were driven by the same passion: to understand human actions and get it right. Secondly, we shared an emotional world due to similarities in the structure of the professional environment. We were driven by high pressure on performance, experienced a lack of job security and were subjected to constant evaluation of our work on the basis of content and placement of texts.

It was this similarity and our closeness that created the dissonance. We persistently acted on the assumption that we knew each other. We had yet to learn that nothing was that straightforward and that there were several ways of speaking authoritatively about the social. However, our tussles were not only a source of conflict, but eventually became the foundation for deep understanding. Journalists were not only irritated by me but were also vocal about their observations. They not only scrutinised my work and their feelings about it but expressed them in elaborate statements about the nature of their profession. It was this intellectual engagement which I began to value most. Thus, when I draw conclusions, I base them, like anthropologists do, on the observation of practices and the narrative appropriation of these practices. The latter gained clarity through my existence as an oddity and the journalists' readiness to engage with me. Mutual reflections, exchange and discussions of images and self-images became an essential part of the research. Together with the journalists of Lucknow, I strived to generate reflexive knowledge about their trade.

The Book

I will unravel my data and present my findings in four chapters. The introduction continues in the next chapter with a more specific description of news-making in Lucknow, the position of the news houses I worked in and the internal structures that organise work flows. It describes the organisational cultures that influence how journalists approach their tasks, accounting for some of the fundamental differences between the vernacular and English-language press. From there I move into the field that is a zone shared by all journalists to explore the cultural significance of news-related encounters.

Chapter 3 is a study of the agency of news in urban environments. The desire of vernacular news organs to offer a local product has turned them into a political instrument that is appropriated by the resource poor for the realisation of their own interests. People lobby through the newspaper to gain status as leaders, to manipulate relations, or to improve their living conditions. Case studies of local citizens' intervention in the news writing process will demonstrate the interactivity of news-making as well as the impact of dense news networks on the news discourse. The characterisation of culturally moulded styles of exploiting news and news networks will lead to a reconsideration of the dominant notions of the public sphere. I describe the public as a communicative network, which people build up, maintain and use in order to secure the attention of the press, as a powerful organ that defines and shapes public concerns.

Chapter 4 investigates the making of political news. The focus is on the relationship between politicians and journalists and its ramifications for news writing and political decision-making. It is obvious that journalists fish for exciting new information and maintain close ties with powerful people. What is not quite as obvious is that most of their time is spent cultivating sources even when they are not 'hot'. I describe and analyse activities of networking in political circles and show that news-making is not only a process of selecting the most important and relevant information, but is also an enterprise in establishing, nurturing, strengthening and repairing relations. News follows expectations in reciprocal relationships, as much as estimates about news worthiness. My analysis of the close-knit relationship between journalists and politicians / the press and politics prompts me to critique the concepts of social fields (Bourdieu) and social systems (Luhmann). I show that the notion of a separate journalistic domain is insufficient to describe the social dynamic of political news-making. I contend that the journalist's activity of assembling texts constitutes a political dynamic. In attempting to unravel the political role of journalism, I distinguish between a moral economy that strives for professional purity (of journalism and politics) and a practice that precludes the possibility of separation.

Chapter 5 describes a dynamic set of practices tied to the commercialisation of the press. The powerful intervention of private advertisers has fuelled a reorientation in themes and styles of news-making. Today reports on show business, consumer products, education and health take their firm place next to political news. While reporting on the government and opposition parties is still the most respected and sought after domain of journalism, political themes now compete for space with other popular news items. More important are changes in styles and perspectives. Infotainment and infomercials are promoted as new models for news writing that clearly favour private business. The reorientation has implications for political reporting. Experimenting with different forms of narrative writing and 'reader friendly' language, journalists configure novel formats for political comment. The inherent devaluation of political actors is aggravated by the ability of newspapers to depend on private money, liberating them from the political patronage that was the rule before 1980 and making them more daring in their political criticism. What comes as a revolution in Indian political writing is simultaneously the re-articulation of a global trend of opposing state institutions and celebrating the market. Journalists appear to trade one hegemonic perspective for another, questioning any naive belief in the possibility of resistance.

As a whole the book constitutes an attempt to come to grips with the significance of news as a cultural tool. The focus is on political developments, at all levels of the social hierarchy. I debate the transmutation of political processes through media relations. Central focus is the re-working of the leader-centeredness of the Indian political space through media networks and publishing policies. I study the mimeses of a leader posture by local citizens, the techniques used by officeholders to manipulate their public images, and the making of new heroes from the private industry in a transformed publishing environment. At all three levels the ambition of individuals for recognition finds expression through re-inhabiting cultural models, while calibrating personal goals in shifting social landscapes. It is a process of re-negotiation of power structures in a network society. News as culture demonstrates the significance of extended news networks in the shaping of an urban public sphere.

Notes

1. For descriptions of these difficulties, see Gamson 1994; Hertz and Imber 1995; Mazzarella 2003a; Shore 2000; Shore and Nugent 2002.
2. The State of Emergency was imposed by Indira Gandhi between 1975 and 1977, thus suspending civil liberties and allowing her to rule by decree. During this period the freedom for political mobilisation was heavily curtailed and many opposition activists imprisoned.
3. The conflict was triggered and kept alive by Hindu radicals fighting for the construction of a temple to Ram at the mythical birthplace of the god-king in Ayodhya. This is a highly controversial issue since the site belongs to the Muslim community and used to host a mosque, which was destroyed illegally by Hindu radicals. Despite archaeological evidence to the contrary, Hindu fundamentalists maintain that a temple to Ram existed on the disputed site before it was destroyed by the Muslim invader Babar, who is said to have built the mosque (Gopal 1991; Elst 2003; Hartung 2004; Nandy 1995 et al).
4. This is not to deny that there were valuable contributions earlier. Visual anthropology especially has been of major importance in the creation of media anthropology, and there are certainly overlapping themes and interests. However, media anthropology developed around a very specific interest in the social embedding of media texts.
5. For an introduction to media anthropology, see, for example, Askew and Wilk 2002; Dracklé 1999; Ginsburg 1999; Ginsburg et al. 2002; Mazzarella 2004; Peterson 2003; Spitulnik 1993.
6. Influential texts are Hall 1992b [1980]; Fiske 1994. Hall also gives an interesting summary of the approach of cultural studies to media 1992a [1980].
7. Beat system refers to an institutional structure within news organisations. Typically all reporters are assigned a certain set of institutions or topics (beat) which they routinely cover.
8. Uttar Pradesh is a state in northern India, the state capital being Lucknow.
9. In an Indian context Mark Allen Peterson (forthcoming) has contributed to such a project. Probing the social significance of newspapers in everyday life, he describes the emblematic character of newspaper consumption. People acquire newspapers not only for their information content, but as means of status assertion. Buying a newspaper is a casual act, motivated by the desire for particular information, to kill time or to be entertained. In contrast, subscribing to a newspaper means engaging in a family tradition and communicating something about one's social standing and membership in a particular community. Strategic newspaper consumption plays a role in the production of social ties and is part of a body knowledge productive of social distinctions (Peterson, forthcoming).
10. The discussions on 'traveling cultures' (Clifford 1997) and 'multi-sited anthropology' (Marcus 1995) are experiments in ethnography. In a world

where people are increasingly building relationships across long distances and are very often on the move themselves, whether voluntarily or not, strategies for research have to change.

11. Several articles were published in the newspaper about my stay in Lucknow and the work I was doing (see, for example, *HT City*, 5 February 2000; *Hindustan*, 1 February 2000).

CHAPTER 2

Lucknow News

In this chapter I wish to broaden the introduction and provide a background to my observations of news networks in the following chapters. I will begin by describing the newspaper market in Lucknow and the rationale for my selection of companies. In the second half, I describe typical work routines of journalists and the internal hierarchies within the news organisations.

This serves two purposes. At a descriptive level I shall provide an overview of press work, describe diagrammatically the local scene, positions and functions of employees and explain the terminology used to refer to them. At the interpretative level I shall demonstrate the significant difference in the internal organisation of Hindi- and English-language news houses and relate these to the processes of commercialisation and regionalisation. On one hand there is the expansive employment policy of Hindi newspapers. This policy creates incentives for building news networks and patronage relations. The social implication of this development are the central focus of Chapter 3. On the other hand, there are the flat hierarchies introduced in the English-language newspapers. The latter have also relaxed the beat system and encourage journalistic independence, which feeds into the process of reinventing journalism under the conditions of commercialisation, the main topic of Chapter 5. At this point I aim to distil the fundamental organisational differences that have implications for news-making practices, giving regionalisation and commercialisation a particular character.

Newspapers in Lucknow

Lucknow is the capital of the northern Indian state of Uttar Pradesh and had a population of approximately 2.8 million at the turn of the millennium, the period of my research. To its visitors, Lucknow is presented as the 'City of Nawabs'[1] whose lively culture and beautiful architecture blossomed under Muslim rule between 1722 and 1857. From 1764 onwards the British East India Company slowly started to take over the city. The 'final *coup de grace* was to come in 1886, when Awadh[2] was annexed and the Nawab deposed' (Graff, Gupta and Hasan 1999 [1997]: 4). Today there are few reminders in the everyday life of the city of its Muslim past. These influences are now kept alive only through monuments, handicrafts and other cultural products that are important for tourism and for the high culture industry. In the newspapers this aspect of Lucknow is treated only occasionally in supplements that offer feature articles on the city's 'culture' and history.

In 1920 Lucknow became the capital of the United Provinces of British India. It continued to be a political centre after Independence and the subsequent reorganisation of the states in India. It is Lucknow's disposition as a political turnstile that was of interest to me. Political observers often view developments in Lucknow as indicators of general trends in Indian politics. From the time of the freedom movement onwards there have been connections between Delhi and Lucknow. Lucknow is a platform where national political trends have been established and made popular (see Brass 1968; Freitag 1989; Graff, Gupta and Hasan 1999 [1997]: 12; Weiner 1957). One important person who re-connected Lucknow to the centre during my research was the then Prime Minister, Atal Bihari Vajpayee. He contested and won all his elections from Lucknow and maintained close ties with the state BJP (*Bharati Janta Party*) after his elevation to the top position in Delhi.

All large newspapers and news agencies have one or more correspondents in Lucknow, and many media companies have opened offices in the city to produce local editions of national or regional newspapers. In 1998 nine Hindi, one Urdu and four English-language newspapers were being produced in Lucknow (Ståhlberg 2002: 31). With its vibrant press activity situated in a central, politically significant location, Lucknow was an ideal choice for a study of Indian journalism. The city is important enough to attract all the major newspapers but sufficiently compact for a visiting anthropologist to get around. I began my work among the leaders in the local market, the *Times of India* and *Dainik Jagaran*.[3] In order to broaden my comparison, I later included the respective number two newspapers in my case study, namely the

Hindustan Times and *Hindustan*. Furthermore, I read all the major newspapers in Lucknow daily and regularly visited meeting points for journalists. Thus, I will also present material from *Amar Ujala, Sahara, Pioneer* and *Asian Age*.

The *Times of India* in Lucknow has been notably successful since opening its doors in the city in 1984. In 1999 daily circulation was 17,000 copies and rose to 50,000 in 2002, by 2004 sales were up to 80,000. The *Hindustan Times* followed with its local edition in 1996.[4] In 2000 around 35,000 copies were sold and circulation increased to 42,000 in 2002.[5] The most successful Hindi newspaper is *Dainik Jagaran*. It came to Lucknow in 1979 and the unofficial 2002 sales figure of the Lucknow edition was 55,000 copies sold every working day. The closest competitor is *Hindustan*, which opened its doors in Lucknow in 1996 and was selling approximately 48,000 copies a day in 2002.[6]

The goal of all these companies is to offer a high-quality newspaper with a local flavour. It is part of the expansion strategy of media companies in India to increase profit by moving into the regions and publish newspapers aimed at local readerships. In Lucknow the two most successful English and Hindi publications are subsidiaries of larger companies. The *Times of India* belongs to Bennett Coleman & Co. Ltd., a Bombay-based family corporation. *Hindustan* and the *Hindustan Times* are part of a Delhi-based media company owned by the Birla Family, while *Dainik Jagaran* is an offshoot of a family-owned newspaper company located in Kanpur.[7]

The 'go local' formula had proven to be extremely successful (Ninan 2007).[8] Of sixteen pages in the *Times of India*, two were devoted to local news in 1999. By 2004 the section for local news had increased to five pages. In addition a supplement called *Lucknow Times* (four to six pages), which was originally a weekly magazine insert is now included six days of the week. Out of its sixteen pages, the *Hindustan Times* offers two on local and state news and also produces a four-page supplement called *HT City*. The Hindi newspapers' bias towards local news is even more apparent. Over the years, *Dainik Jagaran* and *Hindustan* have increased their local coverage to eight pages out of sixteen. They both had a weekly supplement containing city news in 2002. From recent feedback, I have learned that now Hindi newspapers also have several supplements a week, for local news and celebrity culture.[9]

There was also substantial coverage of local news on the front page. On average, one third of news articles on the front page dealt with events observed in Lucknow. The only exception among the four papers was the *Hindustan Times*. Their front page often had no local stories. *Dainik Jagaran* designed page three like a front page in order to indicate the beginning of the local section, making this section look almost like a separate local newspaper within the main paper. All four newspapers distinguished state news from city news. This is reflected in the organisation structure, with journalists working on separated teams, one group concentrating on stories about state organisations, the other looking at the city politics, administration, crime and urban life styles. There is a hierarchy between these two groups. Younger and less experienced reporters work on the city section, while senior reporters research state matters. However, the *Times of India* has abandoned the distinction between the two teams, thus opening up all areas of activity for all reporters.[10]

The work of reporters from Lucknow fills about half the space in the Lucknow editions of the various newspapers. There are pages covering national and international news, sports and the economy, for which information is picked up from agencies or from other offices of the company.[11] Additional pages of local news are prepared for the separate editions produced for outside Lucknow. I have excluded from my analysis all pages that are based only on agency news or information from correspondents, since the aim was to look at news in relation to practices and the news networks that come into being during news-making.

Work Routines and Organisational Context

The work routines of all journalists follow a similar pattern. Most press people begin their day with a detailed reading of the newspapers, comparing their own product with those of their competitors. Decision-makers hold initial consultations over the telephone to set the targets for the day. Around noon journalists reach the offices for the morning meetings, which are devoted to the discussion of the day's work schedule and a short review of yesterday's newspaper. After this reporters swarm out to attend their appointments, visit sources and go to places that are known as platforms for the exchange of gossip and the staging of protests. After 5 P.M. people start to return from the field and discuss the day's events with the editor and other colleagues, write their articles and submit them. The editor or team leader will have an initial look at the incoming articles and sometimes – especially if the news is not routine – there will be some feedback and instructions if parts of articles have to be rewritten. The article is resubmitted and the reporter leaves work.

Editing starts earlier, around 4 P.M. when articles that have already been submitted are distributed among sub-editors in accordance with their anticipated placement in the edition. Each sub-editor is assigned one, sometimes two pages. He or she corrects articles, gives them headlines and decides on their placements on the page. Final page design will depend on the number of advertisements booked, which always get preference over editorial content. Most pages are finalised and sent for production between 8 P.M. and midnight.[12] The front page is decided last, often after a brief meeting between leading staff members.

The work of reporters and sub-editors is supervised by the news editor and the residential editor. Editors, reporters and sub-editors together form the newspaper's editorial section. There are three other departments involved in the production and distribution of newspapers. The advertisement section negotiates with clients on the cost and placement of advertisements. They do this in coordination with the circulation department, which provides sales figures as the basis for calculating advertising fees. The circulation department has several other tasks: organising the distribution of the printed product, advertising the newspaper and collecting feedback from readers. Finally, there is the printing unit – sometimes there are several in different localities in order to keep transport routes short.

The staff members from these different sections have little contact with one another. Every individual has a clearly defined task to fulfil in the overall process for which he consults almost exclusively with his own team leader. Leading members from all sections hold regular meetings in order to coordinate the work and take policy decisions. At times reporters receive direct feedback from the advertising section, when there is a conflict of interests between the two areas. There is also an information flow from the circulation department to members in the editorial teams about readers' reactions.

In this study, which examines the interconnections between reporters and the urban environment, I focus on teams of reporters and their leaders. During my days in the offices of newspaper houses I spent most of my time with them. To complete the picture I also worked in the editing section for some days, conducted interviews with the general management, the leading staff in the circulation and advertising departments, and students who had been employed to conduct surveys. In the following section I will outline in more detail the working practices of the different reporting teams and how hierarchy structures relations and work routines. I shall begin with the Hindi organisations, move on to the English-medium organisations and then offer some comparisons.

The Company as Family (Hindi Newspapers)

Dainik Jagaran and *Hindustan* operate with two teams for reporting: a small group of permanently employed state reporters; and a large, heterogeneous group of city reporters. State reporters (the 'bureau') are in charge of news that originates from the state organisations that are located in Lucknow, while city reporters work for the local pages and report about events in which city organisations or city neighbourhoods are involved. The chief reporter and the city editor supervise the work of their respective teams, both reporting to the news editor and the residential editor. An idealised hierarchy of the reporting section in the Hindi-language press might be depicted as follows.

Table 2.1. Schematic overview of the internal hierarchy of the reporting section at *Dainik Jagaran* and *Hindustan*.

Leader of the local edition of the newspaper	Residential editor	
Co-manager of its editorial content	News editor	
Leaders of teams of reporters	Chief reporter	City editor
Staff reporters	State reporters	City reporters
Stringers		Stringers (freelance reporters, trainees, informants)

Such a schematic representation needs to be contextualised, since concrete tasks, authority and interrelations have their own characteristics at each level of the hierarchy.

Roles and Functions

The residential editor has the main responsibility for editorial output, managing its style and content in coordination with the head office. At *Dainik Jagaran* the residential editor is removed from most routine work and only steps in to mediate during crises, hand out rewards or give direction on policies and philosophy. At the *Hindustan* the residential editor supervises state reporters directly while keeping a distance from all other routine functions.

The news editor oversees the production of all editorial input. This means that he[13] supervises reporters and editing personnel. He collects and checks all articles, coordinates placements on the pages, selects the photographs for publication, and approves and finalises each page before it is sent for printing. The news editor is particularly close to state reporters. He meets them in the morning, has ad hoc discussions with them during the day, and is the first to read their articles in the evening. In contrast, he has little direct contact with city reporters and communicates his instructions through the city editor and only reads reports from the locality once they have been approved by the city editor. At the next level is the chief reporter, who coordinates the work in the team of state reporters. He is an active reporter himself in the state team. Differences of status between state reporters are not emphasised during everyday routine, though there are slight differences, according to the importance of a beat given to a person and his seniority.

The role of the city editor combines the responsibility of the news editor and the chief editor. The city editor does not work as a reporter (though he might write an article occasionally), but invests all his time and energy in instructing, training, supervising and coordinating the work of a large number of city reporters. He takes full responsibility for the work of the city team. His tasks are to distribute themes, control articles and pass on the views of those higher up the hierarchy. News coordination at this level is rather more difficult, since the city editor deals with a heterogeneous and fluctuating group of reporters made up of both staff members and stringers. There are permanent and short-term stringers: these include newcomers to the profession, students doing internships, and informants who want affiliation with the press.[14] Working as a stringer can be a first step toward a career in the media, but it can also be a hobby, a tactic to increase the visibility of a certain locality or organisation, or a means of realising one's interests as a businessman or leader (see also Chapter 3; Tharyan 1999: 162).

Reporters at Work

Work routines for state reporters and city reporters have a different character. State reporters are senior members of their organisation. They are attuned to the needs and styles of the company and have become trusted associates. Thus they are allowed to work relatively independently. By contrast city reporters, especially stringers, are yet to be moulded and fully integrated into the organisation. Routines in the press room produce daily proof of the difference in status.

The state reporters meet in the morning with the news editor (*Dainik Jagaran*) or residential editor (*Hindustan*) in a relaxed atmosphere. All journalists suggest ideas for the day. They listen to criticism of the previous day's coverage and receive instructions from their leaders. This will include directives to write continuations of stories that had been missed but reported by other newspapers.[15] The atmosphere is democratic. Journalists are considered experts in their respective areas and their views are valued. Respect flows up and down the hierarchy. Reporters respect their bosses and bosses treat them as authorities in their fields because they depend on the information available only to reporters. The evening hours are particularly lively. State reporters feed information to their bosses, circulate gossip and current affairs, while designing stories and writing them up. Articles need to be approved by the news editor (sometimes also by the editor) and while there is a degree of discussion and rewriting, articles are rarely rejected. State reporters are experienced enough to know what is desired and expected. They exercise discretion and self-censorship in order to minimise conflict. Once the work is done a spirit of celebration sets in. Staff reporters buy tea and snacks from a stall outside, which they share while narrating the day's events, images and impressions.

In sharp contrast to this cooperative spirit and relaxed atmosphere is the authoritarian atmosphere of the *Dainik Jagaran* city reporters' meeting. Here the city reporters assemble in the news hall at 12 P.M., where they are seated in a semi-circle facing the city editor, who remains standing. There is no discussion, only consultation, during which individual reporters are handed their tasks. In fact, on many days the term 'meeting' appears inaccurate, since people may come late or leave immediately after receiving a task. Journalists do not come to debate, but to be instructed. On some days the city editor uses the opportunity of the co-presence of the city reporters and stringers to educate them about their trade. They are frequently subjected to instruction on how to be a proper reporter and a competent member of the company. Since employees come mostly with no prior training in journalism, these meetings are the main forum for initialising young people into the profession. The following observations from one of the meetings give a good sense of the way in which 'training' is accomplished:

> Deepak, the city editor, held a press release from INTACH (Indian National Trust for Art and Cultural Heritage) in his hand about a Jain temple needing repair. Furiously he turned to Ajay, one of the stringers: 'You are with us now for over four months. How many times did I tell you to make a story about this Jain temple? Now see INTACH has taken the initiative. You should have take up the theme first! How many times did I tell you, there is always a story? You just have to develop it! Remember, the conservation of architecture is *always* a good theme for writing!' After this scolding Ravi, another stringer asked whether he could cover the issue. The Deepak handed him the document from INTACH and then turned to Ajay:[16] 'Now the story is gone for you! Forget it! Whatever happened happened. But from now on you have to be more alert.' Thus, the reporter was doubly embarrassed. He was scolded in front of everyone, but also lost the story and thus the chance to make up for his mistake. (Field notes, 8 March 2002)

As a forum for open praise and criticism, the morning meeting functions to recognise, train and mould new talent. Reporters are praised or scolded for their preceding work, their performance is compared to that of their colleagues, and arrangements for supervision are made. The city editor knows 'his people' and assigns tasks in accordance with talent, regularity of attendance, writing skill and the ability to conform to the policies of the house.

At *Hindustan* city reporters are treated with more respect, and junior reporters are also asked to suggest stories before they are given further instructions. Disciplining and the arrangement of tie-ups are more often handled more discreetly. Yet, there are also occasions for public scolding. In severe cases the editor personally attends the morning meeting, which happened twice during my stay:

> Just when the city reporters' meeting was about to start, the editor arrived. Everyone got up out of respect. He sat down, looked with grave silence at the news editor then at the assembled reporters. He took a deep breath and began to complain that the reporters were not building proper relationships and were not on top of information. 'This is what happens if you keep contacts only via the telephone!' The meeting went on for about 45 minutes. Thirty of these minutes were taken up by the speech of the editor. There was little discussion, though a few reporters

initially tried to defend their work. The real discussion started only when the editor was out of the door and journalists struggled to cope with the criticism. They tried to find out what had gone wrong as well as overcome the tension and normalise the atmosphere. […]. Afterwards the city editor asked Shiva to make friends with a policeman at Cantonment to get stories and information from there. (Field notes, 1 April 2002)

This incident underlines the importance of hierarchy for evaluating work: Reporters look to leaders for guidance and are anxious to please them. Young reporters are easily sacked. If the whole team does not function, pressure increases enormously, and the otherwise invisible editor suddenly becomes a very present figure, threatening consequences if the usual command structures cannot produce the expected results.

Supervision continues in the evening when city reporters write up their articles under the strict guidance of the city editor.[17] He will check all articles, make changes or demand rewriting before approving the texts and passing them on to the typing section. Once an article has been passed by the city editor, it moves on to the news editor for approval, and placement. In most routine situations, there is no direct meeting between the city reporters and the news editor. Coordination is done by the city editor, who acts as a nodal point in a highly structured hierarchical process of communication. Stringers, trainees and newcomers have no guaranteed place in the newspaper. They move up the hierarchy when their articles are published regularly. Those who have been granted a beat have made the first step towards a career. From then on their work becomes easier.

Working Hierarchies

Three principles govern relationships at *Dainik Jagaran* and *Hindustan*: (1) formal and informal designations, (2) performance and (3) seniority.

I have discussed above the difference in treatment between state and city reporters. There are other more informal designations that create hierarchies within the teams: How important is the work assigned to a person? How often are his or her articles published at a central point in the paper? How often is s/he granted a by-line? Has s/he been assigned a separate beat? How important is that beat, and how effective are the connections one can build there? Have younger journalists been put under his or her supervision? The answers to these questions give a clue about who is who in the organisation. They create a flexible hierarchy that is manipulated and contested. Sometimes I was given two or three different descriptions of a person's position.

The manipulation of one's position within teams is closely associated with an evaluation of performance. The performance of people in lower ranks, in particular, is closely monitored and important for possible repositioning. Reporters can easily be laid off, but they can also be promoted quickly, at least in the initial years.[18] Reporters described *Hindustan* as slightly more 'bureaucratic', meaning that roles are more clearly defined and procedures more strictly prescribed. They are less subject to direct interference from their bosses and feel more reassured about their jobs. At *Dainik Jagaran* the residential editor makes sure he remains in control. Although most of the time he is absent from the actual scene of work, everyone knows that he pulls the strings from behind. He keeps himself informed about all his employees, manages relations with other institutions, and makes regular speeches about necessary, desired, acceptable and unwanted forms of journalism. Any journalist who behaves too independently will not remain in his favour for long. Part of his strategy of control is to keep hierarchies flexible, at times obscure: 'Once you give a man a formal designation, I feel that he becomes half as useful to us. He will only look to his own rights, not to his duties. And it becomes a little difficult for us to sack him. The rest of the team suffers' (Residential editor, *Dainik Jagaran*, cf. Ståhlberg 2002: 100). In following this approach, the residential editor has created a 'floating system' (Ståhlberg 2002: 102). Instant punishment and gratification are part of a system in which everyone must continuously prove his worth. Fear of criticism and hope for recognition are factors in the work ethic at *Dainik Jagaran*. At the end of each year, the editor's promotion scheme, called the 'Top 10', is put into practice, with the ten best journalists being selected and promoted at that time.

In both companies, hierarchy is the main principle of organisation. It compels its members to give and receive both instructions and protection. Younger members have to conform with and learn from seniors. Elders discipline their juniors, but are expected to care for them and help them build a career. Typically, journalists call colleagues their (elder or younger) brothers, a relation of affection and control. The model follows the idea of a traditional Indian family,[19] where authority and affection govern hierarchical relations. The ideal traditional Indian extended family has two ordering principles: age and gender. The older members instruct and protect younger members, while men rule over and protect women. The hierarchy among women depends on the status of the men with whom they are associated in the household (Mandelbaum 1989 [1970]; Kakar 1971, 1991 [1981]: 117). In Hindi news organisations the latter principle is of no significance as there are few female employees. If they stayed on and managed to move up the hierarchy, they appeared on an equal footing with men. In contrast, age, or in this case seniority, plays an important role in structuring the hierarchy.

The most senior member is the residential editor who acts as the patriarch. He is a distant authority, instilling respect and fear and is hardly ever approached by junior members. He monitors performance from a distance and regularly scolds, praises and promotes. The news editor and the city editor take on the roles of guides. Like elder brothers they teach reporters all the necessary skills and supervise the day-to-day work. Junior members conform, lobby and seek advice. Sometimes relations are extended into the private realm where junior reporters helped their seniors with domestic chores. Among reporters of a team, relations are governed by a mixture of equality and difference. Within the city and the state team respectively, members complete similar assignments and compete for praise and promotion from the same leader. However, even here reporters are never fully equal. This is particularly obvious in the city team. There are many ways to distinguish city reporters, through seniority, task, regularity or performance. A tutoring system emphasises differences and encourages hierarchical relations.

The simultaneity of equality and difference creates ambivalence similar to what Mandelbaum portrays as a typical characteristic of relations between brothers:

> A major ambiguity and common cause of strain in the fraternal relation is that brothers are equals and yet are not equal. They are all equal in property rights, all equally representatives of the family, all equally bound in with the family's social status and fortunes. Yet an elder brother is also vested with some more authority over a younger and the younger should, in some degree, be submissive to his elder brothers. But sooner or later the question arises of the degree and nature of deference. The uncertainty as to when equality should be paramount and when inequality should prevail tends to rile their relations. (Mandelbaum 1989 [1970]: 64)

In news organisations relationships were progressively adjusted by acknowledging seniority and measuring performance. Together the two criteria are responsible for defining and re-creating formal and informal designations. Thus we find that there is flexibility in the system that may upset the hierarchy of seniority. Younger colleagues can rise fast while others may be kept in the same position for a long time. In this case position overrules seniority. This also happens when members are recruited from outside and put in charge of a whole team.[20]

The system ensures conformity and allows leaders to exercise a great deal of control. Junior members usually enter the organisation with little knowledge about the trade and with average writing skills. They are moulded and trained through years of supervision. Before they are allowed independence, they have become intimately familiar with the internal criteria for the selection of themes and perspectives. Unclear designations and job insecurity ensure that people stay in line with the policy of the news house.

Flat Hierarchies (English-Language Newspapers)

The internal dynamic in English-medium organisations is in stark contrast to the culture of Hindi-medium houses. They work with flat hierarchies, and attribute equality as a basis for competition. *Times of India* has departed most radically from the model of 'company as family' and is credited with taking the lead in revolutionising Indian news-making. The company operates with a very simple structure. There are few positions of authority and little to formally distinguish reporters.

Table 2.2. Schematic overview of the internal hierarchy of the reporting section at the *Times of India*.

Leader of the local edition of the newspaper	Residential editor
Co-manager of the editorial content	News editor
Staff reporters	Coordinator
	Reporters

The residential editor directly supervises, instructs and coordinates the production of all articles. He is very accessible, discusses all details with reporters and reads each one of their articles. He also converses daily with the general management and the advertisement section, keeping in mind the economic interests of the papers. The news editor rarely interacts with reporters. He supervises editing and placement and hence confers mostly with the desk staff. There is little that distinguishes the reporting staff. All reporters are free to work on any theme relating to the state or the city. There is a very basic beat system that covers the political parties and major institutions like the police. Yet even this allocation of work has to be turned to an advantage through performance, since all journalists may also encroach on the beats of colleagues. Two positions are slightly elevated: the coordinator of reporters and the state reporter. The coordinator is a reporter himself and works as a colleague to all others. In addition, he functions as a go-between who channels some of the communication between the residential editor and the reporters. However, reporters are free to address the residential editor directly even for complaints regarding the coordinator's favouritism. Depending on the performance, the post of coordinator may rotate. The state reporter has a special role because he covers news from the rest of the state and enjoys frequent travel. Within Lucknow he competes with all other reporters for state news.

The lack of hierarchy is a revolution in Indian news-making. Older colleagues complained of having been robbed of the privileges they would have earned earlier, while junior reporters objected that the flat hierarchy was an ideal but not a reality. Only the elders, they would comment, receive the interesting tasks and important stories. Thus it seems that seniority still plays a role, but it is more subtle, contributing to daily power negotiations, but no longer providing an institutionalised or guaranteed advantage. Everyone competed with each other on a daily basis and lobbying the editor was an important part of securing a good position.

Table 2.3. Schematic overview of the internal hierarchy of the reporting section at the *Hindustan Times*.

Leader of the local edition of the newspaper	Residential editor	
Co-manager of the editorial content	News editor	
Staff reporters	Coordinator of state reporters	Coordinator of city reporters
	State reporters	City reporters

Hindustan Times is more structured but relations are significantly more relaxed than in the Hindi-medium organisations and reporters at all levels work relatively independently.

The residential editor has little direct contact with reporters. He supervises the making of the final product from a distance, while regularly consulting with the owner and the advertisement section. The news editor is in charge of all reporters, calling the morning meetings as well as supervising their work during the day. There are little differences in the way in which city and state reporters are treated. Both teams are almost equal in size and all reporters are staff members. City reporters tend to be younger and junior to their colleagues from the state team, yet, their views are equally respected. Both teams of reporters have a coordinator who assists in the communication between the news editor and the team of reporters.

Work Routines

The morning meetings of all English-language journalists are democratic. Debate and contributions by all members is actively sought. For the rest of the day, journalists work independently. It is in the evening that the difference between the Hindi- and the English-language news houses becomes particularly apparent: the latter are characterised by the virtual independence of their journalists, their relative equality, and the short line of communication up and down the hierarchy. All reporters sit on separate desks in front of computers, concentrating on their work. While there is some discussion, it does not rival the collegial exchanges and gossip at *Dainik Jagaran* nor reflect the celebration of the approaching end of the day. There is no coming and going of the numerous stringers, no overflowing baskets of handwritten news, no elaborate system of the various stages through which the news passes. Among the journalists there is competition, since status fluctuates in accordance with performance and the preferences of the current residential editor.

In the evening the residential editors and news editors meet frequently. They scan through the submitted articles and review the incoming news from correspondents, other offices of their company and agencies. Together they make a selection from the pool of news and photographs. Without mediating personnel, quality is ensured through their competent leadership and monitoring the work of staff. Leaders depend on reporters for information and stories. That dependence was accentuated by the fact that editors changed frequently.[21] From 1999 to 2002 – the period of my fieldwork – the

Hindustan Times and *Times of India* had three different editors each, while in the Hindi newspapers the leaders remained unchanged.[22] The changes put a burden on journalists. They must be able to operate 'independently' and to help a new residential editor understand the local scene. They also have to adapt to different leadership, and to be aware that their role as a favoured (or out of favour) reporter may not last long. Flexibility and self-assurance are qualities that help ensure survival in companies that constantly re-position their own standards through new leaders.

Work Cultures

The radical difference in work cultures between the market leaders *Times of India* and *Dainik Jagaran* stuck me as extreme and highly significant. To back up my observation I expanded my sample and included the *Hindustan Times* and *Hindustan* in my study. These two newspapers from the Birla Group seemed ideal for comparison, not only because they are the respective number two in the market. More importantly, they belong to the same company and share one building. The editorial staffs of both newspapers are located in the same office space, separated only by make-shift walls. Despite the spatial proximity there is little exchange. The organisation reproduced essentially the difference in organisational cultures I had observed at *Times of India* and *Dainik Jagaran.*

Therefore, the flat hierarchy and substantial independence for journalists in the English press contrasts against the elaborate hierarchies and networks of patronage in the Hindi-language organisations. This difference can be seen in the organisation of office space at the *Times of India* and *Dainik Jagaran.*[23] *Dainik Jagaran* has broken up the working area into various territories. In the multi-storey building the second floor belongs to the editorial staff. Here we find, among other things, the news hall, a separate room for state reporters and the office of the news editor. The room of the residential editor is on the third floor, so that he is not readily accessible. On the second floor we find two doors next to each other, one leading into the news hall, the other into the news editor's office. Moving through the news hall, one reaches a separate room where the state reporters sit. The office of the news editor is accessible from two sides. An ordinary visitor will pass through the main door from the entrance hall, which leads to a secretariat that has access to the news editor's office. State reporters can reach their boss directly through a second door that connects his office with their room.

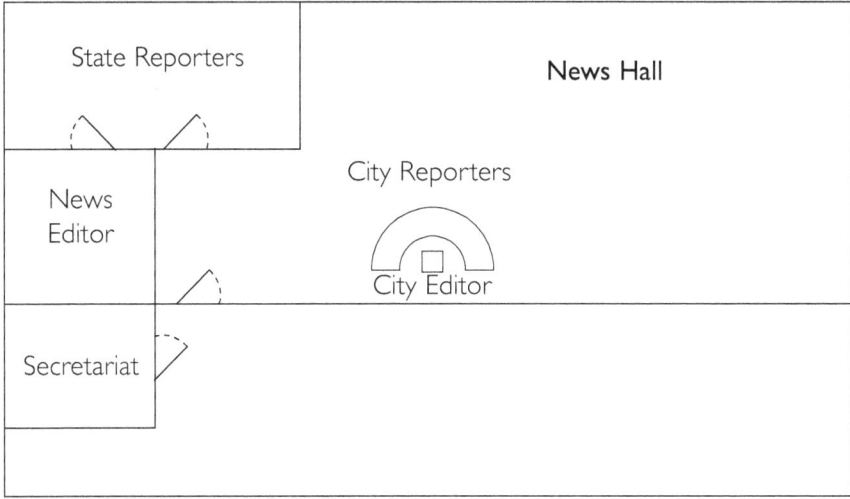

Figure 2.1. Schematic representation of working places given to journalists at the offices of *Dainik Jagaran* (not to scale).

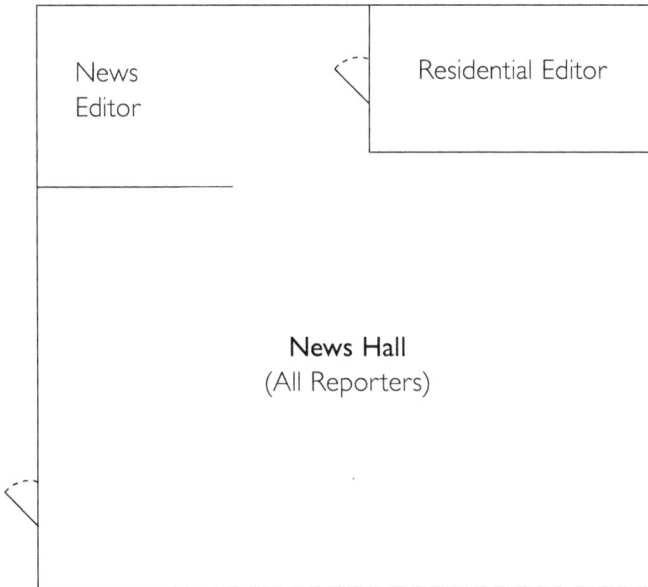

Figure 2.2. Schematic representation of working places provided at the *Times of India* office for journalists working for the main pages of the newspaper (not to scale).

Dainik Jagaran imprints status positions into the space. City reporters sit in a large hall along one big table. State reporters occupy a separate room, where each person has a desk and a computer for his personal use. The news editor and the residential editor have spatially and visually separate offices with secretariats. Every group of reporters has direct access only to their immediate bosses, while persons of higher rank can only be reached by passing through the territory of mediating personnel. This organisation of space supports a rule typical of both the Hindi newspapers I studied. Junior reporters are discouraged from involving senior personnel in routine matters. There is a line of communication up and down the hierarchy.

In contrast, at the *Times of India* editorial staff share one large hall. The news editor and the residential editor are placed separately. They are not, however, shut off from the reporters, who can easily see what they are doing. The news editor sits behind a make-shift wall at one end of the hall. Just across from him is a glass room for the residential editor. Reporters sit in front of their own computers. There is no spatial indication of differences in status between them. Status distinctions are understated and remain subtle.

Staff members themselves are aware of the differences between Hindi- and English-medium news houses. Leaders in the Hindi press justified the need for more supervision with regard to the poor quality of Hindi education. Hindi newspaper editors complained that they could not find high-quality staff, as Hindi-medium education does not attract the best students. Ambitious and well-established families send their children to English-medium schools, which have much higher recognition and better job prospects. Thus, managers of Hindi newspapers produce a tight system of supervision as a means to make up for the educational deficits of those who start with them. This has implications for the size of staff required.

The difference in the two work cultures can be related to the two processes of regionalisation and commercialisation, the latter pushed by the English-language press and the former by the Hindi-language press. Regionalisation is essentially about quantity, an attempt to get as many voices as possible into the newspaper. The idea is that people buy and read the newspaper because they, themselves, and their neighbourhood are represented. As I will show in the next chapter, this process involves a large number of citizens, who make up a dense network through which events are communicated and press releases forwarded. The character of local news is tied to the structure of Hindi-language news organisations.

The patronage structure extends into the public domain. What defines journalists' work processes inside the news house becomes the guiding principle for involving non-professionals in the news-making circuit. Journalists extend the hierarchical structures through which news is generated into the public domain. Their position in internal hierarchies defines the kind of patronage they can exercise outside. Team leaders have the authority to nominate official informants, who through their permanent status and their direct connection to middle-range authorities, yield influence. They turn the privileged media connection into a personal advantage when building their own patronage relations and negotiating with other authorities. They act as external 'sub-stations' that bring a particular newspaper to the attention of locals and connects them to the publishing house. Journalists in lower ranks build informal urban networks. Their efficiency in transforming urban voices into news will influence their position in the press and their stance in the urban community.

The quality of news articles is ensured by their progress through the hierarchy. The main concerns are structure of text, fluency, correct spelling as well as political considerations. The process is one of streamlining rather than diversification. The voices are multiple but the style of presentation shows little variation. Straightforward observations and long quotations are the essential elements of Hindi news. Variations on this are produced only by a small number of long-service staff reporters. They are given the freedom to comment, compare and analyse. Their relative freedom and their ability to negotiate directly with the top authorities make their job profile comparable with their English-language counterparts.

Commercialisation is driven by the English-language press. From the perspective of the everyday life of journalists, there are two important aspects to this transformation. Firstly, the viewpoint of outsiders is not cherished. While multiplication of perspectives is desired, this should not affect the advertiser-friendliness of the newspaper. The task of finding the 'right' kind of stories is entrusted to well-trained staff reporters. Freelancers are not trusted and are rarely published in the newspaper, as their articles are less likely to be in line with company policy and may contain inappropriate material. Hence, staff members are expected to produce new exciting stories. Experiments with content, style and perspective are encouraged and rewarded as long as they contribute to the sales figures and please the corporate sector. Relative freedom coupled with internal competition serves to tap the creative energy of employees while ensuring conformity.

Conclusion

In this chapter I have provided an introduction to Lucknow, the newspaper companies I studied and their internal working structures. The emphasis has been on differences, which are very apparent at this level and follow the language divide. Whereas Hindi-speaking journalists have to learn how to accept and provide guidance, English-language journalists have to prove their independence while remaining in the ideological framework of their company. This material supports Rajagopal's concept of the 'split public'. The notion of the fundamental difference between the Hindi- and the English-language press is justified by what he conceived to be a basic difference in the concept of news. He suggests that while English-language newspapers subscribe to the idea of news-making as rational discourse, Hindi newspapers refer to a variable set of values that are generated from the social settings in which their personnel are embedded.

> English language news emphasised the truth-value of news, as information serving a critical-rational public. This reflected the origins of English language news as an elite form of discourse in liberal market society. Here, any self-consciousness about the story-telling aspect of news gave way to the sense of a transparent communication that was objective and neutral.
>
> Hindi news audiences have a more fraught and contested relation to power, and could not assume a transparent, value-neutral approach to the news in quite the same way. Even as a means of informing citizens for active political participation, then, Hindi news was written quite differently from English news. The narrative aspect of news was much more in evidence, and perhaps understandably so, as the power relations between readers and rulers required constantly to be assessed, dramatised, criticised, or ridiculed, rather than to be taken for granted. (Rajagopal 2001: 152–35)

The same line of argument appears in Gupta's (1995) debate of local newspapers. He attests that they provide local readers with all the details of the complex relations between citizens and representatives of the state. National newspapers, in contrast, portray the state as a monolithic entity, which gains its character from the rationality of the deciding elite.

There is much to be said in support of the thesis that Hindi newspapers are more responsive to activities in civil society. In this chapter I began to establish the readiness of Hindi-language papers to engage with local voices and multiple perspectives, while English-language newspapers prefer an elitist perspective. I will elaborate this thesis in the following chapters and demonstrate the social consequences of the two different ways in which newspapers position themselves in the public. Yet, as I have already stated in the introduction, the concept of the bifurcation is exaggerated and in fact appears very dated when taking contemporary developments into account. The idea of rational and transparent discourse is closely tied to the developmentalist phase in Indian history and, as Peterson (1996) shows, is a hallmark of news-making before the 1990s. Market liberalisation has fundamentally changed English-language news-making. The introduction of infotainment, the great pressure to conform to neo–liberal ideologies and please advertisers, promotes reflectivity and draws practitioners' attention to the constructed nature of news. The paradigmatic shift towards questioning all forms of representation – following on from post-modern philosophy – is today also a standard part of journalists' education in mass communication courses.

It is yet to be seen how future developments will affect employment structures and relations to the urban environment. During my fieldwork I observed a nascent process of the vernacular press of tuning their papers to corporate interests. This development has clearly been accelerated in recent years as Ninan (2007) and Neyazi (2008) show. English-language newspapers will increasingly feel the competition of a reinvented vernacular press. Both of course face a rapidly changing television culture (Thussu 2007a), to which they necessarily react. Hence, the dramatic difference in staff structure may well change in the near future. What I will set out in the following pages is a document about the instantaneous process of change that characterises the social consequences of the two key processes of regionalisation and commercialisation. As such, the book describes significant innovations in the public sphere, which continue to be in a state of flux. The speed of current changes in the Indian media market makes me highly aware that my argument is a freeze frame. I capture a moment in the history of India's media business to highlight how the rearrangement of social ties is entangled with media related activities.

Notes

1. On the history of Lucknow, see Graff, Gupta and Hasan 1999 [1997]; Llewellyn-Jones 1985, 2000; Oldenburg 1984; Sharar 1975.
2. Awadh is a province in Uttar Pradesh. Under Mogul rule and later British colonial rule it functioned as a separate administrative unit. The united

provinces of Agra and Awadh were renamed and became the state of Uttar Pradesh after Independence.

3. A 1999 advertisement for the *Times of India* (Lucknow) was plastered on many big hoardings in the city. The message was bold and simple: this newspaper is three times bigger than any other English-language newspaper in the town (a figure I could not substantiate but it seems grossly exaggerated.) At the entrance of its Lucknow office *Dainik Jagaran* had a large banner saying: 'Number One in the Region'. This slogan was also used in many advertisements.

4. The arrival of *Times of India* and *Hindustan Times* changed the newspaper market in Lucknow significantly. The local editions of the other two English-language newspapers, the *Pioneer* and the *National Herald*, lost readership and today struggle for survival.

5. Sales figures were treated with great secrecy in all companies. What I present here are approximations communicated during interviews.

6. As a comparison, the sales figures for *Rasthriya Sahara* were given as 15,000 and those of all other Hindi newspapers in Lucknow (*Aaj, Swatantra Bharat, Navjivan, Swatantra Chetan, Amar Ujala* and *Kuber Times*) as 20,000.

7. In 2000 *Dainik Jagaran* also had offices in Gorakhpur, Varanasi, Jhansi, Math, Deradun, Agra, Bareli and Jalandhar (Ståhlberg 2002: 39).

8. It is a formula that has proved successful around the globe (see, for example, Franklin and Murphy 1998; Kaniss 1991). This is true not only for newspapers, but also with respect to local television programmes (for an Indian example, see Butcher 2003: 65, 69). Page and Crawley (2001) are more sceptical than Butcher about the future of localised television programmes in South Asia. Although they found several local language programmes, they see it as imperative to promote them in a competitive market, where big companies have enormous economic advantage.

9. I thank Hemand Narayan for keeping me up to date with new developments after I left Lucknow in 2002.

10. The only organisational division is between the *Times of India* and the supplement called *Lucknow Times*. Both have separate teams of reporters and separate editors.

11. In the same vein, news from Lucknow is included in other publications of the particular company if it is of national interest.

12. Because all four organisations bring out several versions of their newspapers every day, one for the city and several others for places in the hinterland, all pages are sent out several times. The work in the afternoon usually starts with the regional pages for locations outside Lucknow. Then early versions of the other pages are produced and sent to printing units in the hinterland. The city edition is produced last.

13. In Hindi news companies women are practically absent and are hardly ever to be found in leading positions. Hence I am consciously using the male pronoun here. There is a significant number of female staff in the English-language press. Jeffrey estimates that in 2000 8% of press employees were female, most

of them working for English-language newspapers. Jeffrey explains the under-representation of women with reference to the attitude of employers, who 'regarded women journalists as a nuisance to avoid if possible' (Jeffrey 2000: 173–76). Joseph (2000, 2004) has given evidence of such differential treatment. Standard complaints were that editors hesitate to employ women, that career progress is slower, and that women are more often assigned 'soft' stories and kept out of political reporting. Complaints against colleagues ranged 'from condescension and belittlement at one end of the spectrum to sexual and professional harassment at the other' (Joseph 2004: 171). There are also a few studies of news content with regard to women. Bathla (1998) shows the marginalisation of women's issues in news reporting. She contends that news-making draws on brahmanical ideals according to which women play no role in the public sphere (see also Chakravarty 2002: 6–27; Joseph and Sharma 1994). None of the women journalists I met complained of unfair treatment or harassment. Yet they did feel that they were assigned mostly to 'soft' stories and were less likely to make inroads in political writing. With the growing demand for essayistic writing about life style, fashion and health the female voice is welcome. This ongoing transformation is likely to improve the employment prospects for women, especially for those who are genuinely interested in the new areas of reporting.

14. There are informants in each quarter of the city, in every large community and organisation, as well as in each district in the state. An informant may not earn much – sometimes he does not get any salary at all – but he can use his affiliation with the newspaper to boost his own importance.

15. There is always something to complain about. There are two reasons for this. Firstly, there is never a complete congruence between different newspapers, and hence there is always a feeling that something was missing in the house publication. Secondly, the chiefs receive regular feedback from people in power, who may not like the way they have been portrayed. Dealing with criticism is part of the daily routine. Almost every day some issues are taken up because other newspapers have already reported them. However, missing important news is a critical omission, and there are consequences for the reporters if it happens too often. Journalists are vulnerable, since short-term contracts are the rule.

16. All names of journalists have been changed to protect informants.

17. At *Dainik Jagaran* city reporters wrote by hand, sitting on the semi-circular table under the gaze of the city editor. At *Hindustan* computer facilities are available for all and city reporters submit their articles through the intranet.

18. While it is easy to rise during the initial years, there is less scope for promotion once a person has reached a middle position. Thus, many Hindi journalists expressed frustration about career stagnation at an age of about thirty-five to forty years.

19. This observation of the parallels between family dynamics and company structures has also been made by Sudhir Kakar, who sees a connection

between the sense of hierarchy inculcated through socialisation in a family and the nature of professional relations: 'The principle of a hierarchical ordering of social dependencies extends beyond its home base in the extended family to every other institution in Indian life, from the jajmani system to corporate business, from the guru-chela relationship in religious education to department staffing in an Indian university' (Kakar 1991 [1981]: 119).

20. The importance of performance as a principle for re-ordering status distinguishes news organisations from families, at least to a certain degree. Even in a family, a younger brother may gain additional authority because he is more efficient in organising family matters and thus may stand above his elder brothers in some situations. Yet, age can never be fully eliminated: it remains significant in standardised situations like, for example, rituals. This is different in news organisations, where respect needs to be earned and seniority is acquired through a combination of age, length of service and performance.

21. The frequent change of editors is also possible because they are considered of little importance for the development of the newspaper's market. The *Times of India* follows a strict division of labour between management and editorial staff, placing the manager over the editor. The management is accountable for the paper's performance in the market. This means on the one hand that the editor is free to do what he wants as long has he does not interfere with the aims of the company. On the other hand, the editor has to accept direct interference when the interests of advertising customers are involved and when the management feels that the newspaper is no longer adhering to set standards or styles.

22. One obvious reason for the frequent rotation of editors in the English-language press is their national agenda. The regional editions of English-medium newspapers are not supposed to be or become regional newspapers. The task of a residential editor is to develop a newspaper with a regional flair without diverting from the policy of the main office. In order to create a truly national newspaper, decision-makers are rotated through the regions, to be informed about various places and to learn how to strike a balance between the national outlook and regional styles. The national outlook of English-language newspapers may not be the only reason for recurring changes of residential editors. However, it was impossible for me to obtain access to decision-making processes at that level, since they take place outside Lucknow.

23. The *Hindustan* and *Hindustan Times* show no difference in the office set-up. However, in observing how people moved through the space, one could clearly discern the difference in authority structures. Hindi-language journalists were much more restrictive in their use of office space than their English-language counterparts.

CHAPTER 3

Local Voices

Empowerment through News-Making

This chapter moves into an in-depth discussion of local news production. The organisational overview drew my attention to the expansive nature of local teams. Hindi newspapers engage large numbers of city reporters, stringers, informants and freelancers to penetrate all corners of the city and ensure a regular flow of information from the grassroots. Moving through the system, this information is turned into local news and offered to urban readers as reflecting their interests and environment. The policy decision to offer the newspaper as platform for local communication is complemented by people's love of publicity. Citizens nurture press connections in order to push their grievances, hopes and achievements into the newspaper. Two trends predominate: firstly, local want-to-be leaders appropriate news production to create fame and importance; secondly, resource-poor people assert their interests by manipulating media relations. Agitated citizens encounter the willingness of newspapers to 'listen'. It is this intersection that is significant and that will form the basis for my argument in this chapter. Exploring the media–public interface, I will develop the notion of the public as network. I will shift the focus from reacting audiences to acting citizens who are drawn towards participation in news-making by a promise of empowerment. Their media-related practices are the basis for a re-creation of a politics of patronage in the media sphere.

The chapter has two parts. The first half introduces local news-making practices through three case studies. I begin with a study of how political ambitions acted as a driving force for the creation of the media hype around the making of the film *Water* (Deepa Mehta). I then elaborate on how members of a local caste group used the newspapers to manipulate their proximate social environment; and finally, I explore the role of journalists as brokers, who occupy a nodal position in media-related urban networks. The second part of the chapter introduces the relevant social imaginaries that empower newspapers and, via newspapers, citizens. My conclusion of how citizens exploit the performative power of news leads to a critical engagement with dominant ways of conceptualising the public sphere. I argue for an analysis that moves beyond text, or the focus on making and reading texts, to viewing news as culture, as a way of theorising the effect of media on the rearrangement of social contexts in an emerging media society.

Local Reporting and 'Open-Door Policy'

In the last chapter I discussed the expansion strategies of newspapers in Lucknow. Investment in regionalisation is a dominant trend. Local news-making is a growth market and vernacular newspapers are particularly keen to exploit it (Jeffrey 2000). The corollary is a rapidly growing number of local pages. In 2002 *Dainik Jagaran* and *Hindustan* reserved half their publications for local news, which is equal to about eight pages. To fill this space an elaborate beat system has been developed that ensures a regular flow of information from a broad range of urban institutions such as: Housing Board, District Magistrate, Co-operative Department, Distribution Department, LDA (Housing department, colony development), Pollution Control Board, Narcotics, Forest Department, ration (subsidies), Cane Co-rporative, Agriculture and Animal Husbandry, Social and Welfare Department, *Vikas Bhavan* (Chief Development Officer), Pension, Scheduled Caste and Scheduled Tribe Commission, Taxes, Minorities, Medical, Electricity, Water supply, Education and Scientific institutions.

This beat system is not fixed but is a dynamic entity that keeps growing with editors and reporters constantly 'discovering' new areas of urban interest. What concerns me in this chapter is a second trend emerging from the investment in local news. Newspapers open up their publications to the influx of information passed on by citizens. The management holds the conviction that people want to read not only about their immediate environment but also about themselves in the newspapers. To ensure wide representation of people and neighbourhoods, three channels are open for the input of urban concerns. These are: high receptiveness to press releases, extensive networks of stringers, and a personalised style of reporting.

Press releases: Newspapers receive a substantial number of press releases from all strata of society. Hindi newspapers publish these with little evaluation or editing and only reject them if there is extreme bias.

On average, twenty per cent of all news items (not news space) in the local pages are lifted from press releases written by local citizens or organisations. When asked about this policy the city editor confirmed my observations: 'We try to print all press releases, even if we have to shorten them. The content is theirs; the words are ours' (City Editor, *Dainik Jagaran*, 27 March 2002).

News networks: Hindi newspapers have divided the city into neighbourhoods and communities (such as religious communities, ethnic minorities) and assigned a stringer to each of these groups and places. Stringers keep the newspaper office informed about local events, may write articles and can be contacted when citizens report on incidents or conditions in their neighbourhood. They fulfil the task of mediating between the local community and the newspaper. This turns them into key people in a network that produces publicity.

Policy of naming: Reporters are instructed to name people whether they were actually seeking publicity or not. Here is an instruction from Deepak, the city editor at *Dainik Jagaran*, who guided a freelancer writing up his report about an annual function at a local school:

> Do not give the content of the speeches at the school function, but mention the names of the children. We should mention those things that really matter to people, and children will be proud to see their names in the newspaper. It will help them progress, and we should always keep that in mind. (City Editor, *Dainik Jagaran*, 27 March 2002)

Besides producing long lists of participants of functions, celebrations or protest marches, we also find articles that enumerate opinions. *Hindustan* has introduced a daily column that consists of a random survey of eight to ten people. They are questioned on topics selected as 'themes of the day', and their opinions are printed along with their picture. The same style is used when covering issues of controversy and the resulting debate and activity in society. Reporters collect random samples of views and reproduce them with little editing.

The policy of news houses to sell a comprehensive picture of local life meets the desire of urban citizens for publicity. The ready availability of news space has encouraged city dwellers in India to engage with news companies and use the newspapers as instruments of power, organs through which they negotiate public and also private concerns. Citizens exploit their connections to news personnel in order to get published. Publication is tied to the desire for social mobility, solving problems, facilitating progress in business, working through the bureaucracy or accumulating fame.

In the following sections I will describe several cases of how personal ambitions drive news-making, and discuss leadership competition, an intra-caste fight and the attitude of journalists towards popular complaints. All cases involve exploiting the newspaper for the production of influence to create an advantage in face-to-face negotiations. They reproduce in a printed mass medium a politics of importance as a pertinent form of public life in India. They also create links between the performative politics and news writing. Analysing the public media interface, I will demonstrate the linkages between readers and writers and their intertwined agency that results in a particular kind of public sphere. My aim is to show the proactive engagement of citizens who create and maintain media networks as channels for public communication.

The *Water* Controversy

In December 1999 Deepa Mehta, a Canadian-based film-maker of Indian origin, and her crew reached the city of Banaras in order to shoot the film *Water*. It was planned as the third film in a trilogy and therefore as a sequel to *Fire* and *Earth*. The story is set in India during the 1930s and portrays the struggle of three young widows against social stigma and a life of deprivation. Even before filming could begin there were protests. Opponents claimed that the film would misrepresent 'Indian culture' and Indian women and would discredit India in the eyes of the world. A struggle developed which for a few weeks involved the film crew, groups of supporters and protesters, as well as the local administration, the national and the state government in extensive negotiations about definitions of culture and the question of authority in the domain of cultural politics (Rao 2005).

Starting from mid-January 2000 till 9 February,[1] all the major newspapers reported extensively in three to five articles every day. Texts[2] covered the initial efforts of the film crew to start filming, the destruction of the set by violent protesters, the introduction of security measures, the ban on shooting imposed by local administrators, who saw law and order as being under threat, and the ensuing negotiations concerning the further fate of the film. There were statements and counter-statements by a wide range of leaders and reports of press conferences and protest marches both in support of and against the film. As a whole, the excessive media coverage communicated the image of a city in turmoil.

This media generated view of massive unrest was in stark contrast to reports of direct observers. Protests in Banaras were highly localised and carried out by a clearly defined group. Here is the reaction of the manager of the hotel I stayed in, who had little sympathy for my research interest in the subject: 'This whole thing is about politics. Anyone can get 200 people together and protest. That comes and goes. It will not have any impact on the city or its name. I personally did not find anything wrong with the story [of *Water*]' (Hotel manager, 7.3.2000).

Members of the film crew were particularly upset about the dust a 'few protesters' kicked up and speculated about who could have had an interest in discrediting the film. They complained that the protests did not represent a common sentiment but the vested interests of a handful of egocentric leaders. Journalists also saw anti-*Water* protests as the publicity stunt of a select few. I had a long debate with Michael, the Banaras correspondent of *Hindustan Times*. Like his colleagues he was cynical about the event: 'They all meet at Papu's tea stall at Assi Ghat [the place where filming was supposed to take place], where they *make* all the news!' (Correspondent, *Hindustan Times*, 8 March 2000). A similar comment could be heard at the *Times of India* head office in Lucknow as a reaction to incoming news from Banaras: 'During the morning meeting at *Times of India* discussion turned towards the *Water* controversy. Maria got angry. She said that she was sick of talking about Deepa Mehta and that all this protest looks so stage-made' (Field notes, 1 February 2000).

Yet newspapers continued to report on the issue, driven by competition for coverage and demands from the state offices. News personnel adopted a style referred to as 'pack-reporting' (Ericson, Baranek and Chan 1989: 181; Pedelty 1995: 31–32; Schlesinger 1978: 163–204; Schudson 2003: 139–40), where all reporters stay and move together, ensuring that they get the same news and share perceptions. Having said that, the question still remains as to why the event became as big as it did and why journalists felt inclined to invest in it for a period of more than two months. In the following pages I will examine the local scene to discuss the reasons for the specific character of press writing. The starting point is the connection local observers make between political ambition and media hype. Exploring this connection, I will discuss the relationship between leadership ambitions, civil society and media that is created and expressed here. I contend that the controversy served as a platform for the display of leadership, the negotiation of public images and the communication of moral issues. It flourished at the conjunction of a particular publishing policy and a culturally moulded style of leadership competition.

It is not surprising that maximum media coverage during the controversy was given to the film crew, the local administration and the major politicians involved in deciding the case.[3] Yet as the conflict dragged on many more people aired their view in the newspapers, even though they did not belong to the key decision-making bodies. While national organisations, politicians, artists and professors can easily attract media attention and have many platforms from which to speak, local leaders are much less likely to hit the headlines. The *Water* conflict gave them a perfect opportunity for pushing their names into the newspapers and promoting their political careers.

The number of local people who managed to disseminate their opinion through the press was impressive. We hear of the *tabla* (Indian drum) master, Padma Shree Krishan Maharaj, and learn about the activists of local sections of Hindu nationalist organs like the RSS,[4] VHP,[5] BJP,[6] *Sanskar Bharti* and the youth wing of the BJP, called *Bharatiya Janta Yuva Morcha*. We are introduced to all kinds of small organisations active in Banaras, such as the Organisation for the Defence of the Culture of Kashi (KSRSS),[7] the Hindu Awareness Platform,[8] the Kashi Scholars' Association[9] and the People's Tradition Platform.[10] Support for Deepa Mehta and protests were expressed by the All-India Democratic Women's Association, *Sahmat*, the All-India Progressive Women's Association, *Nari Ekta* (Women's Unity), SARC and *Parivartan* (Change). We encounter artists' organisations like the Centre for Research and the Application of Folk Art, Film and Theatre, the Indian People's Theatre Association, *Ishta* and Media Talk. There were also comments from the All-India Students' Association and All-India Youth Federation.

The teams of city reporters were highly receptive to the activities of all these organisations and their representatives. They extended themselves and granted publicity to everyone who made an effort to contact the press. The corollary was a large number of long articles listing protest activities and quoting engaged citizens. A text published in *Hindustan* on 31 January 2000 is an excellent example of this approach. The article begins with a summary of the day's events and in its second half reproduces the public statements of various local speakers. The following is a paraphrase of this second part:

> Binda Pandey (ex-BJP Member of Legislative Council and active woman leader) said that the film would insult the culture and women of Kashi and thus will not be made and will never be allowed to be shown anywhere. Sudhakar Pandey (president of the City Progress Committee and a famous writer) elaborated on the history of widow ashrams in the city and complained that Deepa Mehta wanted to make money by inventing an incident that does not reflect the general situation of widows in 1930s Banaras. Five scholars of Sanskrit and the Vedas

threatened to drown themselves in the Ganges if the film was made. Dr Vijay Karn (state assistant secretary of *Sanskar Bharti*) is quoted saying that Mehta will not be given a chance to attack the dignity of the city. Jitendre Kumar (state president of *Sanskar Bharti*) saw the need to protect Indian culture from the attacks of foreign media. Dr Kalmeshvar Upadhyaya (city working president of the VHP) met the district magistrate and demanded that filming should be stopped. The Kashi Scholar's Association (*Kashi Vidwat Parishad*) demanded in a petition to the same authority the right to pass the script before filming be allowed at a sacred place such as the *ghat*[11] of the Hindu poet Tulsidas and the Goddess Ganga. The article then names fifteen men of local eminence who had signed the petition.[12] It then continues to report that Suhel Akhtar (national secretary of the National Hero Abdul Hamid Foundation) commented that a film-maker who made insulting films like *Fire* and *Earth* should not be allowed to continue. A petition to this end has been sent by the VHP and the Shiv Sena to the government and the city administration. (*Hindustan*, 31 January 2000)

The text is remarkable for its assemblage of random voices. In this and similar articles, journalists duplicated as closely as possible what was communicated to them in a flood of press releases, a proliferation of (miniature) press conferences, small protest marches and suicide threats. The English-language press ignored most of these voices, following general policy guidelines to focus on major events and statements by decision-makers. When I visited the Banaras office of the English-language paper *Hindustan Times*, the correspondent pointed at a huge pile of press releases and in a dismissive tone commented to me: 'It is a fashion to give press releases of every small event. I ignore most of them!' (8 March 2000). In contrast, Hindi journalists were pushed to publish on all these grassroots activities. Again a visit to the local office was revealing. *Dainik Jagaran* employs eleven reporters in the Banaras office, all working on different beats. However, during the controversy they all responded directly to the flood of *Water*-related events and announcements, following the imperative to give people a voice. The result is a fantastic redundancy in reporting. The profusion of highly standardised expressions of protest (and approval, or protest against the protest) in articles like the one quoted above add little substance to a debate about the quality of the film. Instead they produce visibility through a practice of naming.

Kaushal Kishor Mishra's *Water*-related activities can illustrate the social rationale that feeds such production of visibility. Mishra was a lecturer of history at the Banaras Hindu University. He entered the debate relatively late, weeks after the local Hindu nationalist organisations had made their opening moves. His interest in the protest was stimulated when he got hold of a copy of the script and suddenly saw the possibility to 'prove' the anti-Hindu bias of the film. From this moment on, he claimed, the attitude of the press changed and now turned against the film:

> In the beginning the journalists were against us. When I showed them the script they joined the fight. Although national newspapers were speaking in favour of Deepa Mehta, defending the freedom of speech, their local correspondents had to write against the film. I pointed out to them that they would lose out on the market if they did not respond to the atmosphere in Kashi [another name for Banaras] and instead write in favour of the film. They would be finished. I made that very clear to them. (K.K. Mishra, 8 March 2000)

Recognising the chance for a successful fight, Mishra founded the Organisation for the Defence of the Culture of Kashi (KSRSS)[13] and elevated it to the status of coordinator and leader of protest activities. An elaborate media strategy was a major part of this effort. The correspondent from the *Times of India* remembered: 'We got daily press releases from the KSRSS. So there was no need to contact Mishra' (8 March 2000). Mishra's efforts bore fruits. During the peak of the controversy the KSRSS and its president were mentioned daily in several newspapers.[14] His opening statement was published on 30 January 2000:

> Dr. K.K. Mishra, the former president of Banaras Hindu University [sic!][15] said that the film 'was a conspiracy of Anglo-Saxon establishment to demean India and brutalise Indian womanhood'. He said that the script suggested that young widows were subjected to prostitution in Varanasi [another name for Banaras] in 1930s. (*Hindustan Times*, 30 January 2000)

This opinion is replicated in different forms over subsequent days. Mishra boosted his media presence by speaking from different platforms, acting not only as ex-chairman of the BHU Teachers' Union, but advertising his position as founder and president of the KSRSS and speaking as a member of the Kashi's Scholars Association.

However, Mishra's prime interest was not the anti-*Water* movement. This was a vehicle for taking a leading role in a 'clash of civilisations'. Quoting Huntington (1998 [1997]), Mishra makes two different predictions regarding the future development of global cultural wars. In one version he identifies a conflict between the major religions of

Christianity, Hinduism and Islam. In a second version he speaks about the need for all to unite against Muslims. This political vision is coupled with personal leadership ambitions. Mishra praised himself for having been able to exploit the *Water* conflict to demonstrate his leadership qualities and expressed the desire to ride on the wave of this controversy to political power. The popularity gained during the *Water* controversy, he hoped, would make him an obvious candidate for the BJP at the next state elections. This would crown many years of political activism.

Charismatic Leadership and the Media

Mishra's appreciation for the importance of newspapers to disseminate a name and create fame is part of an approach that recreates the typical leader-centredness of Indian politics in the news medium. Charismatic leadership is at the heart of the Indian political system, in which electoral success is tied to the ability of individuals to stand out, through a popular image and a network of relations (Brass 1983, 1998; Jaffrelot 2003). Leaders typically build a following by patronising a well defined social group (e.g. caste, ethnicity, class), or set of social groups (e.g. Muslims, Scheduled Castes, Other Backward Classes [OBCs]). They trade patronage and favours for the loyalty of followers, who participate in creating a benevolent public image of him or her. The political field consists of an elaborate hierarchy of leaders, with national politicians depending on local leaders in order to sustain their power through communication with the grassroots. Local leaders are indispensable for the circulation of a positive image, the mobilisation of votes, the initiation of public protests as well as the communication of political ideologies and parliamentary decisions. Supporting those in power, local leaders can negotiate advantages for themselves and their clients, which in turn increases their own fame and may help them to climb further up the ladder of political power (Brass 1965, 1998; Dickey 1993b; Eckert 2003; Mines 1996; Price 1989).

The making of leaders is closely tied to public arenas.[16] Official functions, rituals and festivals host a plethora of occasions for the public display of status, social engagement and eminence by selected individuals. The connection between political power and performative politics reaches across several historical periods (Price 1989). There is ethno-historical evidence for the role of temple rituals for royal authority (Dirks 1987; Eschmann et al. 1978; Stein 1978). In colonial society festivals bore a whole new set of leaders engaged in the independence movement (Freitag 1989; Cashman 1970). Today party leaders also invoke deities, undertake pilgrimages, attend temple festivals or organise devotional events as part of their (electoral) campaigns (Davis 1996; Kaur 2003; Rao 2003; Schnepel 2006). The central element of all these events is the creation of visibility. Organisers, sponsors and special guests crowd the stage to perform rituals, give speeches, be thanked and garlanded. Names of eminent persons are disseminated through announcements, pamphlets and banners. The order of appearance and the role of individuals in the performances communicate something about their status, their networks and position in social and political hierarchies.

While this display of leadership is regularly part of religious celebrations, there are also secular occasions for the ritualised production of status, like Ambedkar's or Gandhi's birthday, laying the foundations of new buildings, anniversaries of public institutions, annual functions at schools or universities, the opening of conferences and fairs. Films and film clubs also offer political opportunities. From the 1960s onwards a set of political leaders in South India have been recruited from the film industry (Agnihotri 1998; Dickey 1993b; Hardgrave and Neidhart 1975). The ascent of actors and actresses to power is tied to the activity of fan clubs widely active in the urban landscape. Fan clubs are founded mostly by lower-class males, who organise around a movie star to celebrate him, watch his films and arrange social activities in his name. The self-declared reason for such activity is the desire to participate in social uplift and thus add to the fame and positive image of the hero. However, engaging in 'altruistic' social activities, young men also create a platform for expressing social distinction. Activists stand out in the crowd and build their own fame and reputation in the shadow of their star. Such fan activity blurs the borders between media reception and political activism, which is fully transcended when fan clubs are recruited as part of the cadre of an actor-turned-politicians (Dickey 1993a, 1993b, 2001).

The intimate connection between image making and political ascent as a pertinent form of Indian political leadership has given mass media a strong role in the design of political careers. What some big stars practise at the top end of the political hierarchy is replicated by 'small people' at the local level since the opening up of the news media to local news. At this level ambitious personalities create an image and spread their fame, not through the embodiment of archetypical characters in fictional genres, but through continuous investment in the making of a heroic, real-life image, disseminated through the press and stabilised through personalised networks.

The connection is very clear in Mishra's case. Motivated by political ambition, he continuously invests in this strong position as 'institutional big man' in a universe of organisations (Mines 1996).[17] His social engagement connects him to the university elite of the region (KSRSS, Banaras Hindu University Teachers' Association), the main religious authorities in Bananas (Kashi Scholars' Association), the cadre organisation of the Hindu Right (RSS) and its parliamentary wing (BJP). Ideologically he acts as a fighter for the preservation of a 'pure' Hindu culture in an emerging 'clash of civilisations'. Mishra regularly speaks as a representative of these organisations in the press and thus continuously keeps his name in the public sphere.[18] In an effort to build up an image as an efficient leader, Mishra joins in a competition that is acted out not only in the public arena but more and more in the media. This was obvious in the case of the *Water* controversy where the hectic media activity was at odds with the rather limited commotion in the public arena. While direct observers dismissed the event as media hype, local leaders purposefully directed their activity more at the press than the observing public, thereby acknowledging the influence of the medium and appropriating it for their own purposes.

The leaders' appreciation for the press is mirrored by reporters' recognition of leader-centred organisations in the political process. It is a well-established finding in journalism studies that in order to select relevant speakers, journalists rely on validating contexts, such as status positions, connectedness, money and power. Newspapers favour authorised speakers, whether from the political field, the police or the courts.[19] In turn, non-authorised speakers need to invest more in order to generate press attention. They are also more likely to be subjected to cross-checking of their information and run a higher risk of their activity being criticised or portrayed in a negative or de-legitimising light (Ericson et al. 1989; Fishman 1980; Goldenberg 1975; Tuchman 1978).

In selecting news for the local pages, journalists depended on classifications produced in the public arena. Leader-centred organisations are then not only a prerequisite for recognition in the public arena but are also exploited as legitimising contexts vis-à-vis reporters. Every speaker during the *Water* conflict was mentioned with his affiliation. Interestingly, there was no discrimination between them with regard to significance or influence. Little did it matter that the Kashi Scholar Organisation had only five members or that the KSRSS was founded only for the sake of anti-*Water* protests. This lack of differentiation in the local news discourse creates a process of *circular authorisation*. Leaders use the press to elevate their organisation to a status of significance, while journalists rely on organisational affiliations for singling out authorised speakers representing groups in civil society.

This dynamic of mutual empowerment is an acknowledged and even anticipated part of public activity. The centrality of the press as a means to increase the effect of social engagement is confirmed by the fact that those who are attempting to win a leading position collect articles in which they are mentioned. This archive of articles is on view to substantiate their status, for example, when meeting with a foreign anthropologist. Ambitious personalities may even start newspapers of their own. K.K. Mishra made just such an attempt. In an interview he mentioned that he had been the editor of a news magazine. Further enquiry exposed the fact that the organ was a self-published magazine, the first and last edition of which appeared in 1986. However, what is at issue here is not the success of Mishra's news magazine, but rather his attempt to become famous via publication. Starting a news magazine was part of his political strategy of authorisation of his role as leader through the written word. Such strategies carry into the newspaper a technique well established in public performance, where visibility is tied to the making of leaders. In the process of pushing for media recognition, ambitious personalities carry leadership competition into the written domain. Offering local personalities a medium for publicity, newspapers contribute towards the perpetuation and remaking of the typical leader-centredness of the Indian political system.

The *Water* controversy is not an isolated event. The entanglement of local reporting with leadership competition is also evidenced in Rajagopal's analysis of the press coverage accompanying the Hindu nationalist movement for the construction of a Ram Temple in Ayodhya. The movement aggressively acted out opposition against the Babri Mosque situated at the site designated to be the birthplace of the God Ram. On the basis of this religious myth, Hindu fundamentalists demanded that the site be handed over to the Hindu community. Force was added when Hindu fanatics attacked and destroyed the mosque illegally in December 1991. In the aftermath Hindu–Muslim riots and pogroms against Muslims spread throughout India. Rajagopal (2001: 151–211) notes that the Hindi press – unlike the English-language press – was actively engaged with the movement, bringing it close to the people and making it intelligible through extensive reporting from the grassroots. He attests reports in Hindi newspapers to have been 'subjective' (p. 167), including extensive quoting of statements from leaders and the printing of direct propaganda. Rajagopal explains this style of reporting with reference to the greater familiarity of Hindi journalists with the symbols of the movement, sympathy for the movement and economic interests of proprietors. My analysis of the production processes provides a further explanation. The open-door-policy of Hindi newspapers promotes the newspaper as a place for leadership competition. City reporters are thankful for ready-made statements, a sentiment that resonates with ambitious personalities who have learned how to formulate press releases successfully.

Exhibiting local leadership in the news media is not an exclusive attribute of reporting dramatic events like the *Water* protests or the Ayodhya campaign. Daily reports highlight a fantastic array of activities and statements of local activists. Any random examples can demonstrate this. Here is a summary of activities in civil society featured in *Hindustan* on just one day (3 April 2002):

- The president of *Airid Bharat* and the citizens of Gomti Nagar protest against trees being cut down in their neighbourhood.
- The Indian Exploited Farmers' Trade Union will launch a protest against the destruction of a ten-year-old wall in Om Puri Colony.
- Members of the State Youth Industry Trade Association met the chief secretary regarding a case lodged against them by the tax department.
- The International Krishna Consciousness Society will perform a *Jagannath Yatra* on 20 April.
- The Citizens Safety Association, Chinhat Division, will meet today to discuss the celebration of Holi and Moharram.
- A celebration of Vaishakhi in *Naka Hindola Gurudwara*.
- A religious programme at *Nimanath Digambar Jain Temple*.
- Ex-MLA und social worker Prof. Khan tells the RSS to clarify how they want to develop trust between Hindus and Muslims.
- Members of the Middle Vocational Teachers' Association met the governor with a demand to regularise service.
- People in Asharfabad protest against the efforts of the head of the Police Station to prevent the burning of Holi effigies.
- The meeting of the People's Movement will be organised at state level on 7 April.
- An advocate from Lucknow sent a letter to the state president stating that he would like to form a democratic government in the state, complaining that power has been always in the hands of a few parties and is thus not a true representation of the people.
- The City Bus Owners' Association complains that the city administration has not kept its promise to build a bus terminal and provide tax benefits for buying and running buses.
- The Awadh Sahakari Bank Investors' Forum has demanded that the prime minister should consider their problems.
- Junior engineers, selected by the Public Service Commission but not integrated into the departments, conduct a sit-in strike (*dharna*).

- The sixth meeting of the Indian People's Society, which helps victims of the Gujarat riots, was held today.
- A meeting of the National Gandhi Oil Merchants' Association took place today.
- The Uttar Pradesh Middle Teachers' Association will enter their candidate for the MLC elections.
- The Hindu-Muslim Unity Association and the Congress Committee organised the Id and Holi celebration today.
- The Mulayam Singh Yadav Youth Brigade organised a Holi celebration today.
- The Lucknow Merchants' Association will conduct a sit-in strike (*dharna*) against objectionable rules of the business tax department.
- The Uttar Pradesh State Electricity Consumers' Board demands that the increase in electricity charges be revoked.

The articles name individuals who are presidents or members of these organisations and have become active as participants in civil society. They use the newspaper in much the same way as Mishra and other minor leaders, as a means of becoming recognised in the city and trying to influence public opinion in favour of their own projects. In the absence of the craze created by *Water*, these articles have less chance of being widely read. They all face the danger of becoming lost in the ocean of local issues published every day. Yet, this does not necessarily make them ineffective. The following case of an intra-caste fight demonstrates that publication as a political tool may have very specific addressees, and is not always necessarily directed at the general public.

Intra-Caste Fight and the Press

The following case illustrates a sequence of media-related activities that were part of an intra-caste fight among Khatiks in Bhopal.[20] Khatiks are a caste of former 'untouchables'. Most Khatiks in Bhopal are illiterate and survive on a very low income, which they generate from their traditional occupation of meat and vegetable selling, or new occupations such as operating a bus service. In Bhopal two organisations represent Khatiks: the city-based community (*panchayat*) and a state-wide caste society (*360 Gautriya Kshatriya Samaj*).[21] However, not all is well between these two organisations. Although membership overlaps, the organisational differentiation marks a rift between two factions in the Bhopal caste community. The local Khatik community is headed by the traditional authorities of *patel* and *barhkul* and has a management committee (*panchayat*), into which all male Khatik adults from Bhopal are born as members. The men meet regularly to discuss and decide caste matters. They organise festivals and caste-based rituals, settle conflicts between caste members and nurture economic ties.

In the 1970s, for the first time in the history of the local Khatik community, there was a small group of young males who had completed a college education. They benefited from privileged access to education that the Indian state grants members of scheduled castes.[22] The educated men entered prestigious positions in state institutions and private companies. On the basis of their acquired status, several members of this new caste elite claimed rights to leadership in the local caste community, against the *patel* and *barhkul*. Most successful in this enterprise was Shiv Narayan Singh Bagware. Today he is the head of a caste society (*360 Gautriya Kshatriya Samaj*) as well as the prestigious caste temple. He founded and designed these institutions as an alternative platform to replace the traditional *panchayat*, while putting him in charge of caste matters. These new organisations broaden the scope of caste politics by involving Khatiks from all over Madhya Pradesh. Bagware's organisation enables him to celebrate his solidarity with other 'forward' members of the Khatik community from outside Bhopal and organise programmes that patronise Khatiks across the state.

However, the new institutions have not – as Bagware hoped – replaced the *panchayat*. The 'traditional' institution owes this survival to the engagement of another faction of successful Khatiks, who gained middle-class status by exploring new business opportunities in the growing city of Bhopal. As prosperous members of the local caste, they also wish to represent the whole group and oppose Bagware as leader. In order to do this they use the traditional structures, their influence over wide sections of the community in Bhopal and the traditional authorities and thus are able to dominate *panchayat* decisions.

The main locus of this competition between Bagware and the 'business faction' is the Kali Temple, the most prestigious caste institution in Bhopal. The temple started as a small wayside shrine in 1968 and is now one of the biggest and most popular temples for Goddess worship in the city. One important moment in the history of the temple, decisive for its future growth, occurred in 1974, when the illegal shrine was turned into an official temple by registering a temple trust (Shri Kali Temple Religious Trust). These were the days of the 'bright young men' who were at the forefront of this activity, foremost among them Bagware, who drew up the trust deed to his own advantage. He became life-president of the temple trust and tied the temple to the simultaneously founded Khatik state society, of which he became lifetime chief advisor. He encouraged all other Khatiks to become members of the society and won over the traditional authorities and other educated members of the caste as trustees for the temple. Yet his position in the two institutions was never as secure as the statutes may suggest.

As the temple became an important religious site, a major centre for Khatik social activities, and an institution with a significant income, it turned into a heavily contested institution. Leading members of the *panchayat* criticised Bagware for his dictatorial management and demanded regular elections for the post of president. Bagware rejected this demand, insisting that the temple needed a visionary leader from the 'forward' faction of the caste. He considered himself the only suitable person in Bhopal. The struggle has gone on for many years now and is still unresolved, with both Bagware and his opponents trying to outdo each other. Negotiations have alternated with acts of force. Ritual boycotts, a mass exodus of members from the state caste society, Bagware's excommunication from the caste and his readmission, official complaints and court cases have been the main elements in this struggle. During the whole process the *panchayat* faction appeared to be in the weaker position, trying ever new techniques to get rid of Bagware as leader, so far without success.

While the conflict goes on, all members of the caste voice their discontent with the situation. Khatiks in Bhopal express a strong sense of belonging to one community and regret the rift. There is also a fear of violence. Khatiks share a stereotypical depiction of their (male) caste members as uncontrollable and quick-tempered. Many Khatiks have witnessed violence between caste members or communal rioting between Khatiks and their Muslim neighbours. Thus, every meeting between the antagonistic factions produces unease and the fear of an eruption of violence. As a result there are very few meetings, and usually only in official settings (temple rituals, marriages) to restrict the antagonists (Rao, 2009a). The struggle is carried on through indirect ways of communication like middle men, letters or the press. Here I shall recount two particularly sensitive moments in the development of caste relations and the way in which the press was used by the antagonistic parties.

In 1996 the disagreement over the management of the temple's finances turned into an open conflict. Bagware, exercising what he saw as his duty as temple president, called upon all Khatiks to account for the financial grants they had received as members of the various working committees of the temple. At the same time, he also started a state-wide call for membership of the trust and fixed a date for new elections. When the members of the informal working committees failed to submit receipts and did not become members of the trust, he dissolved all the temple committees and removed the office-holders from their posts by letter.

Bagware's opponents felt humiliated and were unwilling to accept him as the final arbitrator of temple affairs. They called a meeting of the local *panchayat* (9 June 1996), at which Bagware himself was not present. In his absence the *panchayat* decided that he should be removed from his office as chief advisor of the *360 Gautriya Kshatriya Samaj* and as president of the Shri Kali Temple Religious Trust. However, Bagware did not accept this verdict. A second meeting (26 June 1996) was called which he attended. The atmosphere was hostile, with neither side wanting to lose ground in this struggle for supremacy. The leaders of the *panchayat* insisted that his removal from the offices was final and that he had to submit all the documents and account for the money of the temple and the society. Bagware became angry. According to him the *panchayat* had no right to interfere in matters of the temple trust or the society, since these were separate organisations. Furthermore he maintained that the *panchayat* had no legal status, while his society and the temple trust were officially registered institutions. When he realised that there was no space to re-negotiate his position vis-à-vis the *panchayat*, he left the meeting halfway through, fuming. Afterwards a debate about Bagware ensued, which ended with his excommunication from the local caste. The next day Bagware received a registered letter informing him of his excommunication. The letter listed as reasons for this decision his arrogance and unwillingness to accept the decisions of the *panchayat*. He was asked to submit all papers and accounts of the temple and the society immediately, otherwise a law suit would be launched against him.

When Bagware failed to comply after a week, the *panchayat* became active again. On 2 July a letter was sent to the registrar informing him of Bagware's removal and requesting his office to ignore all instructions he might issue. The same day an article was published in the local edition of the Hindi newspaper *Dainik Bhaskar*, based on the content of a press release sent by the *patel* on behalf of the *panchayat*:

Shiv Narayan Singh has been removed from the presidency of the trust
The 360 Gautriya Kshatriya (Khatik) Samaj has removed Shiv Narayan Singh Bagware from the post of chief advisor to the society and the presidency of the Shri Kali Temple Religious Trust. This information has been given to the press. It has been announced that the above-mentioned decision has been taken due to arbitrary and irregular actions by Shiv Narayan Singh Bagware and his refusal to submit accounts to the society.

Any activity undertaken by Shiv Narayan Singh Bagware in the name of the trust or the society will be considered illegal. (*Dainik Bhaskar*, 2 July 1996, my translation)

Bagware reacted on the same day. He approached the *patel*, communicating his frustration and asking him to issue a refutation. Since the *patel* himself had little stake in this fight and was trying to maintain good contacts with all members of the caste, he agreed to help Bagware (even though Bagware was officially excommunicated!). Thus a second press release, issued by the *patel* informed the press about a new membership drive by the *360 Gautriya Kshatriya Samaj* and the fact that Bagware was still in office.[23] The news item was published in *Dainik Bhaskar* on 4 July 1996. The second half of the article dealt with Bagware's position:

The election procedures in the society are still in progress. Legal steps will be taken against those who created distress. Some anti-social elements published in the press that Shiv Narayan Singh Bagware has been removed from his office as chief advisor to the 360 Gautriya Kshatriya Samaj and as president of the Shri Kali Temple Religious Trust. This is simply an error, untrue, baseless and illegal propaganda. (*Dainik Bhaskar*, 4 July 1996, my translation)

Although in a weaker position, Bagware's opponents did not accept defeat. They ignored the news article, met again and circulated the news of the reorganisation of the trust. On 23 August 1996 this was published in *Dainik Bhaskar* and *Nav Bharat*:

Reorganisation of the Shri Kali Temple Religious Trust
Bhopal. During a meeting of the Shri Kali Temple Religious Trust, the term as president of the founder and permanent president Shiv Narayan Singh Bagware was completed. The meeting unanimously selected the following persons: Ghanshyam Das Rajor as secretary, Chimanlal Bhilware as vice-secretary, Dinesh Chand Kirar as treasurer, Amarchand Ratkar as vice-treasurer, and as legislative body and group of trustees: Pyarelal Bhilware, Ghanshyam Das Bagware, Shobharam Sapere, Gulab Chand Rajore, Dr Shiv Narayan Nekya, Dhaniram Ratnakar, Tulsiram Ghute, Harprasad Kukrele, Chotelal Nekya, Dr Ram Narayan Nekya, Dr Jaurishankar Shejvar, Rajnish Singh Bagware, Harish Singh Bagwar and Govind Singh Bagware. (*Dainik Bhaskar*, 23 August 1996, my translation)

This list of names is interesting since it contains six persons who are not mentioned in the official membership list that had been submitted by Bagware to the registrar, including those identified here as the new secretary and vice-secretary. This is an indication that the *panchayat* (or the subgroup that was active here) indeed tried to reorganise the trust. However, the effort appears to have been half-hearted, given that the press information does not identify a new president. Furthermore, Bagware's three sons are still mentioned as members of the trust. This appears inconsistent given that they continued to live with their father – who had been officially excommunicated – and should thus also be marginalised.

However, in view of the unequal constellation of power, this inconsistency is hardly surprising. It also shows the limits of using the press as an instrument of change. The hostile faction did not manage to reorganise the trust, even though this change was announced in the newspaper. The press does not have the power to make or unmake trusts. It can only announce the decision of a legitimate body, which the opposing faction was not, its members could not be formally registered nor make deletions from the official list of trustees. However, Bagware's opponents were not so naïve as to believe that publication alone would solve their problems. Rather, they calculated the possible effects of publicity, once they had exhausted all internal means of conflict management.

The first step had been to talk to Bagware, then to remove him from all his posts, and finally to excommunicate him. None of these measures were successful. Bagware remained in office and also led all important caste rituals in the Kali Temple, even while he was excommunicated (Rao 2005). This shows that the excommunication had little effect on Bagware, who did not depend on local caste support. As a manager at the State Bank of India and an active member of various organisations, Bagware is financially independent and also respected outside his caste. His engagement for the state-wide unification of Khatiks has won him many friends among powerful Khatiks outside Bhopal, who supported him by openly opposing the decision of the local *panchayat* to ban Bagware. In view of this situation, his opponents needed to re-think their strategy. They wanted to hurt Bagware by attacking his reputation, adding pressure by spreading the false news of his defeat, and hoping that a public announcement would force him to capitulate.[24]

Failing in their strategy, they then reverted to force. Later during 1996 a few men from the caste looted the donation boxes in the Kali Temple and replaced the locks in order to bring the temple income under their control. Bagware responded by reporting this as a criminal offence and replaced the locks again. At this point communication between the two factions came to a standstill. Things only started to move again when leading Khatiks formerly from Bhopal but now living outside the city stepped in as arbitrators. They demanded Bagware's re-admission, which the *panchayat* could hardly refuse. Secretly many were relieved that relations were normalised, because they had realised that banning Bagware had cut them off from an important source of patronage. However, peace did not last long. The conflict now moved to the courts, where allegations were raised against Bagware. Yet, again Bagware came out victorious.

This example of a power struggle within the Khatik caste shows how people use publishing in a strategic way to negotiate power relations. The articles had little information value to people who were not already familiar with the internal conditions of the Khatik caste. In fact, they were misleading, even false, if one took their content at face value. Only a contextualised reading can bring to light the social meaning of these texts. They did not announce a completed organisational change but were intended to hurt the man in office and destabilise an existing order.

The context for publishing these news texts was, like in the *Water* controversy, leadership competition, however, acted out at a different level of the social hierarchy. None of the actors wanted to make it straight into state politics. They were rather interested in directing the caste group and gaining access to the resources of the most important caste institution. Yet, the enterprise was no less ambitious and followed directly from the logic of a politics of patronage. Caste in India is not only a fundamental category of belonging but also a highly politicised entity (Doron and Rao 2009). The struggle of the 'downtrodden' for social justice in postcolonial India has made caste – especially scheduled castes, but also Brahmanism as a counter-force – an efficient instrument for political mobilisation and an important category in battles for votes (Belz 2005; Omvedt 2006; Shah 2001). This is particularly true for Uttar Pradesh, where garnering support through cast alliances is, together with Hindu nationalist ideologies, the most important feature of state politics (Jaffrelot 2003; Narayan 2006). In this context dominance over a local caste group is highly meaningful. A local caste leader acts as middle man between citizens and the political elite. Command over a particular section of the population turns middle-range leaders into indispensable parts of the political hierarchy and provides them with the resources for trading favours for loyalty.

Aspiring to leadership and a position as influential 'big men', ambitious Khatiks mobilised all possible resources to expand their network of patronage. Unable to compete in the public arena, individuals of the *panchayat* faction manipulated press coverage as a means to authenticate their claims. Like Mishra, Bagware's opponents approached the press because they *did not* have a legal position in a significant institution, which, however, they desired. As an organ with substantial cultural capital, the press was to remedy the situation. A public proclamation, activists hoped, would provide them with sufficient clout to turn a claim into a social reality.

Before debating further the cultural imaginary that empowers the press and through it people who seek its attention, I will move further down the social hierarchy and analyse how the concerns of resource-poor people enter the news discourse. Working procedures of editorial teams not only open the newspaper for the voices of manipulative leaders but also offer the news pages to everybody, particularly people who lack connections. News is an instrument for raising citizens' issues with authorities. However the involvement of newspapers in the business of mediation is not always transparent or democratic, but is entangled with the interests of journalists, editors and proprietors and their way of fulfilling the role of broker.

Journalists as Brokers

Journalists do not only promote 'big men' and 'big women', but also occupy a position as brokers themselves. The press as institution empowers citizens by putting its weight behind their demands and statements. This, I have shown, pushes leadership competition into the newspaper. However, the role of journalists as brokers gains more prominence when considering the engagement of the press with resource-poor people. Reporters become proactive in denouncing administrative inefficiency, political corruption and the unavailability of resources. Such advocacy has two platforms. It is realised on a daily basis through communication in extensive information networks and is advertised during strategic events that popularise the image of newspapers as patrons of the common man. A perfect demonstration of the latter is the programme *At Your Doorstep*. The following analysis of it will serve as an entry to a more general debate about the relation between journalists and resource seeking people.

At your Doorstep is a programme organised twice a year as a joint venture of *Hindustan* and *Hindustan Times*. For one day it puts the infrastructure of a selected neighbourhood in Lucknow on the spot. On a Sunday a camp is set up in an area needy of attention. Representatives of the local administration and selected politicians are invited to listen, together with the press, to the grievances of people and suggesting solutions. Days before, the event is announced in the newspapers and people are invited to come and voice their demands. During the day, reporters take down the stories and put pressure on the authorities to solve them. Newspapers then publish the complaints and follow them up during the weeks to come.

During my field research I observed one such programme on 30 January 2000. A tent was pitched at Aliganj, a neighbourhood in old Lucknow. Inside were separate tables for officers from the municipal corporation, the water, electricity and telephone departments. Punctually by 9 A.M. all officers were present waiting for customers. Because it was still empty then, I had a chance to ask each of them why they attended the programme, instead of spending the day with their families. I received a standard reply: no one wanted to risk negative publicity, and thus all bowed to the pressure of the press. By 10 A.M. the tent was filled with petitioners, lining up in front of each table, waiting to raise their complaints. There was a bit of a stir around noon, when the minister for urban affairs showed up. He was immediately surrounded by residents and reporters, who yelled their complaints at him, also protesting about the apathy of his department. The minister was not very sympathetic towards the requests and responded that people did not pay their house taxes, that they were encroaching illegally on public land, that they did not maintain the facilities provided by the state, and he dictated an order to his assistant that no work should be undertaken in areas were there was illegal building activity.

The articles next day were sympathetic toward the concerns of local people, but different lines were taken in the English- and Hindi-language press respectively. *Hindustan* listed the complaints in detailed articles, filling a complete page:

Municipal Corporation

Satylok Colony, Sitapur – they need sewage and roads in the colony.

Basant Bihar Welfare Association, Aliganj Sector B – complaint of sewage, broken street lights and that complaint books should be provided in the departments of the municipal corporation.

Priya Darshan Colony – since the garbage and waste (*kuda*) has not been removed from the colony, the rickshaw drivers have begun to call the colony '*kuda wala colony*' (colony of waste).

Sector K – lack of speed breakers on the main road is causing accidents.

[...]

Telephone
The section starts with a summary of frequent complaints: the telephone is often dead, the dial tone cannot be heard, and the telephone connection is cut as one is talking on it, telephone bills are higher than actual use, the receiver has been out of order for a long time, and even though money was paid months ago, no telephone has been installed as yet.

Sector J and sector C – as a rule the telephone goes dead while one is speaking and then one has to contact the telephone department. Also the voice quality on the phone is very bad.

Sector E and sector H – the telephone suddenly gets cut when using it and there is a tick-tick sound which can be heard in the phone and the phone also gives electrical shocks.

The Divisional Wing of the Ministry of Energy situated in sector H – calls on telephone number 328825 cannot be transferred within the office internally.

Kendrachal Colony, sector K – receiver spoilt.

Sector D – three buttons on the receiver cannot be pressed and outgoing calls have been cut. Money for phone paid in August 1999 and phone still not installed.

[…]

Water
Again the article begins with a summary of typical complaints. Inhabitants have to depend on hand pumps, because the facilities for water provided by the authorities are insufficient. There are problems with sewage which remain unsolved because of infighting between the water department and the Lucknow Development Authority. Water is only available up to the first floor due to lack of pressure.

Aliganj Sector D – both times when water is made available, additional electrical motors are needed to pump the water.

Priyadarshini Colony in Sitapur Road – a water pipe has been laid but there is no water supply. Drinking water problems are very acute. Roads are also very bad here.

Aliganj Sector D – manholes missing in front of several houses and several manholes have not been cleaned, which results in them overflowing during rain.

[…] (*Hindustan*, 31 January 2000)

Hindustan Times did not give the same preference to local voices. They had two equally long articles. The first highlighted the negative attitude of the urban development minister, Lalji Tandon. The second article summarises complaints about water and drainage problems as well as the bad quality of the city bus services. Unlike in the Hindi newspaper, its English-language sister emphasised the power of the press to solve these problems. Inserted in the middle of the article on urban problems was a box listing all the decisions that were taken *ad hoc* at the camp:

On-the-spot sanctions by the LDA V-C
The LDA [Lucknow Development Authority] Vice-Chairman, Mr Diwarkar Triparthik, who was mobbed by scores of troubled Aliganj residents, initiated measures at the camp and approved several development works to alleviate their problems. The on-the-spot decisions and works sanctioned by him included:
- Construction of drains and roads in Sector-A, Sitapur Road (phase II).
- Construction of a public toilet near the commercial complex in Sect H.
- Development work of the park in Sector-N-2 sanctioned.
- Development and repair of boundary wall of the park in Sector H approved.
- Purania-Sector-Q-Danayia Road to be widened.
- Ravindra Garden Colony to be regularised (the compounding proposal submitted by its residents had earlier been rejected by the LDA).
- Zonal Road in Sector-F to be repaired.
- All clogged drains and choked sewers to be cleaned up by February 3.
(*Hindustan Times*, 31 January 2000)

The message that emerges from these articles is that the city is in a bad condition due to the state's neglect. In this situation the newspaper extends a helping hand to harassed readers. However, the event is not only a selfless commitment to social work, but also a publicity stunt. It is a promotional event intended to boost circulation. The feel good factor is exploited for drawing attention and distributing free copies of the newspapers.

Advertising through brokerage as well as advertising of brokerage is a feature in all newspapers. An interesting example from the *Times of India*, Hyderabad, involved potholes. The newspaper embarrassed urban development authorities by printing on the front page a picture of a particularly obstructive pothole in one of the main roads. The picture appeared every day until the hole was closed. Then *Times of India* published the picture of another pothole and later another. The programme continued for a whole month. The *Times of India*, Lucknow, showed its engagement with middle-class readers by organising a product show for cars. They had invited not only different companies selling cars and motorcycles, but also made sure banks were represented, who offered loans for the purchase of these vehicles (see also Yadava 1991: 135–36 on 'Development Journalism').

In the daily business of publishing, such events are exceptions. Yet, they are important moments for the promotion of a particular image of the newspaper as being close to the people. However, there is a clear class division. English-language newspapers are highly selective in taking up issues, while Hindi newspapers are ready to print them all and their readers will actively participate. Sharing the press room with Hindi reporters one can hear them answer an endless flow of incoming messages about water shortage, electricity cuts, bad roads, the unwillingness of politicians to meet with citizens and the arrogance of the bureaucracy. Daily these items are taken up for coverage. Above I quoted from the local coverage of *Hindustan* on 3 March 2002, illustrating the number of people searching publicity. Scanning through their concerns one is confronted with numerous complaints of state institutions. On that single day the paper announced that in Gomti Nagar people feared for their trees, that in Om Puri protesters worried about the fate of an old wall, that two organisations felt mistreated by the tax department, that teachers, bus drivers and young civil servants perceived irregularities in their employment status, that the police carried out high-handed action and that there were unacceptable hikes in electricity rates.

Communication between citizens and the press is institutionalised through a network of stringers. *Hindustan* and *Dainik Jagaran* compete with each other over the number of freelancers they engage. The number fluctuates between thirty and fifty. Stringers are not employees in any formal sense and are sometimes not even paid at all. They follow another occupation, often as shop-keepers or business persons and in this function they establish contacts that keep them informed about incidents and problems in the area they are assigned to. Freelancers advertise their position and thus ensure that stories will come to them. The reward for their work is status as a 'journalist'. Stringers can exploit their press connection to manipulate politicians and administrators for their own sake or that of their clients. Consider the following statement by Anwar, a businessman who buys and sells vehicles. He acquired a role as informant for *Dainik Jagaran* due to his membership in the Muslim community. His job is to report regularly about the social and religious activity of various Muslim organisations. He receives no pay, but draws advantage from his press connections: 'Journalism is a side business for me. I use it as a platform for my business interests, for example, getting licenses issued. For normal citizens it is very difficult to meet officials. As a journalist there is more scope for being heard and succeeding.'

Almost like a confirmation of this statement, I find the letters 'press' printed on the front of his scooter, a word that opens doors 'magically'. I myself experienced this. Going around with reporters, I learned fast that the word 'press' allows entry into many areas that are closed to the common public. I soon stopped explaining that I was a foreign anthropologist doing fieldwork on the press in Lucknow in order to be admitted to restricted areas. Certainly my self-identification as an anthropologist, with a business card from a western university and an academic title, opened most doors for me, but it did so only after explanations. In contrast, the statement, 'I am currently a guest of the *Times of India*, collaborating with them and writing for them', which was no less true, was like a magic spell which rarely led to further questioning and which opened the door to interviews, discussions and favours (see also Rajagopal 2001: 179; Ståhlberg 2002: 125–29).

Full-time journalists are no less skilled in utilising their position for private gain. It is almost a standard routine to persuade politicians to allocate state-owned flats to journalists. Reporters also lobby for seats in overfilled trains, to be granted state sponsorship for elective surgeries, to obtain admission to schools for their children or get preferred treatment in the allocation of loans (Ståhlberg 2002: 125–29). Journalists are not always allowed to follow their own agenda. Junior reporters must abide by the priorities of their bosses. At *Dainik Jagaran* freelancers often expressed their frustration at being used for all kinds of errands. I did not have to search long for evidence. Once I accompanied a freelancer whose assignment was to make train reservations for his bosses. On another occasion I went along to negotiate a financial arrangement for a leading figure in the company.

> Today I went along with Guatam. He had been working with *Dainik Jagaran* as a freelancer for four years. He complained that he had to do all the running around for his bosses. 'Even if you yourself have no interest in taking advantage of your position as a journalist, you are made to do it for your bosses.' And indeed we spent the whole day at the Magistrates on behalf of senior staff members (Field notes).[25]

Junior reporters described as one of the differences between *Dainik Jagaran* and *Hindustan* the way in which informal negotiations were perceived. At *Hindustan* reporters were allowed to do their own 'deals' much earlier in their career, while at *Dainik Jagaran* junior members had to follow strictly the priority of the management.

However, more interesting than the well-known fact that status opens up avenues for manipulating services, is the question of whether resource-poor people actually benefit from getting their grievances published. Do the large numbers of articles that denounce the faults in the system every day have an actual effect? Are newspapers and reporters efficient brokers or are issues forgotten as soon as they are exposed? I asked journalists their opinions on this. Most of them remained uncommitted. They hoped that their work would have a positive effect, but they could not allow themselves to worry about it. Their remit was to write, tell and denounce, no matter how often, hoping that someone would take note and act (compare also Peterson 1996: 332–33).

> People feel happy if someone listens to their problems. They have already given up the hope that anyone will really help them, so even this much, publishing their grievances, is a lot for them. These people don't say: 'The leader does not listen'; they say: 'The leader is not available to us! He does not see us!' We believe that we have to *hammer it in*, in order to be effective. Even if only one out of ten cases gets solved we are happy. (City Editor, *Dainik Jagaran*, 9 March 2002)

My observations during the daily work routine also tell another story. Journalists distinguish or are instructed to distinguish between cases which are simply reported and those in which they or the company actually intervene. Consider the following observation from a morning meeting at *Dainik Jagaran*:

> During the morning meeting Deepak the city editor spoke of complaints concerning sewage problems in one of the neighbourhoods in Lucknow. He selected Sonal for the task of investigating the situation. Just before leaving, Sonal was reminded: 'We are journalists and do journalists' work! This means ask a few questions and that is that. Do not go too deep, don't get involved!' Immediately after he turned to Mina. She was instructed to go to the court and fix a hearing for a person who had requested help. 'Fix the date a few days ahead', she was told 'otherwise you will not know anything about the case when it is heard.' (Field notes, 8 March 2002)

The primary message here is that city reporters are supposed to listen to people, to take their complaints seriously and consider them news. At the same time they must be detached. Underlying this is the message: 'Get involved only when we tell you!' While Sonal is directed to look on from a distance and make an impassive report, Mina is instructed to actually solve a problem, while making sure she gets the story.

Journalists as brokers are part of the network of patronage that extends into all parts of Indian society. Publication of grievances may or may not solve a problem, but direct intervention or recurrent coverage can be very effective. Journalists are well aware of their powers and their choice of profession is often linked to the desire for an elevated position (this is particularly true for vernacular reporters who are usually underpaid and depend directly on income from their brokerage). As privileged observers, journalists participate in the world of the rich and powerful and thus become influential middle men, able to build a following among those who wish to participate in the participation.

Being a journalist means having a position in a network of patronage. As stated at the very beginning of the book, the self-description 'journalist' does not always signify a fully employed professional. If it appears opportune, anyone who has ever written in a newspaper – if only a letter to the editor – may call himself/herself a 'journalist'. There is no absolute distinction, just gradual differentiation that constitutes a continuum. At one end there are the fully employed journalists who work for prestigious newspapers with a large circulation. Then there are stringers and the representatives of small, local newspapers. There are also the editors-cum-publishers-cum-reporters of self-produced newspapers (sometimes of not more than 100 or 1,000 copies), informants, occasional writers, former journalists with good connections and regular writers of letters to the editor. Such people are found throughout the city and support networks that reach out to many other (non-writing) citizens. Hindi newspapers nurture such press–public connections. The expansive local teams described in chapter two create hierarchies through which residents are reconnected to the media. They open channels for communication through which urban concerns reach the newspaper. At the same time these networks constitute an interactive sphere through which the character of a mediated public sphere is created that is highly relevant for the shaping of power struggles.

The print medium is used to empower citizens. I have described two different dimension of this dynamic. Mishra and Bagware rely on established social and political institutions as well as leader-centred organisations to build and maintain their pre-eminence. Access to the media is just one among a number of factors that boosts their importance. In turn, the power of journalists is a direct result of their ability to produce or refuse publicity. Employment with a news company is the journalists' main asset when exercising patronage. Their command over the publication process makes them nodal points in a network of influence that serves as an alternative to the political system of patronage and is used by citizens to manipulate relations.

The observation that journalists are empowered through their professional activity is not new. It has been explored systematically in studies about negotiations between journalists and politicians (Hasty 2005a and b; Manning 2001; Sigal 1973). The significance here is that my study breaks with the notion of an elite space, shared by politicians, administrators and journalists only. I argue that the newspaper boom in India has extended media-centred networks for empowerment beyond an elite circle. The making of local newspapers and local news pages opens up new avenues for communication up and down the social hierarchy. This alternative network emerges as a result of the social significance of news. It is tied to the notion of the press as a major social institution that controls those in power. The following section will explore these imaginaries and their impact on social relations.

The Performative Power of News

Empowerment through publication in newspapers is tied to a communicative processes that transforms information into news. Media publicity produces the authoritative speakers in society and turns their statements into the 'facts' of life. It is in this sense that the media possesses performative power. This formulation draws on Austin's famous theory of the performativity of speech acts. In *How to Do Things with Words* (1990 [1962]), he argues that speech not only reflects the world, but some speech acts are constitutive in nature, bringing about what they proclaim. This happens when a judge says 'I sentence you' or a registrar declares a couple married before the law. The meaning of such speech acts cannot be assessed with reference to the dichotomy true / false. Speech acts can only be successful or unsuccessful.

Bourdieu (1990) has adopted this linguistic argument for the analysis of social situations. He investigates the social conditions which make speech acts, or other symbolic acts that possess performative power, successful. He argues that the structure of a social field defines positions which enable office-bearers to complete performative acts successfully. In order to be successful a performative act needs to be part of a legitimate context and performed by a legitimated person.

> The authorised speaker [of a group] can exert an influence on other actors through words and via their participation in the events and outcomes, because there is a concentration of symbolic capital in their words, which in turn has been absorbed and accumulated by the group thus lending the speaker authority and making them their representative. (Bourdieu 1990: 75, my translation)

In this formulation Bourdieu draws attention to the symbolic capital accumulated in recognised positions, which empowers speakers to successfully complete a performative act. This power is mediated through the existence of a socially shared and generally accepted social 'knowledge' of positions and their powers. The weakness in this formulation is that it does not account for the possibility that subversive acts can be successful even though they do not rely on authorised contexts. Judith Butler (1997) voices this critique and proposes a more dynamic view, asserting that there is a particular subversive potential in those performative acts that are successful although or because they break with established rules. A case in point is the black American fighter for civil rights, Rosa Parks, who in the 1960s provoked other commuters by sitting in the front of the bus, where seats were reserved only for white passengers. This act of civil disobedience attacked rules of racial discrimination at work in American society and became part of a larger struggle that ultimately led to the abandonment and even prohibition of racial discrimination. In this sense Parks's action was successful, although it was not performed by a legitimate person in a legitimated context.[26]

There is common ground in Bourdieu's and Butler's argument. Both show that strategies of authorisation are necessary to make performative acts effective. Bourdieu emphasises collaboration generated in structured universes, in which shared notions of reality verify mechanisms of power. Butler extends the argument by drawing attention to the uncertainties inherent in performative acts. As quotations they may re-enact previously successful performative acts, or they may provoke unexpected results and the formation of new authorising contexts and thus invite shifts in meaning and structure.

This argument about the performative power of symbolic acts is directly relevant for news-making. It accounts for the force that drives the social life of news. The press is a social institution of significance. Its envisaged role is tied to the project of enlightenment. Habermas' historical study of the bourgeoisie public sphere in seventeenth- and eighteenth-century Europe illustrates this beautifully. While his articulation of the historical condition has been thoroughly deconstructed,[27] his formulation captures a widely shared notion of the press that continues to inform an ethic of journalism. The press is believed to be an institution located in civil society apt to criticise and control political power through rational argument. Habermas idealises the bourgeoisie public sphere as an arena of public reasoning that is virtually free of vested interests. It is a shell separated from the world of power in which rational debate leads to an unmasking of political power, a forum purely for the exchange of views (*Meinungspflege*).

This liberal ideal of the press as a forum for interest-free deliberations that control state power is a normative standard in contemporary democracies. It is inscribed in the institutional set-up of modern states, is prominent in the educational material for new media elites, and is part of a standard rhetoric in the public sphere itself (e.g. Gripsrund 1999; Johnson 2006). The argument is also frequently rehearsed in popular publications about the Indian press (Kohli-Khandekar 2006 [2003]; Parathasarathy 1989; Raghavan 1994; Sahay 2006). A typical example is in the introduction to the book *Muddled Press* by Padhy (1994), a longstanding academic observer of the press in India. Here I quote only the first and last sentence of the introduction:

> Shaping the opinion of the public and directing their attention to matters it thought fit; exerting an influence on them too powerful to be disregarded; assisting them in understanding their problems; enabling the electorate to hold the government responsible; protecting the people against corruption, incompetence and despotism; projecting a representative picture of the constituent groups; clarifying the goals and values of the society; identifying itself with the public interest and serving as a forum for the exchange of comment and criticism, the Press provides the variety, quantity and quality of information and discussion which the country needs. [...]

> A participant in the democratic governmental process, a bulwark of democracy, a censor and critic of government, a public protector and indispensable institution of a free people, an adviser to them, the Press keeps a close watch on government, that ever-dangerous foe of freedom, and sounds the alarm whenever the citizens' right are infringed. Scathing criticism and constant surveillance of actions of the authorities by an alert and intelligent Press, established as the cornerstone of the democratic society, is essential to the successful functioning of a government. (Padhy1994: 1, 3–4)

In the moral economy of the Indian press this ideal of journalism as scrutinising state powers is married to another imperative: that the press should act as an educational institution pulling the 'uneducated masses' into the enlightenment project. Journalists are members of the progressive elite responsible for shaping a nation in the making. Together with politics, the press is said to possess the power to transform Indian society by promoting the political projects of unification, modernisation and education. As an instrument for social transformation, the press can also be used in negative ways, to endorse narrow ethnic identities, trigger violence between communities, or create social unrest. Following this logic, the engineers of independent India called for a responsible press. The press should circulate such information, or information in such a way that it promotes positive change (Peterson 1996: 22–69).

While in theory these two positions of the press as controlling and simultaneously supporting the state may be in conflict, in practice together they circumscribe the ideals that inform journalists' self-perception. Press people describe their role as educators of society and as guardians of citizens' rights (Ståhlberg 2002).[28] This is not to say that press people are not aware of what appear to be faults in the system: corruption, bias, pressures, self-interest, as well as, more generally, the constructed nature of news. Yet in spite of, and in opposition to, the practice of muddling through, most journalists uphold the ideal that the press should circulate objective information about major social concerns.

Of course, this argument can be and is turned around. If the press circulates significant information for popular consumption, then an alternative conclusion is that everyone and everything mentioned in the newspaper is important. In this sense the newspaper is a medium for the intensification of a message. The issue here is not only about circulation, but about the authority the newspaper lends to a speaker or actor. Being quoted in a newspaper increases visibility and importance, simply because the statement or topic is being heralded through journalistic processes of selection (see also, Ericson, Baranek, Chan 1989: 3–5). It is in this sense that the written word in the newspaper produces social relevance. The press can make people into opinion leaders simply by quoting them often enough and can also turn the city of Banaras into a place of unrest, even if there are only 200 people protesting. This power that transforms ordinary citizens into relevant actors is a result of the symbolic capital (Bourdieu) accumulated by the press.

Becoming a journalist and being cited in a newspaper are two ways of drawing upon the authority of the press as a collective agent. A journalist is recognised as a powerful speaker. Similarly, urban citizens use newspapers to become relevant speakers. The urgency with which individuals engage journalists and try to convince them to mention their names or investigate their cases is connected to the enormous power of the written word, which makes the issue real by turning it into a social fact and a common truth.[29] While the newspaper acts as an authorising institution in Bourdieu's sense, people also exploit it for subversive projects. They use the institution to attack the working of other institutions, for the sake of personal gains or as part of striving towards a transformation of the system. A return to the case studies can demonstrate the point.

Mishra, together with a number of other political activists from the Hindu Right, fuelled a controversy and made sure the press got to know of it. Once the press was interested, it became almost irrelevant whether the public in Banaras actually participated in the protest and supported their particular vision for an 'Indian society' through mass activity. As long as journalists were ready to take the concerns seriously and give credence to the message, treating it as front-page news, it could be seen as an important issue and would certainly impress political circles. While people in Banaras made contradictory estimates of the level of support for the anti-*Water* protests, events seemed to have intensified when seen from Lucknow. Through the lens of news reporting, it appeared that the whole city of Banaras was in arms. During a press conference the chief minister picked up this clue when he stated that he would leave things in the 'hands of the people of Banaras' (press conference on 7 February 2002, see also the press coverage on 8 February 2002), meaning that he would not allow shooting as long as protests continued. He accepted the media 'truth' that law and order was in danger in Banaras, and through his interpretation of press reports conflated it with *the* voice of the people.

The press in turn focused on Banaras because protests were a confirmation of a stereotypical image of the city as a traditional religious site with a mostly conservative population, where people are still living according to 'ancient' religious laws. Following this logic, anti-*Water* protest expressed sentiments typical of what would be expected from a local resident. The local administration contributed to this narrative by repeatedly emphasising the threat to law and order, playing on the notion that Banaras was a stronghold of radical Hinduism and thus a place prone to religious violence.[30] Eruption of Hindu nationalist unrest in Banaras was news because it fuelled the fear of the disruptive forces of Hindu nationalism or enshrined the hope for a true transformation of the Indian nation. Scale seemed of secondary importance. Protests were relevant because they contributed to hotly debated positions in the process of Hinduising India.

This was the key for Mishra who jumped on this bandwagon and skilfully positioned himself within these powerful meta-narratives, calling his struggle a contribution to the unfolding 'clash of civilisations'. For him, mass circulation was a major issue. It mediated a national debate in which Mishra, an otherwise insignificant figure in some local place, became a major speaker who reached and was understood by many people because he could be fitted into an established category within the political landscape as belonging to the Hindu nationalist movement.[31]

Mishra thus became important because the press circulated and authorised his voice. The press made him out to be important because he stood at the forefront of a movement that proved in a powerful performance that Hindu nationalism is a force to be reckoned with. For the moment the press made a new leader – as a copy of so many other leaders – and confirmed the image of Banaras as a stronghold of the Hindu nationalist movement. It can be believed; it had to be believed, because as an authorised speaker, the press creates the very reality it proclaims. Through extensive coverage, mostly on the first page, all newspapers produced – for at least two months – daily proof that this issue was of major importance. The hype was an effect of a mutual process of authorisation, through the press and organisations respectively. Ambitious leaders and journalists worked in tandem, on the basis of shared assumptions about the nature of Indian society, to re-create this reality, from which each side drew its own advantages.

The issue is quite different in the case of the intra-caste fight in Bhopal. Here we find only three small articles somewhere on the local pages, which would have escaped most people's attention and produced little resonance in the urban community. The articles were directed at and could be understood only by a small group of insiders. Yet going public was a strategy. In a situation in which members of the *panchayat* were unable to push through their claims internally, they approached the press to add power to their demands. They used the newspaper as an intermediate agent, hoping that the declaration of change in an official medium would bring about social movement leading to the desired transformation.

Although the rivals have not succeeded so far, their action was not in vain. Cuttings of the articles are circulated among those who are unfamiliar with intra-caste relations to 'prove' membership and positions. As a curious anthropologist I was among those who triggered the production of such 'proof'. My inquiries about the structures of the caste prompted several individuals to tell their story and present their evidence. After long months of fieldwork, when I had managed to work through several layers of narrations, letters, press releases and articles, I discovered the many contradictory readings of the history of the Kali Temple and realised that there was no one 'true' version, but several perspectives reflecting the political rivalries in the Khatik caste.[32]

Newspaper cuttings as a source can be expected to gain credibility with time, considering that at some point they turn into historical documents.[33] Thus, when the conflict is retold years later, each side can 'prove' its own version of the truth through article collections. When the details have been forgotten or cannot be recovered from the depths of history, something that was not successful in 1996 may suddenly become real. The rivals may finally become what they never were, managers of the temple, even if only as an imaginary memory building on a written 'fact'.

The power of journalists to mark issues as important and authenticate them serves them well and makes them brokers. Journalists use this power in official, publishable ways by rushing to the service of the common man. A hierarchically organised network of journalists is spread over the city. This news network is quite distinct from the one described by Tuchman (1978). It is not a beat system responsible for structuring news around a predictable number of institutions. The news network I am describing makes channels available for communication through responsive mediators who turn the newspaper into an organ that absorbs an astonishing plurality of urban stories. The agents of this news network are not neutral individuals. They personify different shades of grey on a scale from journalist as heroic helper of the resource poor to master of corruption and self-serving practices. Public service and private advantage amalgamate when journalists use their power over news to systematically build up a position in a system of patronage.

The three examples demonstrate how people create, maintain and activate channels for communication through the press. These analyses shed new light on the intricate relationship between common people, state institutions and the vernacular press in India. Akhil Gupta (1995) has explored this relation from the perspective of reception. His enquiry into corruption in rural India demonstrates the role of local newspapers in exposing and influencing the relations between citizens and the state. He recounts the countless details published in local pages about concrete conflicts between citizens and state institutions and attests that vernacular newspapers provide valuable moral tales about corruption as well as helpful descriptions of the working of the many institutions that can make life difficult for people. Local newspapers service the people by supporting their claim to a right of service and their outrage at the many ways in which state institutions exploit and harass citizens.

Analysing what remains invisible during reception, I have produced evidence of a split agency. Gupta emphasises the activity of media personnel who use rhetorical strategies 'to galvanise into action citizens who expect state institutions to be accountable to them' (Gupta 1995: 388). I show that the agency of reporters is interlinked with the activities of citizens, who complain, report, inform, propagate and write. Thus, while reporters may create subjects, urban residents also create themselves as subjects by using the press as a medium for expression. Local citizens prompt the press to recursively bring to public attention their difficulties, hopes, ambitions and ideologies. In this process the news discourse absorbs a cultural technique of visibility well established in public performances. Popular ways of creating a public for personal concerns by appealing to news media carries performative politics into newspapers, which has a formative impact on the public created by local media. In the following section I will spell out the idea of the public as network and critique the text-centrism of most studies on media publics.

Connectivity in the Public Sphere

In this chapter I elaborated on the fact that the attractiveness of the news medium is only partly a corollary of its wide circulation. More importantly, it functions as an authorising institution. Its power emerges from the notion of the newspaper as a medium for rational debate and controlling state powers. As such it is part of an emancipatory project tied to modernity. Public performances, in contrast, follow a distinct cultural model. They are not idealised as providing 'objective' information or critical evaluation. They are the deeds of politics. They introduce and create powerful individuals and highlight their position within political hierarchies, serve party mobilisations and express the demands of those who lack privileged positions in society.

What in an ideal imaginary and moral economy may appear to be distinct is entangled in practice. News writing, as I have shown, can become a function of performative politics. Leaders at times substitute activity in the public arena with the production of news texts (press releases that become news texts). Where performative politics is retained, it is proliferated through mass media. Able organisers ensure that their performances generate media coverage and may even directly influence it by providing press releases. What serves leaders also galvanises citizens who have no leadership ambitions but many concrete problems. People amplify their demands through public protest and / or news coverage. The sheer quantity of incoming news makes it difficult for journalists to catch up with the stories. They print them mostly unchanged, allowing newspapers to serve the self-presentation of publicity-seeking individuals. A technique well developed in the public arena is transported into a different medium and can reincarnate as news.

This conclusion reverses an argument made by Ramdinder Kaur (2001, 2003) in her study of the Ganapati festival in Mumbai. She shows how changes in the festival facilitated rational debate – associated with the news medium – in the performative domain. In the 1980s newspapers in Mumbai began to sponsor competitions between different temporary shrines – dedicated to the Hindu God Ganesha – set up during the festival. Prizes were given for decoration, artistic style, educational message, social engagement of committee members, cleanliness and discipline at the shrines. This changed design and content of these shrines. More and more often they now comment on ongoing political events and thus turn into a medium for the negotiation of national values. Kaur concludes that rational debate, associated with the public sphere of the newspapers, spills over into the performative domain. The Ganapati festival connects the political debate of the literate – in the newspaper – with reflections in the religious domain, consumed by the masses.

I agree with Kaur that the boundary between performative politics and news media is fluid. However, my reading of the local pages takes the opposite direction. I perceive a cacophony of voices and a build-up of publicly voiced interests in the mass media, rather than the promotion of 'rational' debate outside a media sphere. In stating this, I am not joining the ranks of culture pessimists, who lament the deterioration of the public sphere due to popularisation. I rather shift the focus from debating a cultural ideal to analysing a social practice. Approaching the contextual production of a concrete public sphere, my study adds 'ethnographic flesh' to a theoretical concept.

With this approach I propose a radical departure from the dominant way of theorising the relation between media and the public spheres. I argue for a broad analysis of media orientations developed at the intersection of different social contexts. I investigate the contribution that potential readers make towards shaping newspaper discourse and explore how networks of relations and techniques of visibility become tied up with the making as well as the usage of news texts.

Typically the analysis of media generated publics starts from a highly professionalised media system in which journalists act as privileged observers of society. Consequently their action is treated as fundamental for the making of the media generated public. Citizens are given the role of consumers, and questions arise only with regard to access of information and reading traditions. From this vantage point, the input that feeds the public sphere of the media is generated by professionals, who digest activities in society and make them available to the masses (Imhof and Schulz 1996). The sense of totally emerging from such perceptions has been critiqued by scholars who debate the complexity of real publics. Studying the mobilisation of citizens outside state institutions has led academics to acknowledge the plurality and fleetingness of public spheres. The terminology is pluralised and we encountered micro-publics (Berger 2000) and alternative publics (Fraser 1992) as well as sub-publics and counter-publics (Warner 2002a). Robbins (1993) contends that the public is not a social entity but a phantom, an imaginary construction that conceives of the attentiveness of people as an ideal rather than a reality. In real life attention is difficult to get, fleeting and easily diverted. The resulting public is unstable and incomplete.

While mass media are a highly effective means of creating a public, and have played a significant role in constituting what is conceived as a political public in modernity (Habermas 1992 [1962]; Warner 2002a), there are other public arenas. Warner (2002b) distinguishes between three ideal public types: (1) the public as an imaginary construct circumscribing those belonging to a predefined entity like a city, a state or any other community; (2) a concrete public as experienced in a face-to-face encounter in a public event; and (3) a public created through the production of text. Disciplinary division has promoted a scholarly discourse that tends to look at these different publics or dimensions of publics separately and hence fails to discuss their interconnections. I concur with Dahlgren (1991, 1995) that there is a need to connect the analysis of civil society with that of the media discourse in order to deepen our understanding of public sense-making processes.[34] Dahlgren advocates research into sense-making practices in reception contexts, the contribution of activities in civil society towards shaping the public, as well as the historical context of social relations and their impact on sense-making activities.

I have quoted Kaur's study as an Indian example that makes sense of the connection between co-presence in a festival and mediated public sphere. While her study bridges the gap by demonstrating the relation of two organisationally distinct forms of public, the focus remains on the writing elite as essentially shaping the character of the public sphere. What I have shown in this chapter is that an essential link between the media and its addressee (the public) is missed, when only the agency of professionals is considered. Citizens galvanise the media through activity in the public arena, while at the same time using the media as an authorising institution.

Warner reminds us that the concept of the public sphere contains a relationship. The public encompasses more than a speaker (writer), a speech (text) and its addressee. The public is an 'ongoing space of encounter for discourse' (p. 62):

Between the discourse that comes before and the discourse that comes after, one must postulate some kind of link. And the link has a social character; it is not mere consecutiveness is time, but a context of interactive. The usual way of imagining the interactive character of public discourse is through metaphors of conversion, answering, taking back, deliberating. The interactive social relation of a public, in other words, is perceived as though it were a dyadic speaker-hearer or author-reader relation. (Warner 2002b: 62–63)

A study of a public sphere that moves beyond the writing profession needs to make sense of this connection and characterise the nature of the 'dialogue' between producer and consumer, positions which in a media saturated world increasingly overlap.

Public as conversation has been a central theme in the analysis of electronic media. Various studies have shown how popular participation in blogs reinvigorates the idea of an ongoing democratic debate. Critical voices raise objections, saying that the multiplicity of voices in the internet does not constitute an effective debate or challenge power relations (Barnett 1997; Noam 2004). However, there are others who praise the internet as a democratic platform for controlling elite institutions, like politics and also the press. Interconnectivity between professional journalists and bloggers, as well as between mainstream media and marginal publications, enriches the debate and creates new mechanisms for practising democracy (McNair 2006).

Such research is a return to the question originally asked by Habermas (1992 [1962]) who analysed public spheres not as discourses but as media-related practices in society that connects citizens in social relations.[35] I share with Habermas a desire to understand the multiple social agencies that produce the particular characteristics of public spheres. In this chapter I have discussed popular participation in a local Indian mass medium, and described local newspapers as a site for the amassing of subaltern voices, evoking the city as a patchwork of interests, views and activities. One could easily argue that there is no conversation at all. There is certainly no coherent debate focusing on a limited set of themes of major importance, but rather a fantastic array of concerns disseminated through local papers.

To discover the conversation that keeps the discourse going, we need to move beyond the printed product and the activity of the writing elite. The discourse of local pages originates in a network of relations, producing connectivity between local speakers, hierarchies of mediating personnel and the political elite. The conversation exceeds the printed product. It includes a range of social actions that are 'before' and 'after' the text. There is the identification of key informants and the regular exchange between mediating personnel and local inhabitants. There is also the systematic collecting of printed evidence, the privately extended circulation of the written fact and its continued use in social negotiations. It is a social dialogue of power acted out in the performative area and the written domain. While organisationally distinct from political institutions, newspapers are not separate from the power networks that feed organised politics. Newspapers contribute to the open-ended social 'dialogue' productive of social hierarchies.

This public is a far cry from the Kantian project of an ideal public sphere, as a space for pure reasoning. In complete contrast to the ideals of rational debate, local news pages revel in subjectivity by circulating personal opinions and promoting the visibility of ambitious or aggrieved individuals. They are appropriated as a medium for the expression of (collective) outcries against the state, its institutions and representatives as well as a wedge in leadership wars. In this sense local newspapers open up a space much closer to Habermas' notion of the public in times of modern mass mediation.

> In the course of the shift from a journalism of private men of letters to the public services of the mass media, the sphere of the public was altered by the influx of private interests that received privileged exposure in it – although they were by no means *eo ipso* representative of the interests of private people as the public. (Habermas 1992 [1962]: 188–89)

For Habermas the work of contemporary media appears far removed from the historical ideal. Public relations managers of leading companies and dominant political players are seen as manufacturing made-for-media events in order to push their concerns into the spotlight. Hence, those who monopolise private capital and political power stabilise their dominant position through the manipulation of public organs. Habermas shared this pessimistic version of contemporary media with other scholars from the Frankfurt School, who argued that the mass media are an instrument for the creation of a false consciousness and a medium for dominant classes to drown the oppositional spirit of the subaltern (Horkheimer and Adorno 1998 [1944]).

The Indian example presents us with the fact that 'small' people (Guha 1996) have taken on board media strategies stereotypically ascribed to spin doctors acting at the behest of the big and powerful. Subalterns and local leaders succeed in a media landscape that invests more and more in local news. Through local pages and by supporting the making of news networks, Indian newspapers offer institutionalised 'social capital' for democratic circulation. It is the door to a 'parallel' universe of connections and influences. The desire to become connected, and the reality of having to work through relations, turns newspapers into a local organ. Newspapers achieve what Berger (2000) has called the democratic participatory role. It opens the newspaper to popular voices. Audiences are addressed 'not only as consumer of politics but producers' (p. 86).

The characterisation of the local pages as a democratic organ needs to be put in context. It does not replace the elite bias of media, but complements it. A democratic participatory approach in local reporting adds a new facet to news-making, but does not erase other tendencies, such as a preference for elite voices. A whole range of studies on journalism in Western countries confirms the tendency of newspapers to stabilise the status quo, proving that it is those with significant amounts of money, power, and status that dominate newspaper content (Fishman 1980; Goldenberg 1975; Golding and Elliott 1979; Hall et al.1978; Schudson 2003; Tuchman 1978). In India the influence of the political and economic leaders is obvious and all pervasive. It is the theme for the remainder of this book. I continue with a debate of the political elite in the next chapter and move on to the influence of advertisers in the subsequent chapter. However, it would be false to assume that the possibility of public reasoning in the press is exhausted by the powerful intervention of dominant actors. At least in the Indian case we find that the desire of newspapers to increase sales by appealing to local citizens has given resource-poor people an official instrument of power. The character of local reporting in Hindi newspapers transforms urban citizens from readers to potential subjects and even writers of news texts.

Citizens have acquired a tool for manipulating relations perfected by the political elite; they copy mechanisms of empowerment typical for the Indian political culture. Hence, some of the key techniques introduced in this chapter will resurface in the discussion of the political elite. Prominent leaders are reconnected to the population through networks of patronage. They form the top end of a hierarchy of leaders, who compete for public attention as one condition for political ascent. Manipulating media coverage for personal promotion is part of the standard toolkit in politics. Unlike subaltern actors, politicians are in a position to offer return 'gifts' for media attention. As patrons they are the equal of the journalists. Hence, journalists are keen to respond to politicians' media initiatives. By keeping leaders in the news, they consolidate a network of political connections. While the motivation for leader-driven reporting differs at the top and bottom end of the political hierarchy, the effects cumulate in one important point. Reporting reinforces the leader-centrism of the Indian political system. The practices that bring about and shape leader-centred reporting of state news is the focus of the next chapter. It interrogates a zone of contact, where journalism and politics overlap.

Notes

1. On 9 February, the media announced that Deepa Mehta and her team had given up and left Banaras without having shot the film. Subsequently the coverage started to decline. For three more weeks there were occasional reports about Deepa Mehta's future plans and the possibility that she might find other locations in which to produce *Water*. Mehta finally produced the film in 2004, filming it in Sri Lanka without any publicity. It opened the Toronto film festival in 2005 (www.rediff.com/movies/2005/sep/02ajp1.htm, accessed on 5 September 2005). Her daughter published a book on the dramatic events that accompanied the making of *Water* (Saltzman 2005).

2. The following analysis is based on the news coverage in the Lucknow editions of *Hindustan Times, Times of India, Pioneer, Hindustan, Dainik Jagaran, Sahara* and *Amar Ujala* between 30 January and 9 February 2000.

3. Statements were made by the BJP, the party in power in Delhi at the time, as well as Lucknow. We heard statements from the following parties: Congress, the Communist Party of India (CPI), the Marxists (CPI–M), the Loktantrik Congress, the Lok Dal, the Bajrang Dal, the Alkali Dal and the Trinamul Congress.

4. The RSS (*Rashtriya Svayam Sevak Sangha*) is a paramilitary cadre organisation. Its aim is to train Hindus to become active, able and aggressive fighters for a Hindu state. Officially it is portrayed as a cultural organisation that serves the preservation of Hindu traditions (Anderson and Damle 1987; Basu et al 1993; Goyal 1979).

5. The VHP (*Vishva Hindu Parishad*) was founded in 1964 in an effort to create a global community of Hindus. A central focus is to reconnect migrated Indians to their homeland and their 'traditional' religion and involve them in the political project of the Indian Hindu Right (Omvedt 1990: 723; Basu et al 1993).

6. The BJP (*Bharatiya Janta Party*) is the parliamentary wing of the Hindu Right. It has served terms in power in the national government and in many northern Indian state parliaments (Hansen 1998; Jaffrelot 1996).

7. *Kashi Sanskriti Raksha Sangharsh Samiti.*

8. *Hindu Jagaran Manch.*

9. *Kashi Vidvat Parishad.*

10. *Jan Sanskriti Manch.*
11. These are stairs leading down to the Ganges river. They are – among other things – used for religous rituals and are considered part of the sacred territory, which is marked by the holy river.
12. Narayan Mishra, Dr Kaushal Kishor Mishra, Ashok Pandey, Nagendra Gandhi, Dr Raj Kishor Singh, Dr Ram Ji Ray, Dr H.N. Ray, Acharya Radheshyam Pandey, Acharya Shiv Prasad Pandey, Dr Shailendre Upadhyaya, Suresh Chandra Chaube, Dr Bhanu Pratap Singh, Dr Sarita Gupta, Dr Mohini Shrivastava and Rajendra Singh.
13. *Kashi Sanskriti Raksha Sangharsh Samiti.*
14. See the coverage in *Hindustan Times, Times of India, Pioneer, Hindustan, Dainik Jagaran* and *Amar Ujala* between 30 January and 9 February 2000.
15. Mishra was former president of the Banaras Hindu University Teachers' Association, not of the whole University.
16. Sandria Freitag (1989) introduces the term in her study of colonial India to capture the character of performative politics acted out in public places. Public performances offered an alternative realm for political activities outside the state during the late nineteenth and early twentieth century.
17. Mines (1996) borrows the term ‚Big Men' from the ethnography of Melanesia (Sahlins 1963; Godelier 1986; Godelier and Strathern 1991).
18. A recent publicity stunt was a staged fight for the right of state employees (which here refers to university teachers) to join the Hindu nationalist cadre organisation RSS (http://www.secularindia.com/news/2006/11/30SANGH%20LINK.htm or http://news.oneindia.in/2006/11/30/bjp-mulls-national-movement-on-bhu-rss-issue-1164961134.html, accessed on 15 July 2007).
19. Goldenberg 1975; Glasgow University Media Group 1976; Hartley 1982; Manning 2001; Rajagopal 2001: 172; Sigal 1973.
20. The material was collected during an earlier study focusing on Hindu temples, which I conducted in the middle Indian city of Bhopal in the 1990s and followed up in 2002 and 2003 (Rao 2003).
21. The name indicates that some Khatiks claim a high status as Kshatriyas (warrior caste), which they are said to have lost due to their low level of sophistication and education (Rao 2002).
22. Former untouchable castes are officially registered as Scheduled Castes. This guarantees them reservations in educational institutions and state employment.
23. Due to time constraints and the flood of petty concerns that reach the newspapers every day, city reporters do not have the time to check the accuracy of such statements or research the context of the cases. In the case of the temple trust controversy, it is interesting to note that the journalists apparently did not notice or did not care that both the initial letter and the refutation were sent by the same person, which under normal circumstances should have made them suspicious about the content. There is no time to indulge in such local issues. Press releases are

published as they come, in accordance with the policy that it is important to provide citizens with information about events in their locality.

24. This strategy of planting news as a political instrument to influence ongoing power negotiations is described in a different context by Sigal, who shows how state officials use their media connections to circulate information or disinformation in order to influence perceptions to their own advantage (Sigal 1973:163–74; see also Roshco 1975: 80–101).

25. I do not quote the whole case in order to protect the anonymity of the individuals involved.

26. To ground her argument theoretically, Butler refers to Derrida's (1988 [1972]) notion of iterability. Accordingly, the power of the performative speech act stems from a break with all previous contexts, which – according to Derrida – is necessarily part of every act of re-appropriation. Based on this idea of difference, Butler asserts that a speech act is never fully identical with previous speech acts. It may consist of quotations that refer to past acts, which are, however, re-contextualised in the present. Yet unlike Derrida, Butler does not stress the paramount importance of this shift. She takes a middle road between Derrida and Bourdieu when she states that it is the particular combination of contexts – previous and current – in which a 'citation' becomes meaningful and effective. The social context is an important parameter in this negotiation, but it does not necessarily determine the outcome.

27. Habermas has been criticised for overstating the difference between the various forms of the public sphere, as well as for his clear-cut distinction between the state and civil society. Objections have also been raised regarding his concept of rational debate, his idea of media-manipulated masses and his singular emphasis on the role of the media that ignores other forms of social communication like gatherings, festivals, rituals, etc. (see, for example, Dahlgren and Sparks 1991: 5–6; Hartley 1996; Jeffrey 2000: 11–19; Kaur 2001: 25–26).

28. Berger (2000) offers a helpful classification by describing journalistic practices as variously informed by four guiding principles. Journalism functions as a watchdog in the political process, as an educator, as a medium for the proliferation of multiple viewpoints and as a channel for popular participation. In the course of the chapter I argue that local pages strengthen popular perception and hence add a new dimension to a traditional liberal and educational ideal.

29. This argument relates to recent debates in the anthropology of the advertisement. Several studies showed that in an age of advertisement, power lies – more than in the production of goods – in the circulation of signs that give value to a person, a company, an agency or a product and thus create their status (Malefyt and Moeran 2003; Mazzarella 2003b; Rajagopal 1998). Similarly, one could argue in the field of politics that the circulation of a name and the making of fame through the media has become central to establishing and maintaining a particular social status.

30. See here Brass's argument about the function of 'riot-systems', institutions and images that fix a city within a particular history of religious strife that works as a self-fulfilling prophecy. According to this argument the fear of communal violence and the measures taken to prevent riots are part of the very reality that creates this religious violence (Brass 1998).

31. Rajagopal makes a similar argument about the power of the press to create leaders. In his study of the Ayodhya conflict and its political implications, he notes that the press played an important role in selecting the BJP and its leaders as main actors in the controversy, thus simplifying but also restructuring the movement (Rajagopal 2001: 171–86).

32. For a similar point, see Lotter (2005). In the article the author shows how historical narrations about a temple are used to manipulate caste relations in contemporary Nepal.

33. See also Gupta's ironical suggestion: 'Treated with benign neglect by students of contemporary life, they [the news articles] mysteriously metamorphise into invaluable "field data" once they have yellowed around the edges and fallen apart at the creases. And yet it is not entirely clear by what alchemy time turns the "secondary" data of the anthropologist into the "primary" data of the historian' (Gupta 1995: 385).

34. See on this point also van Dijk 1988.

35. This perspective has been taken in an edited volume by Calhoun (1992), focusing on activities that contribute towards creating publics and position in publics.

CHAPTER 4

Political Reporting

Sites of Engagement – Performances of Distance

This chapter continues the debate about the effectiveness of press work in the structuring of social relations and the production of a public sphere. From local news-making, I now move on to investigate writing about established political institutions and their representatives, this being the most popular and most sought-after domain of reporting. The argument focuses on the involvement of journalists in political negotiations and their active contribution towards bringing about the very results which they are reporting. The working days of political reporters are dominated by an unspectacular routine, the tedious exercises in networking and the requirement to turn redundant and unspectacular political routines into exciting news. In the following chapter I will analyse the social space shared between politicians and journalists. I will continue the argument that news-making is not always a process of selecting the most important and relevant information, but is also an enterprise in establishing, nurturing and repairing relations. Networking in the political domain poses specific challenges. Unlike local reporters, state reporters work with informants from the elite. In this context, engagement with leaders is driven by the desire to gain admission to the inner circles of political power and turn social closeness into a career advantage.

Sociological accounts recognise the importance of reciprocity in exchange relations between politicians and journalists (Manning 2001). In writing up reports news personnel take into account their obligations to their sources. I push this argument further and treat news as objects of exchange. Rather than arguing that coverage is influenced by sources, I will show that the desire for intimacy produces news. Journalists invent news where they see none and offer it as a commodity in exchange relations. Acting as masters over the product that is news, journalists receive respect. Their knowledge and influence is valued which gives them significant influence over politicians' practices of public image making. The mutual desire for closeness, as well as the eagerness of both sides to engage with each others' priorities, creates a shared arena. The reasoning in this shared area influences political dynamics and press coverage. The political is invented at the intersection of two institutions. This conclusion contradicts those sociological theories that stress the independence of social institutions, especially Bourdieu and Luhmann. The hypothesis that the salient feature of modernity is a clear and transparent delineation of social domains takes borders for granted and obscures practices of transgression. Such theories miss the significance of non-conformist practices which undermine the purity of institutions and make strategic use of border violations.

I propose a shift in perspective, focusing not on the imaginary centre of any particular field but on practices of boundary making and unmaking. Inter-professional engagement constantly threatens to destroy an ideal order – in which politics and journalism perform different functions – and requires intensive maintenance of boundaries. Through the creation of a shared ground, politicians and journalists can assert their independence and declare the separation of their professions. Border control keeps in check exaggerated expectations in exchange relations and undermines reciprocity. It reintroduces a strong element of contingency in a relation that threatens to impose undue constraints on news-making. The oscillation between the professional distance of journalists and politicians and the personal closeness of informants and reporters emerges as a significant feature of news-making. It produces news discourses and impacts on the structure of the political field.

The debate reinforces the theoretical orientation established in the last chapter. The focus is on news as practice rather than text. In a different arena, I will spell out how the agency of journalists and informants overlaps. Again news-making appears as a collective effort of people who are entrenched in power negotiations. The chapter furthers the argument that the newspapers do not just represent political action but also reflect the character of a political culture. News-making is a tool for the exercise of patronage and the newspaper a platform for exhibiting patronage as a system for organising the social. What happens at the lower end of the political hierarchy reappears in a different avatar at the top.

I begin with case studies which demonstrate how the friendly meeting of politicians and journalists during meaningless press conferences and private interviews produces a social closeness and creates a shared social arena. A second set of examples will illustrate social interactions at the other end of the spectrum of possible relations. It demonstrates the strategic use of social distance, motivated by a professional ethic that sees the press as a political watchdog. Summing up my empirical findings, I then debate social techniques used to navigate the uncertainties in a field characterised by the simultaneous closeness and distance of participants. The chapter ends with a theoretical debate that critiques concepts of social fields and social systems by exploring the notion of border. Treating news as objects in exchange relations, I demonstrate the relational surplus of news-making, that impacts on political structure and the news discourse.

The Agency of News

In the previous chapter I elaborated on the appropriation of news-making by the urban community as an asset in power contestations. People value news articles as a commodity to enhance their claims to status and their demands for recognition. A systematic investigation of how often the publication of concerns in the press delivered the demanded outcome may yield depressing results. However, such reasoning may not capture all the intentions invested into news publishing. The value of a news article exceeds its content – and the intentions communicated through its content. A news article is an object for self-promotion and is used to boost prominence and consolidate status. It is a commodity fetish that foments social relations.

Karl Marx (1976 [1867]) uses the term fetish to describe the social imaginary that transforms a physical object (a product of labour) into a commodity. The value of the commodity is detached from the material thing, rooted solely in a belief system that defines social relations via the object and thus constructs the object as meaningful to people (p. 163–65). Marx's distinction between the 'use value' of a good and the 'exchange value' of a commodity provides a matrix for appreciating the significance of published articles. The worth of the printed news as commodity is generated in social actions reflecting the assumption that access to mass media augments influence. News releases its power to act as a catalyst in social relations.

I propose that news is an object which exercises agency. Anthropological debates inform us that objects are enlivened by collective assumptions prompting people about the power of things. In his pioneering study Marcel Mauss (1996 [1950]) explores the social intentions that inform gift giving, making the gifts objects in a chain of exchange relations that demand return gifts. If recipients fail in their obligation to reciprocate, they experience the malevolent power of the gift to poison their social existence. Arjun Appadurai (1986) expands this perspective by advocating an economic anthropology that follows the trajectory of things and explains the 'regimes of value' (p. 4) that they embody. He identifies the need to move beyond a mere focus on products, production or intentions of producers to analyse chains of exchange relations in which objects structure exchange and exchange enlivens objects. In a similar vain, Alfred Gell (1998) defines the anthropology of art as 'the theoretical study of social relations in the vicinity of objects mediating social agency' (p. 7; see also van Binsbergen and Geschiere 2005, Raheja 1988).

Treating news as agent creates an appreciation of its exchange value in social negotiations. The popularity of journalism as a profession is also a result of the structural advantages gained from producing such items of power. The promise (or the threat) of publicity is an effective puissance, bringing numerous advantages to journalists. They are well accounted for and range from privileged access to information, to advantages in using institutions and services, to material gains (Bhandari 1998; Sahay 2006; Tharyan 1999). The practice of trading publicity for favours is especially pronounced in the central and highly developed domain of political reporting. Here I am referring not so much to the personal advantages journalists draw from their professional engagement, but rather the favours of preferential treatment in information sharing. A number of studies have elaborated the struggle for control between journalists and sources over information (Ericson et al. 1989: 199–204; Hasty 2005a; Manning 2001). Reciprocity figures as an important social technique which is instrumental in manipulating coverage and securing information. The giving and receiving of information and the exchange of favours serve to manage uncertainties in the news business. They help contain the subversive effect of the principal independence of sources and journalists, the imperfect control over information flow as well as the interpretative freedom derived from the equivocation of statements and actions. 'Gifts' and 'return gifts' put a check on the disruptive potential of uncontrolled actions in the relation between power elites.

In the following pages I wish to take up this theme and turn it on its head. Instead of treating news writing as the core activity influenced by rules of reciprocity, I focus on reciprocity as productive of coverage. This reversal in perspective is motivated by the following observations. While at the end of each day reporters have to submit articles, much of their day is not spent seeking information but in cultivating sources. The advantage is apparent. Well-connected journalists will be clued-up by their informants when events happen. This ensures that they do not miss news opportunities while doing their routine work, but rather are pre-informed and prepared. Knowing the right people increases reporters' chances to break news and get exclusive stories. To augment their effort in labouring the field, efficient journalists write an array of news texts purely devoted to this end. Many activities and statements are covered not because they adhere to a journalistic sense of news-worthiness, but because of their strategic importance in securing long-term privileged access.

The exchange value of the commodity – news – in political writing differs from that in local news-making. While in the last chapter I focused on the way in which subaltern actors exploited news to build up their position, I will now explore news as trade object in political relations. I contend that the ensuing closeness between journalists and politicians demands a rethinking of assumptions about politics and journalism, as constituting two separate, though interlinked domains. I will argue that while politicians and journalists uphold and perpetually emphasise the fiction of separation, their activity is complementary and constitutive for their respective professional activities.

Weaving the Web of Relations

During the period of my fieldwork, the government in Uttar Pradesh was a coalition between the BJP and several smaller parties – the Loktantrik Congress Party (LCP), the Janatantrik BSP and the Janta Dal (RRP). In November 1999 the BJP installed Ram Prakash Gupta as the new chief minister, as Kalyan Singh had become too controversial. This change of leader led to a renewed round of discussions about the distribution of ministerial posts among the coalition partners. Several discontented MLAs urged the new chief minister to restructure the cabinet. Finally, after a number of announcements, on 8 February 2000, the departments of twenty-four ministers (six cabinet and eighteen state ministers) were reshuffled. The newspapers printed the list of new ministries on 10 February, along with the bitter comments of the displaced ministers. Subsequently, on 10 February all newspapers started printing complaints from disgruntled MLAs, who lost positions or complained that they did not receive adequate consideration. The debate about who received what and why continued to appear in the newspaper – with short interruptions – for ten days. It was front-page news for three days, until 21 February when the press reported on a meeting initiated by the chief minister to communicate a code of conduct for MLAs and ministers to stop the infighting.

Journalists had several reasons to jump on this issue and keep it alive for as long as possible. First, the news was easily available and in part exclusive. The grievances were not publicly announced and thus were not available equally to all press people. Reporters made private appointments. Thus their articles contained details about behind-the-scenes negotiations, which justified them being printed on the first page, showcasing the newspaper's good connections. Secondly, reporters followed the 'pack',[1] making sure they did not fall behind their colleagues in reporting the event. Finally, the occasion was a perfect opportunity to establish, strengthen or reconfirm friendly relationships with selected leaders, which could be exploited again at a later point.

By covering the dissatisfaction of some ministers, reporters could easily integrate two demands that at times pulled them in two different directions: they satisfied the employers' desire for 'exclusive' news while simultaneously doing selected leaders a favour. The peak of coverage was reached on 10 and 11 February, when the six newspapers *Hindustan, Amar Ujala, Dainik Jagaran, Times of India, Hindustan Times* and *Pioneer* covered the issue on page one and printed a total of eleven articles on the first day, and thirteen articles on the next. By-lines give a further indication of the favourable evaluation of interview-based articles. P.B. Varma of the *Times of India* received a by-line on 10 February 2000 for his article on the resignation of two ministers, news that was also printed in all the other newspapers. On 11 February 2000 both Manoj Shrivastava from *Amar Ujala* and Deepak Gidwani from the *Hindustan Times* received a by-line for similar articles about three more ministers who had threatened resignation. On 12 February 2000 the *Hindustan Times* printed M.A. Hafiz' name along with an article about Triparthi's complaints that contained information also printed by *Aj* and *Sahara*. There was another article on 13 February 2000 by Deepak Gidwani in the *Hindustan Times* that once again summed up all statements, accusations and threats. It is interesting to note that here by-lines did not mark exclusive news, in the strict sense of the term. They rather rewarded reporters for their efforts to obtain personal interviews, which politicians were only too happy to give.

The leaders themselves seemed to have little to lose and much to gain from this public battle. Publicity appeared to be the only instrument left in this bid for power. By calling on reporters individually, dissatisfied politicians made the news look exclusive, which it was not, since leaders fixed several appointments a day on the same topic. Yet, the personal touch secured prominent display, drawing attention to the leaders' grievances without fixing complainants in a particular position. Politicians could always retreat from their demands by claiming that they had just expressed a spontaneous emotion that had subsequently been blown up out of all proportion by the press. In this case the chief minister did not give in and made no further changes and the whole thing was dismissed as media hype.

What emerges in this situation, and later in many others, is the struggle for the right balance between the ideals of news-making and obligations in exchange relationships. To come close to leaders without becoming involved (corrupt) makes the task of reporting difficult. Journalists need experience or at times imagination to generate news from often vague allusions. In order to elicit statements, be able to interpret them correctly and predict future events, reporters stay close to leaders. To know, understand, respect and trust each other is the key to obtaining political insights. Hence, reporters spend a lot of time with leaders and party workers.

However, even if there are many informal meetings that may appear to outsiders as friends drinking tea, the contacts are always goal-oriented. Neither journalists nor politicians have time to waste. Thus, at the end of a meeting, no matter how meaningless it was, something has to be written. Newspapers are full of articles portraying leaders, replicating their views and describing their activities.[2] Writing extensively about politicians and keeping them in the news even in event-less times, journalists fulfil their promise for reciprocity, which is implicit in every acceptance of an invitation. Politicians present their hospitality, information and friendship as a gift. It demands a return gift which materialises in (friendly) articles and (continuous) publicity.

There are at least two frequently occurring settings that primarily serve relations: the routine press conference which has little news value, and personal interviews of top leaders. Politicians woo journalists in casual press conferences. A jovial tone and excellent hospitality keeps reporters happy and leads to positive publicity. In turn, journalists woo politicians in private interviews. Here subservient behaviour and leader-centred articles express sympathy and remind politicians of their obligation towards particular media representatives. What makes these events important is the regularity with which they occur. They are not occasional episodes squeezed into tight schedules, but are part of the daily routine, taking up much time as well as filling substantial space in the newspapers.

Meeting the Leader

The BJP leader, Om Prakash Singh, organised a lunch for journalists on 21 February 2000, to present himself officially to the press as the new president of the Uttar Pradesh BJP. With forty reporters present, the event was well attended. All were looking forward to a relaxed celebration; news collection was more of a side issue. In keeping with precedent, the event started with a press conference. The leader gave a long speech about his strategies for rebuilding the party after major electoral losses. The journalists were bored, but patiently listened for at least half an hour. Finally, Sanjay, a senior reporter from *Dainik Jagaran*, interrupted the leader and asked about the upcoming by-elections and the seat-sharing arrangement of BJP with its coalition partners. This issue was on everybody's mind. However, Om Prakash Singh was not interested in talking about ongoing decisions. He was evasive and stayed 'on message', even when the questioning became more provocative, for example, when he was asked who had been responsible for the weakening of the BJP, or why the Chief Minister, Ram Prakash Gupta, would not stand in by-elections.[3] The state president did not part with any information. He did not want to talk politics, but to build relationships. He had made that clear in his introductory statement: 'I have invited you for a lunch, but it will be an advantage for you and me if we talk a bit before we start with the food.'

After the formal part, the journalists proceeded to have lunch. Intermittently several reporters approached the state president personally to request a private interview. They were all referred to the politician's secretary to check the schedule, except for Sanjay from *Dainik Jagaran* who was given a time for later that day. Sanjay was proud to have outdone all the others and boasted to me of his exceptionally good connections with the BJP. The interview was scheduled for 5 P.M. Sanjay and I went together. Sanjay repeated his questions from the morning, with no result. Next he put down his pen and paper and asked for confidential information, again with no avail. In the end Sanjay had spent several hours that day without getting anything, let alone anything exclusive. In spite of his disappointment, he wrote a supportive article. In four paragraphs he summed up the leader's critical remarks on the state of the party organisation and his plans for rebuilding the BJP from the grassroots (*Dainik Jagaran*, 22 January 2000).[4]

There are many more such occasions that occupy the time of journalists without delivering hard news. For example, Ajit Singh, the national president of the Janta Dal party, paid a visit to Lucknow as a special guest to the 'India Festival' organised by the Sahara Company. On the day of his arrival he used the time for a press conference, attended by approximately thirty reporters. After a few minutes it became clear that the politician had nothing new to say. He expressed his opinion on some of the ongoing political issues and gave forewarning of a future announcement on a seat-sharing arrangement for the forthcoming by-elections. A reporter next to me commented dryly: 'See, that is what they do. They have a meeting somewhere and couple it with a press conference, no matter whether they have anything to say or not.' The arrangement was one of convenience. It got Ajit Singh into the newspaper, even though he had not put forward anything. With the exception of the *Times of India* all the newspapers reported the various comments of the leader the next day in long articles.

Pedelty has described the organisation of such 'pseudo-events'[5] as well-planned performances that present a particular institutional point of view. Through the frequent organisation of pseudo-events, those actors with the most resources can monopolise the time of journalists. Tied up in pre-scheduled meetings, journalists are prevented from investigating other incidents and perspectives (Pedelty 1995: 120–23; see also Ericson et al. 1989: 202–03, 227; Gans 1979:121; Schudson 2003: 137). My argument follows a slightly different path. Although I share with Pedelty the perception that press conferences represent a (more or less successful) effort to get the organiser's point of view into the newspaper, here I would like to emphasise their function in an exchange economy. By rushing to politicians' self-promotional events reporters make themselves available. They demonstrate their willingness to pay respect to leaders in situations with limited functional utility. They invest in a relation for the later procurement of news.

During the time of my stay, the Samajvadi Party (SP) was particularly active in securing press attention through meaningless press conferences. As an opposition party, the SP was of little news value for journalists, who are naturally more interested in the activities of the government. To counterbalance this structural disadvantage, the SP organised a press conference almost every week, where a major leader commented on all the current debates. These meetings were very informal. Reporters joked with the leaders, listened to comments, discussed political issues, enjoyed tea and sweets, and afterwards wrote short articles about some of the statements made. The meeting on 17 February 2000 serves as an illustration.

Journalists and politicians alike were excited about the imminent by-elections. The question of who would win was on everyone's mind. The topic dominated the discussion during the SP press conference. The SP spokesman declared that the party would secure the Kannauj seat. The issue was exciting because the state president and former chief minister, Mulayam Singh Yadav, had for the first time fielded his son, Akhilesh Yadav, in this constituency. It was a question of prestige for him and the party to lead him to victory. Like most election talk, the discussion focused on 'vote banks'.[6] Who would get the Muslim votes, Yadav[7] votes, OBC (Other Backward Classes)[8] votes and Brahmin votes? The SP speaker declared that Akhilesh was bound to win, since he could break all vote banks by exciting young people and attracting voters from all castes and classes. The discussion was fun. It added to the excitement of the elections, allowing everyone to speak from an equal position and to experience the satisfaction of sharing a common space for reasoning. The writing of an article was routine. *Dainik Jagaran*, *Aj* and the *Times of India* (18 February 2000) all carried short articles on the inside pages spelling out the SP speaker's speculations about the elections and the election-related accusations against other parties. A few days later, when election results were declared, beat reporters met again at the SP office. Together with party members, they celebrated the victory of Akhilesh in Kannauj. The television set was running, informing the gathering of the latest results. An abundance of sweets added to the festive mood.

Such an amiable atmosphere is typical of many meetings. Politicians and journalists portray themselves as members in a community of communicators. They get to know each other well, express respect and esteem and develop common interests as well as collective forms of reasoning. Ståhlberg gives a potent description:

> [T]he informality and relaxed atmosphere struck me [...] when I accompanied reporters to encounters with the most powerful politicians of the State. The journalists never conformed to the usual procedures of showing respect to people with power – no bowing or feet touching. Press conferences at political headquarters were often held in a quite joyful and egalitarian mood. The politicians and the reporters engaged themselves in conversations on various issues, exchanged jokes and laughed together. On the other hand, challenging or intricate questions to the politicians were rather uncommon. (Ståhlberg 2002: 125)

Journalists were lucky when such meetings produced exciting announcements, but they were not a precondition for a successful meeting. The desire for cordial relations is mutual, and journalists are responsive to politician's courtesies and ready to reiterate their statements in articles.

Where the objective is good relations, journalists can tame their behaviour significantly. The following interlude during the Om Prakash press conferences – narrated earlier – is a case in point. During the question-and-answer session one freelancer wanted to spice up the meeting with a provocative question. He directed the host's attention to the former chief minister Kalyan Singh, who was also his predecessor in the office of state president and had been removed in disgrace from all his posts in November 1999. The reporter wanted to know how Om Prakash Singh could accept an office that had been occupied by his mentor and main supporter, who had been removed against his will. The implication of the question was that Om Prakash Singh was showing a lack of respect towards his mentor and simply forging ahead, egoistically building his career. After this question the atmosphere was frozen. No one said a word for a while. Everyone felt the insult, which seemed to endanger the good mood. Finally, Om Prakash Singh spoke. He normalised the situation through some general remarks, which explained the circumstances that had led to Kalyan Singh's removal, for which he personally was not responsible.

It was clear from the shocked silence and the unwillingness to follow up the theme (journalists can be very ruthless if they discern the potential for breaking news) that the junior reporter had acted against an unwritten code of conduct that keeps critical questions under control in a friendly meeting. Adjusting their behaviour to the occasion is part of a professional habitus, which reporters learn over the years. In this situation the speaker easily re-established the balance. He used a technique that Goffman called a 'corrective process' (1955: 219).[9] An attempt was made 'to show [that] what admittedly appeared to be a threatening expression is really a meaningless event' (1955: 220). Om Prakash Singh's intervention was successful because it fitted the mood of reporters, who were not interested in stirring up a stale history. The theme threatened the good relations with the host while having no potential to produce a sensation.

Journalists do not stop at accepting friendly invitations. They also actively seek out politicians, pay regular visits to party offices and lobby for private interview time. Interviews with major leaders are scheduled whenever possible to maintain contact and make sure that the politician remembers the reporter when an issue is hot and forgives any negative publicity. The following examples demonstrate how journalists woo politicians.

On 25 January 2000 I arranged an interview with Mulayam Singh Yadav, former chief minister of the state, leader of the SP and UP strong man. On arrival at his Lucknow mansion I was admitted into an inner hall, given tea and snacks, and made to wait. An hour later I was joined by the well-known senior journalist Shekar. Without knowing it we had been scheduled together. I was pleased about this opportunity to observe an experienced professional conduct an interview with one of the most powerful men in the state. Shekar grabbed this occasion to meet Mulayam Singh Yadav during one of his rare visits to the capital, to remind him of his presence and confirm their exceptionally close relationship, about which there was extensive gossip in press circles.

The situation was typical. As soon as an important leader showed up in Lucknow, reporters made a bee line to fix appointments for a personal interview. Themes were decided later; one could always talk about current events. This was also Shekar's approach. He had no particular reason to meet Mulayam, except to meet him, which was apparent in his interview technique. Shekar refrained from asking direct questions. Instead, he offered comments on the political situation, which gave Mulayam a chance to react and talk about the themes he liked. The narrative approach was remarkable and struck me as unusual, as I had previously clashed with journalists over this technique. On several occasions reporters gave me very negative feedback when in joint interviews I had encouraged politicians to follow their preferred narrative approach. I was scolded for my inability to control the interview, and had been exhorted to prepare precise questions that would produce good news. This time I had come prepared, but found that Shekar did not wish to impose an agenda. If there was an issue that he did want to pursue, he chose to quote others, such as 'People say there is a danger that fielding your son will lead to dynastic rule!' I tried to push the point by asking Mulayam about his motive for introducing his son in Kannauj. I was immediately cut short by Shekar, who told me that this was done in response to public demand. It was obvious that my intervention had made the question too aggressive. Thus, Shekar preferred to drop it altogether, rather than risk Mulayam feeling hurt and retreating into a more formal exchange. By then I understood that the aim of the meeting was not to provoke interesting answers but to cultivate a relationship.

Shekar used his chance to show himself in a good light. While talking about the imminent by-elections, he skilfully inserted an apology for his wrong election prediction during the last state elections. Like all other newspapers his paper had anticipated a devastating defeat for the Samajvadi Party, which, however, did not materialise. The case was mentioned frequently by SP politicians as proof of the press bias against them.

> It is during elections that the media comes out most clearly with its leaning. We endured this during the 1999 elections. I estimated that we would secure between 25 and 32 seats. But the media put 12 seats in their prognosis. I rang up media people, but no one was ready to listen to me. I have good contacts in the press, but even those close to me said: 'We

have raised the figure to 18, but we cannot go beyond that. It just doesn't match the impression of our management from Bombay.' We won 27 seats!! (Press advisor, SP, 24 January 2000)

Referring to this situation, Shekar commented now in front of Mulayam: 'I have to cross out my assessment for the last election. I have to admit that I totally misjudged the situation. We all did not expect that the SP would be so successful.'

Shekar interspersed the interview with regular praise for Mulayam. He assured the leader that he was so successful because he could attract voters from all strata of society. This interpretation, of course, was contrary to the common notion that Mulayam's strength results mainly from his firm control over Yadavs and Muslims. There were other pro-SP statements. Several times Shekar reminded the politician that he was the first to call him a 'UP strong man' and thus made public his enormous influence in the state. Mulayam responded positively to the courtesies. Not only did he spend two hours of his valuable time with Shekar, but when I asked Mulayam at the end of the meeting whether I could meet him again if I had more questions, he pointed to Shekar and said, 'Ask him; he knows everything about me!'

The next day Shekar wrote a very long article of eleven paragraphs, which reproduced Mulayam's statements on the by-elections, his candidate son and his anger about the fact that the BSP had been declared a national party, while the SP was only registered as a regional party. The text starts with an introduction by the author and then has short comments in between long quotations from the politician, which take up more than half of the text. Here I quote the first part of the article:

Mulayam to see son's smooth sail in by-poll
Lucknow, January 25. Unmindful of the Opposition's accusations against him of promoting dynasty in politics, the national president of the Samajwadi Party, Mr Mulayam Singh Yadav, is diligently working out strategies to foil opponent's schemes of stalling his son's maiden entry into Lok Sabha from the Kannauj Lok Sabha constituency in Uttar Pradesh.

Moreover, he has a definite role defined for his son in his ambitious plans of the expansion of the party during the next five years. 'He has long years of struggle ahead of him', Mr Yadav said in an interview while unfolding the dreams he has for his son as well as for the expansion of the party at the nation level.

However, nothing piques him more than the fact that while the Bahujan Samaj Party with barely 10 MPs in the Lok Sabha has been recognised as national party, the SP, with a strength of 26 in the Lok Sabha and six in the Rajya Sabha, is still a regional party.

'I am writing a letter to the Election Commission demanding him to change the norms for the recognition of a national party. The commission should decide the minimum strength of MPs for a national party instead of the existing norm, which specified six per cent vote in four states', Mr Yadav is demanding the Election Commission to convene an all-party meeting to change the 'ridiculous' system.

However it is Kannauj first.

'How can the Opposition accuse me of promoting dynasty in politics? Ram Gopal Yadav's political journey began from the Block level, Shiv Pal Singh Yadav has long years of struggle behind him, he was jailed, he contested elections. It has not been a case straight from Pilot to Prime Ministership like Rajiv Gandhi,' said a fuming Mulayam Singh Yadav. 'The dynasty charge would have had some base if I had appointed him the Chief Minister while I was in power. I am instead propelling him into a life full of struggle.' (26 January 2000).

None of the themes was new or dealt with in surprising ways. Yet, the text was a subject of debate the next day among colleagues, not for its content but because it confirmed once again what everyone seemed to know: that Sehkar was close to Mulayam. It is not easy to get a private interview with the latter, especially one of such length. The article proved Shekar's special connection, whereby the great length of the article could be taken as an indication of the length of the interview.

After the successful meeting with Mulayam Singh Yadav, my fame also started to spread. Press people respected me more now. My meeting with the leader came up later again when I had a chance to interview Mulayam's son, Akhilesh. He too was aware that I had been allowed access to his father. Experiences like this taught me a communicative technique of journalists that is instrumental in making oneself important and famous in the press community. Like all the others I now ensured that everyone knew all about my major meetings, and I advertised my skills in meeting powerful leaders. I was supported by Manoj, with whom I conducted a series of interviews. Manoj was a young upcoming journalist who was keen to establish himself at the centre of political reporting. We both linked up for a round of interviews. His aim was to impress his editor, his colleagues and to achieve a rapport with leaders. I was interested in observing an interviewer in action. We both exploited each other's status – his as journalist from a major paper, mine as a foreigner and employee of a renowned university – as bargaining points for negotiating interviews.

We started our joint work on 24 January 2000 with an interview with Kalyan Singh at his residence. The atmosphere was relaxed, and there was plenty of time to talk politics, and to exchange courtesies and personal comments. Before the meeting Manoj had made sure that I knew my role. He insisted that I prepare questions and gave me particular things I should ask, because they were too sensitive for him to address himself. He also told me to praise him in front of the politician, to remind the leader of earlier meetings with Manoj and to provide evidence of Manoj's excellent work as reporter. Manoj dropped hints during the interview to make sure I did not mess up my job.

The meeting with Kalyan was a great success. We stayed for two and a half hours, talked about BJP politics at the national and state levels, and the events that led up to his removal as chief minister. We also discussed the electricity strike, Kalyan's preparation for the by-elections and his relationship with the corporator[10] Kusum Rai. Manoj prompted Kalyan about things that would make good publicity. He asked him for his 'philosophy' on electricity and about personal relationships and intrigues. In the end Kalyan showed us around his garden, confirming his trust in us. The article the next day only replicated Kalyan's attack on the government for their way of handling the power reform. When I asked Manoj what the news value of this information was, he insisted that it was interesting to hear Kalyan on the issue since he was the father of the reform. Manoj did not mention this bit of information in his article. To remind readers that Kalyan had master-minded this policy would have weakened the credibility of his critique and exposed his opportunism. This was not the intention of the report. Manoj explicitly told me that he was determined to build good relations with Kalyan. This and other articles were a means to that end.

At the beginning of February 2000 we did an interview with the BSP leader Mayawati. Fixing a date was part of an internal battle in the news room. Sitaram, the BSP beat reporter, had tried to get a private interview with the leader while she was in the city. Manoj was determined to outdo him and was proud that he succeeded and could thus prove to me and the editor that his contacts were excellent and better even than those of the beat reporter. The interview was difficult. Manoj tried a personal approach, but it did not work. Instead of directly answering the questions or engaging in personal talk, Mayawati gave us ideologically laden speeches. Several times she fell into a general attack against the press, which, according to her, is an instrument in the hands of the upper class (and thus also upper castes) and biased against all activities that empower low castes. Manoj became angry. His visit was supposed to prove the opposite, namely that, although he was a journalist from an elite newspaper, he was ready to give her a voice. It was obvious that he did not get his point across. This failure occupied his mind for quite some time after the interview. In spite of the difficulties during the meeting, Manoj wrote a supportive article in which he portrayed Mayawati as a strong and determined leader who was confident of obtaining a good result in the coming by-elections. The first half of the article gives an idea of its overall tone and the extensive use of direct quotations:

> **Naak ka sawaal in Kannauj [A matter of honour in Kannauj]**
> [...] 'Kannauj is a matter of prestige for us', declared a combative Mayawati on Wednesday. The Bahujan Samaj Party (BSP) would pull out all stops to ensure that Mulayam Singh Yadav's son, who is the Samajwadi Party's candidate, loses from there. She also exuded confidence that the BSP candidate Akhar Ahmed Dumpy would win handsomely.
>
> 'Mulayam Singh has exposed his *soch* (ideology) and *charitra* (character) by fielding his son instead of Chote Lal Yadav who vacated the seat for him in the last elections', Ms Mayawati exclaimed and added that the BSP was looking forward to Akbar Ahmad Dumpy's victory from Kannauj. 'For this I will give extra time and attention to Kannauj during the campaigning,' Ms Maywati informed. Upbeat at the prospect of the BSP in eight other constituencies where by-elections are being held, the BSP vice-president maintained that her party would make major gains in the polls. 'Since we held not a single seat we have nothing to lose... every single seat would be a gain,' she said. (3 February 2000)

The strategy of reporters in all these cases was to get close to leaders by giving them what they wanted, namely positive publicity. Journalists could only hope that their investment would later pay off. Promoting a politician is not uncontroversial and is at time frowned upon by editors, yet it is accepted as a necessary part of press activity. Good connections instil respect among colleagues. Yet admiration is coupled with envy and even disgust, especially since articles written after such courtesy meetings tend to be biased toward the politicians' preferred self-image. They introduce the respective leader as a determined fighter for clearly defined (benevolent) social causes. They are hardly surprising and rarely ironic or subversive. Their news value is ambivalent at best.

Needless to say, news and news-worthiness are not clearly defined categories. As a newspaper acts as an authorising institution, everything it prints is news. However, as professionals, journalists certainly develop hierarchies of news-worthiness. As a guideline for the practitioner, the acclaimed American journalist Jack Fuller describes news as a report about something 'a news organisation has recently learned about matters of some significance or interest to the specific community that the news organisation serves' (Fuller 1996: 6). He emphasises novelty and relevance for the audience as salient features. Sociological accounts of news-making arrive at similar conclusions. Schudson defines news as something that is 'publicly notable' (2003: 6). More elaborate lists include the criteria of novelty, suspense, importance, unexpectedness or negativity (Golding and Elliott 1979:114–23; Hartley 1982: 75–79; Manning 2001: 60–65; Ruhrmann 1994; Tiffen 1989: 52–69; Watson 2003 [1998]: 134–47).

The meetings and articles discussed in this section had none of this. Their news-worthiness resulted solely from the status of the speakers. Elite persons undoubtedly rank high in evaluations of news-worthiness. The interest in politicians is highly developed in a leader-centred society like India and fuses with 'traditional' forms of leader-centred performances in the public arena (Rao, forthcoming). What I have defined as the pertinent feature of 'big men politics' at the lower level of the political hierarchy is even more pronounced at the top end. Uttar Pradesh proves a good example of leader-centred politics, with the SP and the BSP built around one prominent, extremely powerful charismatic individual (Jaffrelot 2003).

Thus, the treatment of state politics in newspapers can be accounted for as another instance of leader-centred reporting. A further analysis of the *Water* coverage would support this line of argument. The obsession with individual opinions could be found not only on local pages; it actually dominated all coverage. Yet, while the style may coincide, the implications are entirely different. Journalists gain little from covering minor leaders. In contrast, investment in key politicians delivers insiders' knowledge, elevates the status of political reporters and promises personal advantage. High-level political reporting is unsurpassed in its ability to fulfil the promise inherent in the reporting profession – to become one among the powerful – and hence it is a highly favoured career option. Taking this into account, it is not surprising that journalists invest heavily in the top leaders, hanging out, making friends and writing leader-centred articles.

The desire for intimacy and recognition has consequences for the news discourse. Coverage is driven not only by judgements of what is exciting or interesting for readers, but what fulfils the professional needs of reporters and newspapers. In return for being admitted into the inner circle of power, journalists act as conduits for politicians' promotional activities. News discourse is a function of leader competition. It not only promotes individuals but also perpetuates the cultural assumption that progress follows from the intervention of visionary leaders.

However, journalists are not just obedient servants of dominant political agents or adjuncts in the grip of a political structure. They are in control of a much sought after commodity that is at the heart of political life. Hence they have significant powers themselves. This is recognised by politicians, who dance to reporters' tunes. Journalists receive and demand respect and authority and their interventions significantly impact on the structure of political communication.

Journalists as Informants

Journalists are information people: this is a typical assumption of media professionals and a carefully cultivated image. Reporters take it for granted that political moves should be made intelligible to them and claim an institutional right to break the news. The following statement from a reporter working for *Asia Age* is revealing:

> We have to make predictions, but sometimes we get it wrong. Take, for example, the crowning of a new chief minister. Other names [than that of Ram Prakash Gupta] were in the game. And by that night I had received a call that Kalraj Mishra was final. This is what I wrote. But then this was cancelled again. Ram Prakash Gupta became the new leader of the state. Politicians themselves were confused. So how can we have a clear picture? (Journalist, *Asian Age*, 28 January 2000)

The reporter assumed that he (his profession) should be informed in advance as to who would become new chief minister, even before the result was announced officially. The desire to know first is a corollary to the competition between journalists and newspapers for breaking news. This strategy was also employed to bring respect and invite further information-sharing.

It is considered a lack of professional respect and a source of annoyance when reporters are prevented from accessing information, or presented with information not tuned to their needs.[11] Experienced politicians know this and offer journalists VIP treatment. In order to get it right, they acquaint themselves carefully with the priorities of media people, allowing them to come close to them and build up a special relationship with them, confiding in them and giving them the feeling that they are participating in the glamour of their profession. They do not usually ask them to go beyond their professional routine. Many meetings are specially structured to keep press people in a good mood and retain their attention. It is rare for boring speeches to come without a sweetener. They may be coupled with a lunch, such as Om Prakash Singh's press conference, or other enticements may be offered. Mayawati, for example, aware that Dalit ideology would not excite reporters, began her hour-long principle speech with the announcement that she would reveal the names of candidates for the by-elections at the end, making sure no one left halfway through the press conference.

This normal and unspectacular routine is a well-tuned synchronisation of performances. It is based on an adjustment of perspectives vigorously promoted by journalists who offer advice and spread information that is to their advantage. For example, a meeting initiated by the UP Youth Congress in Lucknow, called *Agenda 2000*, attracted a large audience, but little could be read about its content in the newspaper. The Congress beat reporter from *Dainik Jagaran* later talked about the reasons for this publicity disaster during a press conference at the Youth Congress office. He explained to the leaders that the meeting was too much like a conference. Journalists would have needed more readily available material and more drama to merit a headline. There were other situations where reporters adopted a pedagogical tone. Manoj instructed Akhilesh Yadav on strategic ways of interacting with media personnel. The beat reporter from *Dainik Jagaran* urged Om Prakash Singh to confide more information and to meet press people in small groups rather than at large press conferences.

Journalists are not always quite as open about sharing knowledge and strategies. They may stubbornly refuse cooperation where long-term advantages and news value are in question. The director-general of police experienced this the hard way. On 18 February 2000, he invited journalists for a meeting followed by a lunch. The promise of exceptionally good food and the novelty of entering the normally inaccessible fortress of the police leader attracted an unusually large number of journalists (approximately 200). The meeting began with a one-hour power point presentation, which was followed by another hour filled with a principle speech and a question-and-answer session. Reporters were informed about community policing as a new security strategy soon to be implemented in the state. The director-general explained that the success of such a policy would depend on the trust of citizens in the police. Thus, he wanted to win over prominent citizens, who would promote the project. The press was supposed to play a central role here by advertising the new policy and identifying eminent citizens who would support and popularise the move.

Journalists were bored. The meeting was far too long and the topic anything but exciting. Most of the information was available from the police webpage. Guests also felt intimidated by the probing questions of the host, who wanted to extract from journalists ideas for the best public relation strategies. The event had little news value and there was no indication that community policing would produce good stories in the near future. In other words, the director-general offered nothing and demanded a lot in return, namely feedback, ideas and publicity. This was a bad way to start a relationship. Journalists resisted. They covered the press conference but did not return for the follow-up meeting a few weeks later and wrote no further stories on community policing.

The director-general had invited journalists because he valued them as masters of the process of public communication and as sources of information. Yet, he had to experience that journalists make strategic choices. The resentment that reporters developed towards the director-general was in stark contrast to the cooperation extended to top politicians. Journalists calculate that major leaders are always worth the investment, thus they show off, appease, make friends and solicit information. Informal meetings in particular have no clear protocol and the roles of information-giver and information-seeker may be swapped several times. Journalists gain respect and make themselves indispensable by demonstrating their inside knowledge. Shekar readily fed Mulayam Singh Yadav information about Kalyan Singh's political prospects. His opinion on this matter was highly relevant to Mulayam, since a recent turn of events saw his long-standing political rival from the other side of the party divide competing for the same 'vote banks'.[12] Similarly, Manoj conversed with Akhilesh about the prospects of his political opponent in the constituency, making sure that Akhilesh would remember the conversation as being useful to him. During a press conference at the SP office, one reporter spoke of a neighbourhood dispute that involved accusations of illegal building activities. The SP state president admitted that he had not heard about the incident, asked for the details and announced that he would immediately send someone to enquire and, if necessary, intervene.

In all these situations journalists participate in the circulation of political information. Journalists become partners in communication. They carry information and are the harbingers of news. They are the ever-present alter egos, forcing leaders to make ideas tangible and announce political moves. They are the embodied reminder that politics needs drama and they act as catalysts to bring it about. They function as a political conscience, dragging out past promises and announcements, setting agendas or at least reminding politicians of the set agenda. Journalists demand communication and entangle politicians in dialogues that move beyond sharing prefigured knowledge. Politicians are seduced into engaging in a communicative act that bridges the professions and produces valid ('objective') political perspectives at their intersection. A further example will consolidate the argument.

In January 2000 Ram Prakash Gutpa went on his first official visit as chief minister of Uttar Pradesh to Delhi, where he met his party colleagues in the national government. He had invited journalists to a press conference for this occasion. There were no pressing issues; the conference was a courtesy to the press, an occasion for the two sides to get to know each other and discuss political views. Towards the end of the meeting, however, a reporter raised a question regarding the Ayodhya controversy. He wanted to know whether Gupta supported the demand for a temple to Ram at Ayodhya.

The question touched upon a highly sensitive issue. For many years the BJP had encouraged and actively created a movement to demand the construction of a temple at the mythical birthplace of the god-king Ram in Ayodhya. This agenda resulted in much unrest, violence and great suffering by the Muslim community in India. The supporters of the Ayodhya project wanted a Ram temple to replace the Babri Mosque at the site which was, according to the claims of the activists, and contrary to archaeological evidence, built on the ruins of an earlier temple to Ram. On 6 December 1996, the disputed mosque was illegally destroyed by Hindu fundamentalists; the BJP government of UP remained silent and did not intervene, thus both sanctioning and encouraging the violence. This event was followed by riots and systematic pogroms against Muslims in many parts of the country. Even after these dramatic events, Hindu radicals continued to demand the construction of a temple and undertook building activities near the contested site (for details of the Ayodhya controversy, see Brosius 2005; Davis 1996; Elst 2003; Engineer 1990; Hartung 2004; Nandy et al. 1995; Rajagopal 1994, 2001; van der Veer 1997).

This question was unexpected by Gupta, who had not prepared himself for a critical line of questioning. The request for a comment was an enquiry into his political philosophy and designed to enlighten the community about what to expect under his reign. The Ayodhya issue was significant to journalists as the destruction of the Babri mosque was associated with Kalyan Singh, chief minister at that time and the predecessor of Ram Prakash Gupta. Kalyan was notorious as a vigorous fighter for Hindu fundamentalist issues. Unlike his predecessors (from other parties), he did nothing to ease the tensions between Hindus and Muslims and tolerated the illegal destruction of the mosque by radical Hindus.[13] The question now arose whether the pro-Hindutva policies would continue in UP under the new chief minister. Om Prakash Gupta was considered close to Prime Minister Atal Bihari Vajpayee, one of the moderate figures in the BJP,[14] and lent support to the prospect of change in policy.

The question of the fate of the temple took Ram Prakash Gupta by surprise. The chief minister had only recently returned to active politics after twenty years of absence. He had been introduced as a consensus candidate after Kalyan Singh had become too controversial. Gupta's appointment to the highest office in the state was intended to discourage further intensification of hostility between the various factions in the state BJP and their ambitious leader.[15] However, Ram Prakash Gupta was poorly prepared for his new job. His reaction to the question on Ayodhya was only one of his many mistakes. Instead of giving a well-calculated diplomatic answer, he openly admitted that he personally supported the temple project, even saying that 'the temple should be built as peacefully as the mosque had been destroyed [sic!]'.[16] The TV journalists had their quotation of the day, and the press a perfect headline.

This brief statement from a visibly overburdened chief minister left an imprint on the political debate. It became the 'split in the façade' through which the true intentions of the BJP became visible. It appeared to confirm the dissenting opinion that did not believe in the tame face of the BJP. Of course, the central government immediately issued a disclaimer, calling the statement a private opinion. The prime minister personally stressed that the BJP had no intention of starting any construction at the disputed site. However, these efforts only reinforced the view that the construction of a temple in Ayodhya was part of a hidden agenda.

It was hardly surprising that a representative of the BJP would make a provocative statement in favour of the Ram Temple. The news did not lie in the novelty of the event; on the contrary, the statement was singled out and publicised as 'news' because it confirmed preconceived notions of the structure of the political field, which is often blurred through the contextual activity of politicians. In this case the image of the BJP assumed clarity with a statement that confirmed the established perception of the BJP as a Hindu nationalist party. It has been blurred by the moderate tone adopted by some party leaders since forming the central government.

While all the newspapers highlighted Gupta's statement on Ayodhya as the main news of the press conference, they gave a very different evaluation of the event in internal debates. During exchanges among colleagues, journalists asserted that the statement was the *faux pas* of a helpless chief minister. Journalists acknowledged that Gupta was unable to cope with the responsibility of his office. He seemed too old and too long out of the business to be able to meet the requirements of a political struggle that had changed, not least because of the increasing presence of the mass media. Gupta was unable to react quickly and to make calculations at the same time, partly because he had lost touch and no longer had an intimate knowledge of relationships, issues and the distribution of power. Journalists were convinced that Gupta made the statement because the situation of the press conference had stressed him and because he had lost control over his performance at the end of a tiring session, admitting to a personal opinion which was not necessarily a political project sanctioned by his party. Bombarded by many critical questions, the chief minister was unable to meet the requirements of the 'press conference' format.

The consequences of this slip of the tongue were severe and the press took ample advantage of it. Publishing it provided a forward pass to politicians. To make sure leaders used it, the theme was brought up during interviews and press conferences, extracting strong anti-BJP statements. The ensuing public debate not only discredited the chief minister but also destroyed the confidence in all political moves forwarded by the BJP in the following months. Each instance was portrayed as part of an agenda to Hinduise the state. Consider the following statement by the Congress leader, commenting on the state government's announcement to set up a committee for the review of the constitution, fifty years after it had been drawn up:

C.A. Singh: There is no need for a committee. The constitution has to be amended constantly. This is an ongoing process. Why have something special now? If you want changes, discuss them in the political circles. That they have a committee means they have some hidden agenda. The RSS is behind this.

Reporter: Do you think the idea is to create a Hindu Rashtriya [Hindu reign]?

C.A. Singh: Yes. They know that they do not have a three-quarter majority. This is why they experiment with a committee. (Press conference with Janta Dal leader Chaudhri Ajit Singh, 29 January 2000)

The comments of the BSP chief followed the same line:

The BJP wants to change the constitution. We believe this is an attempt to create a Hindu Raj. Finally the BJP has come out with their hidden agenda. We will challenge such a move. The hard work of Ambedkar shall not be destroyed. [...] Changes in our system will endanger democracy. (Press conference with the BSP leader Mayawati, 30 January 2000)

Both statements were made during press conferences in which the leaders reminded the audience that Gupta had clearly exposed the hidden agenda of his party. His unguarded fundamentalist statement guided their perception. It would be stretching the point to say that the vociferous opposition to the review committee and other BJP policies was only an effect of Gupta's controversial announcement. However, it was obvious that his testimony for a Ram temple heightened sensitivity over the Hindu nationalist agenda of BJP politics.

My argument is not that journalists purposefully promoted an anti-BJP stance. This was not partisan reporting but a means-to-an-end calculation. The quotation could be exploited for increasing circulation figures and it served as a welcome peg in leader-centred interviews. Making public a controversial statement about an extremely sensitive issue was an invitation for oppositional leaders to produce pragmatic speeches for the media, covered by reporters in personalised articles. The discursive effects were significant. A professionally clever and shrewd move influenced the political atmosphere for months to come. Journalists did not create the fear of the Hindu nationalist agenda of the BJP. Yet, they brought it to the forefront and kept it going as long as it served them.

Journalists' manipulation of political manoeuvres is a regular feature of a mass-mediated democracy. Two earlier examples support this point. Journalists most certainly provided the anti-*Water* movement – discussed in the last chapter – with the necessary force. The willingness of leaders to exploit the event was welcomed by journalists who were happy to quote an abundance of voices from civil society and politics. The sheer quantity of articles turned the event into a major movement and uproar by the people of Banaras. The prospect for publicity prompted more and more national leaders to comment or even travel personally to Banaras. For journalists this was a wonderful opportunity for more leader-centred articles and personal interviews, now also at the top end of the political spectrum. The frantic press activity delivered the clue to the chief minister in Lucknow who justified his decision to ban filming with reference to the widespread opposition. By adopting the perspective of the media – that filming promoted unrest – he could sharpen his profile as defender of Hindu culture at no apparent cost.

Similarly, the reshuffle of portfolios was pushed by journalistic activities. When Gupta took over the government in November 1999, he reacted to the demands of his coalition partners by promising that he would give them a greater share of ministries. After the initial assurance the theme disappeared from public gaze. However, journalists were convinced that it was simmering and speculated about when the reshuffle would take place and who it would involve. Afraid to miss the decisive move, they brought up the theme at every possible occasion. The following dialogue concluded a press conference held to discuss the *Water* controversy:

Reporter:	Will you reshuffle the portfolios?
Gupta:	Yes. I want to.
Reporter:	When?
Gupta:	Soon!
Reporter:	When?
Gupta:	In one or two days. I am not able to do as much as I want to do.

(Press conference, 7 February 2000)

Gupta's elusive answer is a clear indication that he did not wish to be reminded of the theme, with other urgent problems to solve, like the energy crisis and the *Water* controversy. Some journalists even speculated that he might have wanted to drop the item from his agenda altogether. While nothing definite can be said about Gupta's hidden strategies, it is clear that the press kept the topic present in everyone's mind. Reporters rehearsed their standard question about the reshuffle at every single meeting with Gupta, till he finally announced the new posts.

While journalists never directly demanded action, they were nevertheless instrumental in bringing it about. Motivated by the professional desire to triumph in the race for breaking the news, reporters became allies of disgruntled coalition members. When changes were announced, journalists immediately 'changed sides' and now sought comments from those who had lost power. Reporters arrived at selected politicians' houses even before the leaders could call them (or reflect on whether they would want to call them). Journalists had every reason to believe that the losers would be in a mood to complain and thus made sure they would get 'the quote' first. The reshuffle galvanised reporters to open up a new round of collecting comments in personalised interviews, feeding into the leader-reporter exchange relation.

Blurred Boundaries

Journalists are key players in the political arena. This is implicated in the notion of the Forth Estate. It is also part of the everyday experience of citizens, who observe in a cursory manner how the media exert pressure on political actors. Sociological accounts demonstrate that journalists function as relevant audiences for politicians and representatives of the public. Their activity of eliciting, sharing and displaying information impacts on the structure of political communication (Ericson, Baranek, Chan 1989; Golding et al. 1986; Schneider 1997; Sigal 1973). Typically, sociological accounts assume the perspective of journalists or sources and investigate how the 'other' is appropriated and integrated into their own work flow. However, in order to appreciate the depth of interconnection between media and politics, we need to move beyond explaining the activity of politicians and journalists with reference to an idealised division of labour. There is no doubt that politicians and journalists are driven by the agendas of their respective professions and develop strategies of how to utilise neighbouring institutions as efficiently as possible.

Yet trans-institutional communication is not just an arrangement of convenience, where professionals engage in mutual exploitation. It is also a shared arena of knowledge in-the-making that is formed in a process of adjusting priorities and forging relations. My research demonstrates how in friendly meetings, journalists and politicians purposefully underplay their idealised roles for the sake of relations. Political images are forged through negotiations taking place at the interface between two professions, whose representatives are ready to engage with each others' priorities. In the arena shared by politicians and journalists, communication has an agenda-setting function, prescribing ways to embody the political and patterns structures for evaluating political performance.

News-making validates and reinvigorates the leader-centeredness of the Indian political system, as both sides like face-to-face meetings and personalised articles are excellent trade objects in an exchange economy. The flow of journalists between politician's houses acts as a barometer for updating the measures of power. Where news-worthiness is traded for closeness to leaders, the political flourishes not only as a series of events and decisions (and debates surrounding these decisions) but as endless commentary, with all decisions, events and movements being viewed through the lenses of all the available ideological positions embodied in the political structure. This exercise of collecting comments hardly realises the ideal of a liberal press promoting a rationalisation of politics through public deliberation. It is rather a recursive updating of an essentialised version of the social, as split in discrete units of caste, religion and region, each represented by a leader and / or a party. Leaders' comments recursively refresh ideologies of caste, religion and region. They delineate political identity groups and recreate them as the most relevant social entities. The parliamentary struggle conflates with identity politics at the grassroots as part of a dialogic enmeshment of journalists and politicians.

Getting involved with each other is not without drawbacks. It promotes a dubious image of the press as being corrupted by power. Confronted with corruption charges, media professionals invest heavily in 'border control'. Thus, while there is much hob-nobbing between politicians and journalists, both sides remain conscious of professional boundaries and are determined to portray a sober image. Movement in a shared territory is punctuated with performances of distance, creating an ideal division of labour. Performances of distance keep at bay unrealistic expectations in exchange relations. They establish journalists' independence and function as repair mechanisms for the chronically difficult relation between the press and politics. They are used to prove independence and repudiate corruption charges mounted against journalists by colleagues and bosses. The acknowledgment of the intersection between politics and journalism needs to be coupled with an appreciation of their social distance. While practices bridge the gap between professions, there is a stubborn insistence on separateness. It invigorates the notion of the division of labour as a salient feature of democracy.

Performing Distance

Everyone in the reporting profession concedes the need for closeness. Yet, the trade-offs are problematic and frowned upon especially by bosses. These are the thoughts of a news editor.

> I encourage my men to have contacts everywhere. But we also have to think about why these people want to say something. What do they expect in exchange? Maybe special coverage, or that negative news about them would be withheld. I am ready to support these sources when I see that they are supportive of my journalists. [...] Of course there are planted stories and open lies. (News Editor, interview 9. February 2000)

The ideal of an independent press promotes a movement contrary to that described in the first half of the chapter. Performing distance is crucial in a profession accused of corruption and admired for yielding influence. The Janus face of power surfaces as a demon hunting journalists at every stage of their work process. The press is the hero fighting for political honesty, objective reporting and social justice. It is also the villain following a trail of corruption and self-indulgence. In chapter three I described how I began to appreciate the simultaneous co-existence of two moral codes. One sees journalists as un-involved observers, the other sees them as brokers. To counter the negative connotations of the strong-man image and to retain a certain freedom, journalists routinely perform acts of distancing – an acknowledgement of the oppressive presence of powerful intervention and the demands for reciprocity. Reporters are instructed early in their careers on the necessity of proving their independence:

> A young man came to the office at *Dainik Jagaran* today. He approached Anil and told him that he wanted to join the company as a freelancer. Anil asked him to send a text at the weekend and then come back on Monday to be assigned a task. Just before leaving the applicant was called back and told 'And let me tell you, all this doing a favour and going after persons and politicians is not our job! It does not work here!' (Field notes, 8 March 2002)

In this and similar statements, old and new members are frequently reminded not to throw independence overboard in view of the omnipresence of 'corruption'. The message is that exchange relations are not the raison d'être of journalism and that the profession must control power from a distance. Anti-corruption rhetoric obviously does not erase obligations in news relationships or remove the temptation to take advantage of connections, yet it is a strong reminder that journalists inhabit a bifurcated arena and have to develop their skills to navigate the minefield of appropriate and inappropriate favours.

Manoj's trip to Kannauj is a good example of how journalists accomplish the difficult task of negotiating social distance. The trip was part of pre-election reporting. Manoj wanted to observe the election campaign of Akhilesh Yadav, obtain a private interview with the prospective member of the national parliament and make sure he got close to him before he became big and powerful. The young politician excited the press. He was a fresh face in politics, a member of an extremely powerful family and a professional educated in Australia. He was perfectly suited for extensive news coverage. Whatever could be said about him would be new and at the same time significant, since Akhilesh could be expected to become a powerful leader soon, due to the influence of his father, Mulayam Singh Yadav.

Manoj and I decided to go together. We left Lucknow on 2 February 2000 at 6 p.m. and reached Kannauj at 12:30 a.m. It was difficult to find accommodation so late at night, especially during an election campaign. However, Manoj made sure that we did not depend on the party, and found us a suitable room through the district authorities. We requested a jeep from the police to bring us to the interior where Akhilesh was campaigning. However, there was no spare car as the police were using all state-owned cars to patrol election areas, and all the taxis had been booked by the political parties. In the end we had to ask the party office and accept a car and a driver paid for by the SP. This made Manoj (as well as his editor, to whom we talked about it later) extremely uncomfortable. During the whole trip Manoj ensured that it was he who payed for the petrol and provided food for the two drivers.

What was thought of as an interview turned out to be a major trip, since we had to follow Akhilesh for nine hours through the interior of the province, meeting him again and again at different campaign locations till we finally convinced him to set aside time for a private interview. It was a tedious, tiring and arduous job. While Akhilesh and his crew moved by helicopter from one area to the next, we had to race after him, crammed in a Maruti van, driving on mud roads. We barely managed to catch up with the team of politicians, reaching each station of the journey only shortly before Akhiliesh's departure to the next place. We went through the same ordeal several times. Stressed by the worry that we would not make it, we pushed our way relentlessly through the tight security, bodyguards dashing after us demanding evidence for our status and proof that we were entitled to meet the leader. Luckily Akhilesh spotted us every time from his elevated position on the stage. He would give us a benevolent smile, waves us up on the stage and quieten down the security people. Seated next to Akhilesh we managed to exchange a few sentences before we were stopped by PR people. Our recurrent request for an interview was referred to Mulayam Singh Yadav. We would then sit quietly and listen to the end of speeches and see the leaders depart without getting an answer. Finally, at the last stop, we were given the message that we could meet Akhilesh at his father's house at 8 p.m. for a private interview. We were overjoyed! We did not mind another twenty kilometres of travelling and rushed to the car to be in time.

We reached Mulayam Singh's residence promptly at 8 p.m. We settled down inside a spacious, beautifully furnished, cool hall. For the first time that day we felt a little relaxed. We were given tea and were asked repeatedly whether we were having dinner. We had not eaten the whole day and were starving. However, Manoj sternly refused a meal and settled for snacks (fruit!). Manoj instructed me to eat as slowly as possible, showing no sign of hunger or greed. The interview lasted for about two hours and was a great success. Akhilesh was very relaxed and talked about anything we wanted to engage. We were proud and happy to be the first press people to get a glimpse of this political personality of the next generation. We finished late and had to leave immediately in order to be back in Lucknow as soon as possible. The editor in Lucknow had thrown a tantrum earlier during a telephone call, rebuking Manoj for not having filed any article that day and urging him to fax something immediately. He refused to write on that day but was nervous to rush back to the office and resume his duties. Travelling back to Kannauj half the night in a region notorious for its criminality was a gloomy prospect. However, Manoj did not accept the offer for transport (and protection) organised by the Mulayam family. His stubborn resistance reinforced the image he had built up during that day of a dedicated newsman, who puts up with harsh conditions to acquire exciting news and stay independent at the same time.

However, while Manoj refused any offer of greater comfort, he had no problem in demanding attention in return for all the pains he had taken to follow the candidate for a whole day. Negotiating a chance to have an interview alone with Akhilesh (who most of the time was kept away from the media by his father), he went on at great length about all the difficulties we faced just to meet him: how we braved the dusty and bumpy roads, bore the heat, had no food, no rest and hardly any sleep. The self-portrait of a tough newsman merged with self-praise for his professional achievements. Manoj boasted about his qualities as a reporter and also asked me to support this line. He also repeatedly reminded Akhilesh that they had been to the same school, promoting a sense of acquaintance and comradeship. Akhilesh responded positively to the informal tone and engaged in a stress-free exchange of ideas. Back in the office, Manoj bragged about our two-hour private interview with Akhilesh. He proclaimed that he was treated like an acquaintance and that we were invited into the inner part of Mulayam Singh Yadav's private home (not just his residence in Lucknow!) and offered dinner (which we of course rejected!).

By way of negotiating his relation with Mulayam and his son, Manoj distinguished three types of favours. He tenaciously insisted on a private interview and keenly accepted an invitation to the politician's private residence. He reluctantly agreed to a party van for transport in view of the acute vehicle shortage. Finally, he resolutely refused a private dinner and private transport. The explicit differentiation serves the demarcation of professional positions. As I have argued earlier, private interviews are a place for journalists' self-promotion and the forging of relations. They are instrumental in blurring professional boundaries, which makes them ambiguous and dangerous, an activity that may encourage unrealistic expectations and can border on corruption. The resolute refusal to cross a certain boundary re-establishes distance and introduces an element of indeterminacy in the relation. It counters the overall impression of a chummy meeting, asserting that this is not friends drinking tea, but a professional exercise with an unpredictable outcome.

Practices of closeness are regularly coupled with such explicit performances of distance. There is always a cohort of reporters leaving a press conference just before lunch or snacks. At times journalists turn down invitations to be given unofficial information or they purposefully wreck press conferences with aggressive questions. Journalists can refuse to sacrifice at the altar of leaders. An interesting case was the *Times of India*'s refusal to treat the visit of the Prime Minister to Lucknow as front page news, as all other newspapers did. The editor saw no news value in the story and argued that in order to progress, India should stop the meaningless hero worshipping of leaders. Journalists can decide to rebuff a request for the dissemination or strategic veiling of information and their articles are often far more critical than leaders would like them to be. All these actions highlight professional distinctions. They reinstate an ideal order in which the press acts as a critical, outside observer. Performances of distance nurture the awareness that professional duties do and in fact should pull politicians and journalists apart. Here the concept of distinct social fields comes into its own as an abstraction validating practices. It enables journalists and politicians to re-emerge as role-players with a clearly defined duty in a greater moral economy that transcends personal obligations for reciprocity. In marking a boundary, journalists reassure themselves and others that they are journalists and only journalists.

Assurances of distance are directed at informants and colleagues, and accompany the boasting about relationships. While special treatment by leaders forms the social capital of a political reporter, it also leads to rumours. Just before the Kannauj trip, Manoj struggled against the negative evaluation of his coverage of Kalyan Singh. He had written four articles in short succession on the party president without showing any sign of critical engagement. He produced straightforward reproductions of the leader's polemical attacks:

Upbeat Kalyan blows the fuse
Lucknow: […] 'Rome is burning and Vajpayee is playing the flute in Delhi', explained former UP chief minister and Rashtriya Kranti Party (RKP) leader Kalyan Singh on Monday while commenting on the role of the Prime Minister in the ongoing power strike. Ecstatic after the success of the well-attended 'Swabhiman' rally at Etah on Sunday, Mr. Singh charged the state government with mishandling the power strike and also

accused the PM with turning a blind eye to the plight of the people in the wake of severe power cuts.

> Questioning the government's timing of pushing through power reforms, Mr Kalyan Singh said the stir had hit both farmer and students alike as it was harvest time and also exams were round the corner. […] Accusing the state government of being 'ill-prepared' and the central government of being 'hardly bothered', he said, 'the seriousness of the PM can be gauged by the manner in which he dispatched a non-entity like Shiv Kumar as emissary'. He also criticized the Union minister, PR Kumarmangalam's whirlwind visit, to the state. (25 January 2000)

Manoj decided to give no context that might have shed a critical light on Kalyan's statements. He omitted the fact that Kalyan had initiated the power reform. He also made no mention of the opportunism with which Kalyan – no longer a member of the BJP – now tried to attract members of the lower castes and Muslims, who had earlier suffered greatly from his Hindu nationalist politics, especially in the context of the Ayodhya conflict. He failed to explain the transformation of the leader from an arrogant political star who commanded journalists according to his whim, to a nice friendly guy who wooed minorities.

The articles on Kalyan contrasted with other texts in which Manoj critically addressed leaders' statements. The editor liked Manoj's ability to contextualise information and encouraged reflexive thinking, such as this introduction in an article about V.P. Singh:

> Has V.P. Singh ceased to be a political force? Or so it appears on Saturday as the former PM spent a quiet morning at his residence in the state capital. Choosing to hold a 'durbar' [court] with some old-time faithfuls on the lawns of his Raj Bhawan Colony residence, the former Raja of Manda pontificated on economic policies and growing divide between the rich and the poor. Interestingly, politics was a strict no no! (28 February 2000)

After this introduction Manoj proceeds to quote some of the political statements the leader made. However, the intended impact of these statements is lost on the reader, who from the beginning is invited to see them critically, as pure self-indulgence by someone who no longer has any real power or any interest in 'real' politics.

Manoj adopted a similar strategy in an article on Mulayam Singh Yadav's election campaign. Again there are several direct quotations, which are re-contextualised through comments on the setting:

Mulayam pontificates on CTBT [Comprehensive Test Ban Treaty] in the rural outbacks of Kannauj

Umarda (Kannauj): The teacher in Mulayam Singh Yadav has (re)surfaced these days. Having left his job as a teacher at the Karhal college some three decades back, the election campaign of his son, Akhilesh, provides many opportunities to see the Samajwadi Party leader's penchant for his one time profession. Disciplining the crowd, directing his candidate son and waxing eloquent on his brand of international philosophy, it's all there. (7 February 2000)

After some direct quotations from Mulayam, the article continues:

While the junior Yadav prefers to keep quiet, papa Yadav speaks at length from anything to everything – scarcity of fertilizers, lack of toilets, his meeting with the Russian President and fallout of signing CTBT. (7 February 2000)

These intersecting comments ridicule Mulayam's statements and make them appear out of place in a rural setting. While the leader may have impressed his audience with a powerful performance, he certainly has not convinced this reporter, who refuses to support the image of a powerful, effective, fearsome personality which Mulayam tries to represent.

Manoj's writing makes explicit his strategic choices, at least to insiders. It is difficult to hide connections because there is always a public side to them. They become part of an internal struggle for status recognition and career development. Krishna – one of Manoj's colleagues and close competitor – was particularly interested in Manoj's relationship with Kalyan. He had been very close to the leader when he was still chief minister. Krishna demanded confirmation from me about our interview at Kalyan's house. I produced it, prompted by Manoj to tell Krishna everything about how friendly and relaxed Kalyan had been and how he had showed us around his garden. Here I could make up for the terrible inefficiency that had annoyed Manoj earlier. I had not taken my camera to the meeting with the politician and thus could not produce proof of Manoj's success. He had wanted a photograph of himself with Kalyan in the politician's garden, which would have been very exclusive! Without such evidence he could only rely on oral accounts.

Yet such fame is ambivalent. Whenever I talked to the editor about how Manoj's work was developing, he complained that the reporter was becoming absorbed into the political network and thus unable to maintain distance. There was also direct criticism, such as during the morning meeting on 1 February 2000. Manoj said that he would like to write an article about two MLAs who had defected from the BJP to join Kalyan's new party. The editor replied: 'We cannot constantly give Kalyan's point of view. We have to be more critical in order to assess the situation.' In spite of this criticism Manoj assured me that he was doing the right thing and had been encouraged by the editor to build up political connections. He also offered a moral argument about reciprocity. According to Manoj, Krishna was once close to Mulayam but deserted him after he got what he wanted, namely a government flat. Following this lack of respect, Manoj claimed, Kalyan ditched Krishna. Manoj wanted to play fair and repay for privileged access. He was also upfront about the kind of return gift he expected: he also wanted a government flat. When I returned two years later he had managed to acquire one.

The editors of all newspapers expressed knowledge of reporters' favourites and complained about their inability to control their employees, while reporters in their turn accused bosses of using them for their personal interests. Thus, while internal competition encourages the building of relationships, the organisation also puts constraints on their realisation. Journalists build and advertise their good connections. Yet, they make sure to emphasise their integrity. Through calculated performances of closeness *and* distance, journalists negotiate the indistinct border between being well-connected and being corrupt.

Navigating Uncertainty

The examples in this chapter demonstrate the range of relationships that tie politicians and journalists together and divide them at the same time. The exchange of favours is a highly ambivalent activity, because the line between gift exchange and corruption remains blurred. Professionals need to navigate the ambivalence that emerges from a double embedding of their work. Close relations are a *sine qua non* for professional success. Press people and informants share a platform for negotiating political matters. However, they do this as representatives of professions that are idealised as constituting distinct domains. Hence, ensuring closeness is kept under control through the symbolic patrolling of professional boundaries.

An excellent indicator of the oscillation between excessive closeness and exaggerated suspicion is the way in which journalists move through politicians' houses. A politician's house usually has three parts: the inner private core, the rooms for confidential meetings in between, and the halls for public gatherings at the edge. To proceed from the outside to the centre, a stranger needs an invitation for each 'border crossing'. However, journalists are never stopped at the front gate. They freely move through all the public rooms, almost as if they were at home. For interviews they are called – usually before the eyes of the assembled public[17] – into the semi-private rooms in between, where they can talk about delicate matters. Petitioners outside are forced to wait, and hence are shown their subordinate position in the social hierarchy. Yet journalists rarely proceed to the inner part and in any case are likely to refuse any such invitation. There is a certain chumminess but rarely real friendship.

Uncertainty and suspense persist in the politician–journalist interaction and produce a meta-discourse about professionalism. Dissonance caused by professional constraints is reflected and digested in half-serious, half-joking comments about the impossibility of being friends. Journalists fall back on the rhetoric of professional duty to justify critical articles, while politicians use it to counter-balance blatant attempts at influencing the press. The latter is well demonstrated by Om Prakash Singh's remarks during a press conference celebrating a BJP victory. The by-elections of 2000 were a great success for the ruling BJP, the only party that gained seats. While BJP politicians were in a good mood, journalists cared less. They did not 'waste' paper on the BJP, but instead focused almost exclusively on the outcome of the 'royal battle' in Kannauj, where Akhilesh Yadav from the SP had won against the BSP heavy-weight 'Dumpy'. Thus, although Mulayam Singh Yadav's party lost seats in the election, his son's victory made him a winner. The celebration of Akhilesh's triumph constituted the climax of a systematically built-up narrative. Tension was created by the frequent meetings with SP politicians as well as by the regular coverage of campaigning in Kannauj. The BJP party leader did not take this kindly.

> During the press conference Om Prakash Singh received a call for a telephone interview with a news channel. When he had finished answering the questions he turned to the assembled press and expressed his frustration: 'They just wanted to know about Kannauj. What about *our* victory of three assembly seats? There has been too much sensation-making about Kannauj. (Field notes, 25 February 2000)

Later he added emphatically: 'At least today write something positive about us!' (Om Prakash Singh, press conference on 25 February 2000). And again over tea: 'You people in any case write what you want, but at least today you cannot diminish us!' (Om Prakash Singh, press conference on 25 February 2000). While expressing his desire for positive publicity, Om Prakash Singh revealed his disillusionment with the press.

Against the constant flow of complaints by politicians about media coverage, journalists mount their campaign of appeasement.[18] I have narrated two examples of social 'repair' work. Sehkar defended his election prognosis in front of Mulayam Singh Yadav with respect to professional pressures. He claimed that he had expected a better result for the SP than most other media observers, but was prevented from publishing it due to a popular perception that contradicted him. A similar dialogue ensued between Manoj and the BSP leader. Mayawati strongly voiced her disillusionment with 'the press' as a sole instrument of the upper classes and castes for hegemony.

> Mayawati repeatedly attacked the press during the interview and concluded that she would receive adequate coverage only if she founded her own newspaper, which she would do in the near future. Manoj took the attacks personally and wanted to defend himself against the image of belonging to an elite institution that is *a priori* against her.

M:	But I am not against you!
Mayawati:	I know not every reporter is against me, but the machinery is.
M:	I always write fair texts!
Mayawati:	Sometimes it is not even the texts, but the sorting, cutting and collecting of articles by political enemies. You give them all the information, which they then use to discredit our work.

(Field notes, 3 February 2000)

Mayawati distinguishes between an individual reporter and 'the press' as two agents. She asserts that 'the machinery' is against her, even if not all journalists are, but as individuals they cannot change the overall effect of this 'elite institution'. Journalism as a profession appears as a separate institution that can be abstracted and constructed even in partial contradiction with the concrete practice of actual reporters. Here this distinction absolved Manoj as a reporter, but castigated his profession, thereby making his sympathies suspicious. In spite of her negative view of the press, Mayawati did not cease to believe in individual reporters and their ability to make a difference, however small. She used every occasion to hold press conferences, appeased media representatives with elaborate lunch invitations, gave private interviews and emphatically repeated to them at every possible occasion to counter-balance the negative attitude of an elite institution: 'Do not ignore me again. And don't banish me to some back page' (press conference, 31 January 2000).

In order to keep unwelcome publicity under control, politicians distinguish between official and unofficial forms of communication. Leaders exercise very little control over the use of official announcements: they are made to be published, and journalists are free to use them. However, most interactions end with non-publishable off-the-record comments. Journalists stay to the end to be fed this information, yet they feel highly ambivalent about it: 'What should I do with such information if I am not supposed to publish it? I do not want to be told things which I cannot use'. The reporter here expresses his frustration about being condemned to repeatedly write routine news only. To avoid this situation, journalists negotiate a limited use of unofficial statements too. Significant for my argument is the way in which the distinction between official and unofficial communication mirrors the delineation between journalists as role players and individuals. Politicians and journalists confide in each other as persons and negotiate advantageous agreements. As role players they can re-establish a distance, hurt each other and justify infringements. Intimacy between individuals can be replaced by enmity between professionals. The challenge is to get the balance right.

The oscillation between personal closeness and professional distance makes the border between the two professions highly permeable. Performances of distance are important markers reminding journalists to resume a reflexive distance once they have acquired the information. While they express a moral compulsion and a professional ethic, they cannot bring about a disentanglement of fields. The divide remains ephemeral, because mutual engagement punctuates the borders between the two professions. The infringement of the moral order through social practice – of transgressing the border between two fields – demonstrates the ways in which agents appropriate and silently subvert the ideal order. It also challenges arguments about the independence of all social units. Academic accounts that describe press output as driven solely by internal operations miss the significant impact of practices in the border zone.

In the remainder of this chapter I take up this issue in a theoretical debate that assesses the relevance of my data for a theory of news-making. I will begin by outlining the limitation of arguments that turn an imaginary social order into a matrix for the sociology of institutions, especially Luhmann and Bourdieu. I will confront these accounts with an interpretation of practices that accounts for agency as equally relevant elements of a professional culture. I argue for shifting the focus from the imaginary centre of a field to the border zone. This brings a new impetus to the study of news and news sources. Research on news sources investigates the processes of seeking, displaying, manipulating and hiding information (Ericson, Baranek and Chan 1989; Manning 2001) as well as the transformation of knowledge in the news-making process (Pedelty 1995; Schlesinger 1978; van Dijk 1988). These accounts tend to highlight the distinctive operations of professional groups, while paying much less attention to the way in which trans-institutional communication shapes a professional habitus.

Journalism as System and Field

Luhmann (2000 [1996]) offers a radical institution–centric view in his systems theory. He defines mass media as a function system within society, clearly delineated from other function systems like politics, law or the economy.[19] According to Luhmann, function systems are independent entities with definite internal structures designed to solve specific problems. They are autopoietic,[20] self-reproducing, self-organising units and treat all other function systems as external. While input from the environment is essential for many internal operations, it is sought only with regard to the respective system's own priorities. Furthermore, when a system integrates outside information, it reworks this information to fit its internal structures of relevance. A process of adaptation takes place, that reconfigures all inputs according to the particular needs, functions and perspectives of the receiving function system.

　　Luhmann (2000 [1996]) applied this sociological model to news-making and classified it as a sub-system of the media system. As an autopoietic system, the news system has survival as its prime aim. It has to secure the attention of the public which is the fundamental condition for its existence and guarantee for endurance. Continuing interest in the news is produced through uninterrupted communication about infractions, which creates the expectation of the unexpected and with it the need for constant alertness among audiences. The news-generated image of a world in flux does not reflect experience and says nothing about the future or possible developments. In fact, it constructs the world as 'contrary to all evidence of continuity in the world we know from daily perception' (2000 [1996]: 35). The compulsion to persistently invoke discord is a corollary to journalism's dependency on popular attention. It is a social fiction also because the production of uncertainty takes place in definite systems designed to produce tension. Serial news covers sports, the stock exchange, or developments in ongoing conflicts, breaches of rules (criminal offences, corruption) or makes historical comparisons.

The narration of dramatic developments and paradigmatic shifts veils the stability of systemic operations configured to produce commotion and thus secure attention.

Luhmann's macro-sociological theory takes a top-down approach. The aim is to explain the conditions under which modern social organisation, defined by high internal differentiation, thrives. Declaring systemic differentiation as the principle characteristic of modernity, the question arises as to how this differentiation is brought about and maintained in view of the potentially contingent nature of human action and communication. The idea of systemic closure guides the answer. Each system drafts its own distinct internal procedures and ideologies. The discrete structure is responsible not only for the original contribution of the respective social system; it is furthermore instrumental in bringing about the conditions under which this contribution is sought, thus stabilising social differentiation. Luhmann's theory precludes the possibility of blurred boundaries. The concept of systemic closure is the premise, clearing the ground for the particular path of his thinking.

Luhmann mounts his theory of systemic differentiation in contradiction of scholars who idealise society as an integrated functioning whole – like Durkheim or Marx. According to Luhmann the pursuit of one overarching principle governing social organisation fails to account for rupture and complexity as the salient features of modern society. Institutional differentiation secures complexity due to the fundamental incompatibility of the various social units. While Luhmann dismisses the idea of a unified society, he reuses the notion of integrated organisms when describing the sub-systems of society. The assumption that shared 'cultures' are a characteristic of function systems and not societies redirects the sociological gaze towards the sub-units. Internal homogeneity is produced by the coordinated action of individuals, stimulated by a shared moral code that ensures conformity and keeps variation within an assimilable range, leading only to a gradual change (see also Horster 1997).

While Luhmann's own reasoning on the media remains in the realm of macro-sociology theory, his adherents have translated his theory into a tool for analysing the practices of media professionals (Weber 1995; Marcinkowski 1993). Weber in particular targets journalism in his study of the editorial system of the Austrian newspaper, the *Kronen Zeitung*. He assumes – with Luhmann – that journalism is one particular sub-system of the media system and that the *Kronen Zeitung* is a further sub-system of journalism. The principal goal of the *Kronen Zeitung* as an autopoietic function system is survival, which is ensured through a set of discrete practices synchronising output and patrolling borders. Weber interprets survival in narrow economic terms. He deduces that since maximisation of profit guarantees the continued existence of the company, it must be the crucial factor determining all further operations.

> We may well assume that the 'programme for decision making' within the 'Krone' is not normative [...], but based on purely economic reasons, which means oriented towards (augmenting) income and the number of readers. Further we have to presuppose, that this programme for decision making is put into practice within the editorial team through a specific form of social control. (Weber 1995: 163–64, my translation)

With financial fortitude being a condition for the existence of the organisation, the actions of all members must be directed to increase profit. Weber identifies coercion by a decision-making elite ('*Kontrollinstanz*') on the work force ('*Arbeitsbienen*') as the prime instrument in the pursuit of news to deliver profit. Journalists' activities appear as a largely conformist engagement with straightforward and unambiguous instructions by the management. A tightly-knit system of internal communication that moves through several levels of a well-defined hierarchy guarantees that outside information is reworked according to the internal priority of profit maximisation. Information is treated as a trigger that sets into motion the reproduction of fixed and pre-set schemes of news-making (see Weber 1995: 151–237).

Here Weber significantly remodels Luhmann's idea about news-making in the process of adaptation. Unlike Luhmann, Weber does not discuss the (unintended) cognitive effects of systemic operations, but portrays journalism as an interest–driven exercise. His analysis of the working procedure does not describe the creation of shared notions of reality through synchronised, self-referential and repetitive actions. Instead he produces evidence for the exercise of pressure within the organisation that guarantees the reproduction of the 'finance-system' newspaper. In this process he has to assume that everyone involved in the *Kronen Zeitung* submits to these pressures and functions according to the aims defined by the bosses. He further presupposes that instructions are the transparent and unambiguous application of instrumental rationality.

There are several indications in the text that Weber exaggerates the power of the elite to control the content and impact of the newspaper. In fact, he introduces 'irony' and 'passive resistance' as two instruments of subversion used by journalists against the line imposed by the leadership. Weber quotes from texts that offer alternative interpretations. He also shows how political pressure can change reporting. However, his predefined theoretical framework does not allow the author to give importance to such incidents:

> To my mind the functioning of the system 'Krone' is not influenced by such forms of protest within the editorial team. In fact, we even have to assume that, paradoxically, it serves the autopoietics of the medium. After all, the editorial team in Salzburg functions in spite of all its discrepancies. (Weber 1995: 183, my translation)

Weber insists here once more that journalists operate within a well-oiled machine that is not affected by subversive acts. This conclusion is a corollary to the assumption that collaboration in structured universes is a necessary condition for institutional success. Following this hypothesis, journalists appear as role players overwhelmed by the dominant organisational principle.

This image of the newspaper as a thoroughly rationalised, coercive institution disregards the dynamic element in Luhmann's concept, who describes social systems as adaptable entities in which coordination and cooperation flow from a shared assumption, a common morality and reciprocity. While Weber significantly reworks Luhmann's concept of logic governing the internal operations of a function system, he converges on the notion of institutional borders. Weber's reasoning follows directly from Luhmann's argument that all systems are operationally closed and strictly follow their own distinct code. This hypothesis views all products of journalism as adhering to a definite set of internal rules. The postulate of autopoiesis precludes the possibility that there exist shared spaces created at the intersection of officially distinct entities.

This restriction appears arbitrary and insufficiently justified. Luhmann deduced his classification of function systems from an institutionalised division of labour in modern democracies. As a second degree observer, he explains that society has given itself an order. The notion is arrived at by reflecting on a social imaginary and an institutional structure that divides society into functional units with clearly defined tasks. Luhmann assumes that practices are in complicity with this order. Presupposing a convergence between practice and ideal, the independence of institutions is never questioned. This assumption is mirrored in Weber's declaration that all non-conformist acts are irrelevant to the system. The system is independent, hence transgression must be meaningless.

Luhmann's approach is forced to play down the efficacy of individual agency. The notion of strictly governed autopoietic institutions has to assume the silent collaboration of all practices. It obscures the doing of culture. The approach is restricted by its structuralist assumptions. It cannot acknowledge social variations and selective appropriation and neglects the contingency of everyday life. Theories of practice have offered an alternative analytical instrument which is attuned to capturing the complexity of real life situations. The analysis of performance has demonstrated that action is never fully determined by ideological arrangements but flourishes at the conjuncture of various structured universes with the emerging event (Handelman 1998 [1990]; Sahlins 1987; Schieffelin 1998). A bottom-up approach exposes the stubbornness of practice that is unlikely to be fully contained in predefined social universes.

Bourdieu starts his explorations of journalism from the other end of the theoretical spectrum within sociology. He proposes an analysis of practice as a way of explaining the dynamic in a journalistic field; however, he falls short of developing the potential of his concept of 'regulated improvisation'. His theory of journalism is over-determined by economic assumptions. Market logic is introduced as the governing principle that, according to the snowball principle, affects all practices and ensures synchronisation of action inside media institutions and across the field of journalism. Bourdieu pays lip service to the idea of diversity in the field and the equivocation of practices. However, subversive acts are considered marginal and ineffective. Thus, in spite of the fundamental difference in approach, there are clear overlaps in Bourdieu's and Luhmann's theories. Both conclude that social institutions constitute distinct social entities governed by a definite set of internal rules which shape the actions of members and the contribution of the respective institutions.

Bourdieu describes journalism as a social field. It is a space structured through power relations which determine people's position and regulate their relations as well as an arena in which institutions and individuals compete for influence (Bourdieu 1998 [1996]: 57). As a social field journalism is autonomous, by which Bourdieu means that its workings are governed foremost by internal structures of practice, rather than being a direct result of outside intervention. However, interference between fields does take place. For journalism the market development is the single most important determining factor directing all operations in the field. The issue is survival, and the survival of media institutions depends on the popularity and financial success of their products, which makes profit maximising the paramount aim. Journalism also influences other social domains. As a dominant form of knowledge production, journalism (foremost televising journalism) has much relevance for the internal structure of all other fields, e.g. art and science. Thus, scrutinising the forces governing the media elite is a precondition for understanding the way in which the social is constructed in the contemporary world.

Bourdieu's theory of fields is linked to the notion of the habitus. By habitus Bourdieu means an embodied practical knowledge that actors acquire through a process of socialisation. It enables them to produce socially adjusted behaviour without necessarily being aware of it, by repeatedly enacting a set of standardised practices in new situations. The synchronisation of habitus in a field is a corollary to the 'objective conditions' of this field to which the body of knowledge is optimally adjusted and which is continuously reproduced through the unremitting application of this same habitus. Applied to journalism, this means that all actions of journalists are synchronised through the application of a non-reflexive internalised knowledge system that is typical of the media.

> When I asked him why he scheduled one item before another, his reply was, simply, 'It's obvious.' This is undoubtedly the reason that he has the job he had: His way of seeing things was perfectly adapted to the objective exigencies of his position. (Bourdieu 1998 [1996]: 26)

The key factor shaping the habitus of journalists is the rating system (or for newspapers, circulation figures). Popularity and financial success are the supreme targets of media institutions and are responsible for the production of dramatic narrations with a high entertainment factor and little political depth. The instant recognition of the spectacular becomes the second nature of journalists. Newcomers lacking this regulated lens eventually develop one through a process of trial and error.

> The executives who worship at the altar of audience ratings have a feeling of 'obviousness' which is not necessarily shared by the freelancer who proposes a topic only to be told that it's 'not interesting'. (Bourdieu 1998 [1996]: 26)

Thus, while Bourdieu acknowledges that there are innumerable actors with different subject positions within the field of journalism, subversive actions are thought to have little impact on the way in which media institutions work, since deviant behaviour is either forcibly suppressed or else becomes extinct through competition that leaves little space for journalists to realise their own personal agendas.

Weber's analysis of the *Kronen Zeitung* reproduces an idea central to Bourdieu's theory by demonstrating how internal hierarchies are instrumental in streamlining output, governed by the sole goal of capital accumulation. There is also a more general theoretical agreement between the two studies. News production is set within a system that forces participants into collaboration. This may happen through direct coercion or – as Bourdieu sees it – more indirectly through internalised structures (habitus) typical for the field, which are reproduced through the synchronised activities of adapted participants. Social actors are 'accomplices of structure' (Hörning and Reuter 2006: 54).

> Yet it remains true that, like other fields, the journalistic field is based on a set of shared assumptions and beliefs, which reach beyond differences of position and opinion. These assumptions operate within a particular set of mental categories; they reside in a characteristic relationship to language, and are visible in everything implied by a formulation such as 'it's just made for television.' These are what supplies the principles that determines what journalists select as a whole. There is no discourse [...] and no action [...] that doesn't have to face this trial of journalistic selection in order to catch the public eye. The effect is censorship, which journalists practice without even being aware of it. They retain only the things capable of interesting them and 'keeping their attention,' which means *things that fit their categories and mental grid.* (Bourdieu 1998 [1996]: 47, emphasis changed)

The agent in this description is the structure, not the person, who acts unconsciously according to shared assumptions and doctrines. My own data does not support the idea of journalists as perfectly adapted role-players. I have introduced the ideal distinction between the person and the role-player to draw attention to the contradictory forces that impact on the reporting profession. Journalists are socialised into various social fields and are subjected to diverse pulls and pushes. This enables them to strategically position themselves in a power network and forces them to negotiate in a matrix of conformity and subversion.

Bourdieu's theory of journalistic practices is constrained by an overemphasis on unity and consistency. He does not acknowledge the relevance of internal differentiations and overstates the stability and autonomy of the profession. He appears to work with a premise that is closer to Luhmann's than one might expect in a work diametrically opposed to systems theory. Luhmann sketches a macro-sociological theory of social differentiation. He sees modern society as made up of independent units, each with its own specific set of internal operations. Starting from the bottom, Bourdieu explores mechanisms regulating practices. However, his investigation is burdened by the hypothesis of homogenous social fields, producing a bias towards recognising practices that nurture separateness and homogeneity. Variants in this line of reasoning are unaccounted for or are declared irrelevant. The working of the institution – journalism – is deduced from an imaginary centre that orchestrates activities. The border is taken for granted and does not come under scrutiny.

However, social boundaries are not pre-given facts or the unproblematic side effects of sharp differences between 'sub-cultures'. Borders can be vague and are regularly transgressed. The compulsion for political reporters to become political insiders forces them to transgress the ideal boundary. Journalists are drawn into another field in which they are not just detached observers but participants in a shared arena productive of political perspectives. Where an ideal division of labour is in danger, delineation is sought. Controlling the margins serves to reduce (or deny) the subversive effects of border violation.

Academic attention needs to shift to this border zone[21] to avoid a structuralist closure. Professional distinctions are ideal divisions, they are invariably imprecise and permanently undermined by practices. I presented evidence for two different fields. Chapter three described how local news-making circumvents the distinction between readers and writers, informants and journalists, granting a range of local actors status as authorised voices. A culture of display is replicated in the newspapers, due to the press-related activities of ambitious personalities who seek the limelight and desperate citizens who cry out for attention. News gathering techniques encourage popular participation and blur the boundaries between professionals and non-professionals. In chapter four I moved up the political hierarchy to argue that professional compulsions seduce journalists into entering into exchange relations with politicians. This turns them into conduits for leaders' self-promotion. The interpenetration of media and politics flows also in the opposite direction. Advantages associated with publicity direct cultural activities. This makes politicians conduct politics in a certain way and it galvanises citizens to organise power contestation in a particular manner. It is this significant impact of journalists' presence in social networks that tends to be underdeveloped in studies about the journalist–sources interface.

Politics in the Border Zone

From a contemporary social science perspective, the approaches taken by Luhmann and Bourdieu appear extreme in their negligence of the dynamic, contingent and negotiated elements in social relations. However, structure–functionalist thinking emerges as an important guiding principle in many studies of news-making and has had a significant impact on our understanding of the news discourse.

Critiquing a narrow focus on individual decision-making and bias in news selection (Geiber 1956; Lang and Lang 1953; Molotoch and Lester 1974; White 1950), scholars have shifted attention to standardised working procedures in the news room in the 1970s and 1980s. The analysis of ethnographic material collected in the news room reveals the structural conditions that streamline news output. A theory of news values, mentioned above, has demonstrated the underlying logic governing selection processes. Furthermore, it was shown that the beat system regulated the gaze of reporters who routinely favoured dominant institutions in the news production process. Power structures in society are mirrored by the privileging of authorised speakers as news sources. The impact of timing is also significant. Events tuned to journalistic schedules are more likely to receive coverage. Announcements and pre-scheduling of events help to inform journalists about particular events. At times news may also be deliberately released at the last minute to avoid the critical attention of reporters. All these accounts describe news as outcomes of structured work processes. They receive ideological backing through the strategic ritual of objectivity that naturalises a particular narrative order and promotes news as a representation of a factual reality (Epstein 1973; Fishman 1980; Gans 1979; Golding and Elliott 1979; Hartley 1982; Manoff and Schudson 1986; Roshco 1975; Tuchman 1978).

While all these accounts have given important insight into the production logic, they leave little room for appreciating the agency of journalists. Journalists' actions are considered to perpetuate the status quo due to an un-reflected complicity with structures. The shortcoming of these approaches has galvanised scholars to focus on negotiation in power relations. A range of studies highlight how journalists navigate carefully in a field structured by the will of the powerful to dominate image-making. Journalists collaborate and resist the efforts of the government to produce tame reporting through manipulating accreditation processes or by using spin doctors to twist public interpretation (Manning 2001; Scammell 1995; Schudson 2003). Hasty (2005a, 2005b) examines strategies of coercion and persuasion used by the government in Ghana to influence vulnerable professionals. She describes news organisations in Ghana as chronically underfinanced and journalism as a profession with little prestige. Journalists are also subjected to harassment by the political elite. While the government is able to manipulate news emanating from the state medium, these accounts are contradicted by private newspapers operated by oppositional journalists, who are fed with inside information also by state journalists. Finally, there has been research into the media tactics of resource–poor groups. Studies outline the advantages and disadvantages of dramatic action as a media strategy. Spectacles attract the attention of media, which makes them attractive to resource-poor people. However, media attention tends to be short term and the initiators have little control over the way in which their action is portrayed and whether the media legitimise or de-legitimise it in the process of weaving it into reports (Goldenberg 1975; Manning 2001; Schneider 1997).

Another set of studies has emphasised the contextual and equivocal nature of knowledge and the contingencies this brings to news-making. Hess (1984) provides a compelling analysis of the inability of public relations officers to fully control information flows. PR people struggle to grasp what everyone in the organisation is doing as well as suppressing unfavorable news emerging from leaks or pushed by political rivals. He concludes that the multiplicity of voices limits the power to manipulate the public. Ericson, Barnek and Chan (1989) investigate the negotiation of knowledge between journalists and sources from politics, the administration, the police and the court. Regular interaction, mutual dependence and exchange relations create common arenas. They are characterised by a convergence of cultures of knowledge as well as by the institutional independence of all actors, who negotiate perceptions at the intersection of various information networks. These studies capture a process of structures in the making at the conjunction of work routines, professional interests and personal skills and priorities. News-making is not simply a process of reproducing fixed social structures, but a dialogical re-appropriation of social processes by communicating elites (see also Manning 2001).

This is also the starting point of my analysis of the border zone. I have demonstrated how a trans-institutional field contributes towards producing political communication and forging ways to inhabit a political space. However, I have moved the emphasis from news to relations. This is a significant shift. It de-emphasises the 'hide and seek game' that dominates accounts of the reporter–source interface. There is much debate about how people get information, how they conceal it or how they give it a public relation spin. In contrast, I have demonstrated that communication between journalists and politicians exceeds the exchange of prefigured (or manipulated) information. Journalists and politicians engage in a process of knowledge production as part of the negotiation of relations in a shared zone. By focusing on news-worthlessness, attention is directed at the relational surplus that informs political discourses, shapes images of leaders, and nurtures a particular political culture.

At this point the localness of the news discourse must be emphasised. Ståhlberg has rightly pointed out that news-making in India is a concurrence of global media styles and local political practices (Ståhlberg 2002; see also Hasty 2005a, 2005b). At the level of political reporting, we find journalists embracing leader-centrism, by targeting powerful individuals for networking and demonstrating an eagerness to produce leader–centered articles. Yet, this activity is not adequately described as partisan reporting. Journalists play with the sleek images of a range of strong men and women, creating selectively promotional and subversive images and producing ambivalent accounts of 'impressive narcissists' and 'pompous political stars'.

There is an interesting contrast here between my account and Hasty's (2005a) illustration of Ghanaian journalism. Hasty describes 'big English' as an important requisite of power in Ghana. It is a declarational language used by the political elite during official occasions to express their political prowess and benevolence. It is also the language of reporters working for state-controlled newspapers, and they use it when quoting government agents. Journalists rarely have exact quotations and also have to deal with the leaders' flawed use of 'big English'. However, able reporters fill in the language gaps and set right political speech by 'quoting' the leader in the official idiom, regardless of the exact words used by the speaker. Journalists upgrade political performance via reporting and, in cooperation with politicians, forge a language of power.

My account from India sees journalists and politicians in a power balance. Indian journalists do not complete politicians, they complement them. Mutual dependence and the desire to cash in on personal closeness facilitate an open-ended communication that produces powerful perspectives capable of inscribing themselves into political practice. The news discourse reproduces this dialogue in the form of an assemblage of voices which represent the party landscape, and revitalise and perpetually update established templates for the interpretation of society, from the perspectives of Hindu nationalism, socialism and caste-based ideologies. The alternation between personal closeness and professional distance creates an ambivalent leader image. Leaders are omnipresent, powerful and impressive speakers who possess significant powers in shaping society. At the same time they are self-indulged, pompous personalities who force themselves on people and journalists. So far I have emphasised newspapers' supportive engagement with leaders. 'Big men' politics is absorbed into the news discourse and re-invented in the written domain. Reporting practices and media discourse promote a particular kind of 'dialogue' between politicians who learn about the actions of competitors during press communications. Journalists complement political performances by situating them in an endless chain of comments through provocation and appeasement.

However, commercialisation has had a profound impact on political reporting. It is now time to turn to the other image of the leader: as a pompous, self-serving narcissist. As well as promotional rhetoric which sells images of benevolent leaders, newspapers present increasingly bold criticism of the political class. Economic transformation has made newspapers independent of political finances. Hence, there is a significant decline in pressure to produce conformist reporting of government activities. Journalists relish the moments when they break news about political scandals, leaders' lack of education or social commitment. The trade-off is an obligation to treat advertisement customers with respect. While newspapers invent the image of a benevolent market, politicians lose glamour. The next chapter is a warning against exaggerating the notion that Indian newspapers promote the political class. Leader-centrism can be turned against individuals, who are criticised for weak leadership, wasteful spending and castigated as responsible for a decline in the political culture.

Notes

1. For a discussion of pack reporting, see Ericson et al. 1989: 180–81; Pedelty 1995: 31–32; Schlesinger 1978: 163–204; Schudson 2003: 139–40.
2. See the following observation, which Mines makes in a different context: 'In fact, reporting is so highly personalised, it is hard for the outsider – anyone unfamiliar with who these people are and what they do – to make sense of the news' (Mines 1996: 1).
3. Ram Prakash Gupta had recently come to power as a consensus candidate to replace the controversial chief minister Kalyan Singh. He was not a member of parliament. To comply with the rules and keep his position, he would have to secure a parliamentary seat during the first six months of office. The by-elections were scheduled to take place three months into his reign, which was an ideal opportunity to confirm the chief minister by popular vote. However, the BJP recoiled from fielding the chief minister,

causing much gossip in political circles and among journalists (see chapter five for more details).

4. The *Hindustan Times* also thought that the event deserved coverage. The paper published Singh's statements on his predecessor Kalyan Singh in an article about the former BJP leader's new party, the RKP (*Hindustan Times*, 22 January 2000).

5. He uses a phrase from Daniel Boorstin's book, *The Image: A Guide to Pseudo-Events in America* (1962). The term pseudo-event is used for all kinds of pre-planned events, including made-for-press events.

6. There is a common perception among journalists, as well as political scientists, that in India voting decisions are influenced by the social group a person belongs to or identifies with. Such 'vote-bank' reasoning is often applied to religious and caste communities. However, some social scientists have also offered evidence that contradicts this assumption (see, for example, Hasan 1988: 821–25; Jaffrelot 2003; Krishna 1972: 18–21).

7. Yadav is a major caste group in Uttar Pradesh, to which Mulayam Singh Yadav belongs. They are counted among the Other Backwards Classes. Yadav plays the role of a relentless fighter for the equality of subalterns.

8. The category of Other Backward Classes includes economically weak sections of society, which however do not belong to the group of Scheduled Castes.

9. Goffman (1955) illustrates such techniques of interaction in his article *On Face-Work*. He emphasises that face work is not the aim of social interaction, but its condition, a mutual effort in which all participants need to ensure that they are keeping their own face and giving face to others. Goffman discusses various measures adopted in critical situations, when corrective measures prevent the breaking down of an interaction, like ignoring an insult, providing an explanation, re-contextualising a statement, or adding further information.

10. A corporator is the locally elected representative of people in the city parliament.

11. Deepa Mehta felt the vengeance of journalists when she behaved arrogantly towards Hindi-medium journalists. Assuming beforehand that the vernacular media would be biased against her, she refused to make herself available to their representatives and spoke almost exclusively to the English-language press. In return she received what she had anticipated. Hindi-medium journalists were enraged at her arrogance and did not give her any support. Those who wanted to write positively about the project chose the famous actress Shabana Azmi, who made herself more accessible to them.

12. As chief minister representing the BJP, Kalyan Singh adopted a pro-Brahmin policy. When removed from the post and sacked from the party, he founded the RKP, a party designed to hurt the BJP. He then cultivated new vote banks, such as OBCs (Other Backward Classes) as well as Muslims, the traditional supporters of the SP.

13. Kalyan Singh turned his image upside down once he lost power in the BJP. Angry at his dismissal, he quit the BJP and founded his own party (RKP),

launched to attract Muslims and lower castes.

14. Since the BJP had won power at the centre, the national BJP officially maintained its distance from the temple issue, although the construction of a temple had been on the party's agenda during campaigning.

15. Lalji Tadon, Kalraj Mishra and Rajnath Singh were mentioned as being in the race.

16. The statement was extremely cynical when one considers the number of deaths in the Hindu-Muslim riots that followed the illegal destruction of the mosque and the pogroms against Muslims that increased their insecurity.

17. Most politicians have consultation hours, during which the public spaces of their houses are filled with petitioners who want to be granted a particular favour, have an urgent problem solved, or extend an invitation to the leader.

18. For an interesting example, see Peterson's narration of a breach of trust by an Indian reporter who published information given by the American ambassador off the record. When the ambassador complained about this article, which quoted his private opinion, he was not taken seriously. The reporter defended his position, saying that his text was positive and thus in no way unfair (Peterson 1996: 355–61). The two actors here operated with different frames of references. The ambassador insisted that there should be press-free zones, while the reporter felt free to write anything as long as it did not hurt the informant. Such categorical disagreements occur regularly in the field of reporting. In spite of them, and the hurt caused to people's feelings, journalists have to keep up good contacts and build relations of trust.

19. On the notion of a function system more generally, see Luhmann 2002 [1984].

20. Luhmann here is adopting a terminology from Maturana and Varela (1980), who describe biological organisms as 'autopoietic systems'.

21. My argument converges with debates in the emerging field of anthropology of borderlands (Alvarez 1995; Donnan and Wilson 1999; Rösler and Wendl 1999). Investigations show how states orchestrate the flow of people, goods and ideas. However, there has been a growing awareness of the significant role of subversive economies, illegal migration flows and social and cultural ties across borders. These unofficial practices produce alternative realities in the shadow of dominant ideologies.
   An early contribution to this end is Fredrik Barth's (1969) discussion of ethnic boundaries. In an inter-ethnic comparison, he found that there is 'no simple one-to-one relationship between ethnic unity and cultural similarities and differences' (Barth 1969: 14). Despite this situation, inter-ethnic boundaries endure, for example in situations of inter-ethnic communication and exchange. Amongst the major factors for the persistence of ethnic categories, he identified the production of selected markers that lend themselves to politicisation and serve to discriminate between insiders and outsiders (see also Kapferer 1988; Rothschild 1981).

CHAPTER 5

Infotainment

Re-Writing Politics after Economic Liberalisation

In this chapter I turn to commercialisation as the second major trend in news-making, underlying and complementing regionalisation. Newspapers have embarked on a transformation from political organs to infotaining products. How does this impact on media perceptions of the political class? In this chapter I will follow articles which are critical of leaders. I will outline the contours of a news policy that favours the corporate sector and unravel novel forms of political criticism developed in the shadow of the new market friendly approach. Three developments underpin this process: (1) the growing financial independence of newspapers from party funds; (2) the inability of politicians to compete with the refined images of the new heroes; and (3) the mandate to find new entertaining ways to inform.

I will analyse these three developments and the consequences for news-making practices, thereby complementing the argument of the leader–journalist nexus. I have debated how journalists participate in and reinforce the leader-centrism of public culture. I have also demonstrated the complex overlaps and personal ties that bind journalists and politicians together. Now I focus on intellectual rifts and a culture of criticism. I describe a development that challenges the culture of inter-professional collaboration, by demonstrating that politicians find it increasingly difficult to prevent critical evaluation of leadership traditions. The starting points of my analyses are personalised articles that expose the pomposity, inefficiency and criminality of the political class through mockery of individual leaders. Such breaches of taboo are encouraged by the drive towards infotainment. Satire and drama are deployed in essayistic narrations about the poor state of politics. While there is a good dose of polemic in this approach, it does tackle serious issues, by breaking through the 'quoting' culture and impinging on the tradition of leader-centrism.

The argument provokes current academic debates about infotainment. I contend that we need to move beyond the lament of dumbing down, typical of much literature on the commercialisation of the press and media. Such cultural pessimism is in danger of glorifying the media discourse of the past, while missing contemporary forms of critical engagement. I do not present a naïve celebration of a new freedom resulting from market ideology. I rather develop an argument about the critical potential embodied in political infotainment. Journalists contribute to the re-imagination of the political sphere by (selectively) confronting questionable political behaviour. This trend is particularly significant in a writing culture that feeds on leader worship. Commercialisation has shifted the power balance and infotainment has opened an intellectual framework for re-imagining the leader. The unscrupulous and ruthless leader finds a permanent place in the newspaper next to the selfless social worker.

The chapter begins with a general outline of media commercialisation in India. This historicised narrative serves as a background for the analysis of my case studies. I introduce the making and internal reception of leader-centred articles critical of the elite. The case studies demonstrate the structural conditions that prevent negative evaluations of private industry, while allowing new forms of political criticism. Reviewing this development I turn to a debate on infotainment. A paradigmatic shift towards soft news is a multi-directional transfiguration of perceptions, assuming new forms of dominance and resistance.

Liberalising News Writing

Commercialisation has dramatically changed Indian newspapers. I have described investment in local news as being predicated on the desire to increase circulation. Appeasing readers is only part of the new approach; satisfying the corporate sector is even more important. Once heavily influenced by the government and a developmentalist ideology, the publishing sector has turned into an enterprise driven by corporate interests. This has profound implications for themes and styles of news-making. Previously considered to be a hallmark of fact reporting mainly from political institutions, newspapers have moved towards infotainment. In this process journalism appears less a political calling and more an activity of manufacturing a financially viable product

This fundamental reorientation has economic roots. In 1991 economic policy in India performed a dramatic u-turn, transforming

India from a highly regulated autocratic state into a nation embracing market economy. The consequences of structural adjustment are complex and multilayered. Here I focus only on media developments. Liberalisation has promoted media growth and the emergence of new business cultures. News companies began to reorganise their operations, streamlining internal mechanisms and tuning the newspaper to the interests of corporate advertisers. This industry-friendly approach is a diversion from the anti-capitalist ideology the press had inherited from the independence movement.

Mahatma Gandhi was among the fiercest opponents of a consumerist ideology and envisioned the newspaper as a platform for popular education that should abstain from promoting private interests. Jeffery summarises Gandhi's attitude:

> Gandhi (1869–1048), an outstanding journalist in English and Gujarati, had a vision of an Indian tradition revived, cleansed and free. Advertising had no place. Gandhi's newspaper, dedicated to the cause of Indian freedom and deeply suspicious of Western materialism, set standards that other Indian publicists often felt the need to emulate. Gandhi's weekly did not accept advertisements, 'ninety-nine per cent' of which he deemed 'totally useless. [...] If there were no system of advertisements, we are surely to save at least half the price [of any article].' He declared that 'the sole aim of journalism should be service.' (Jeffrey 2000: 54)

The first Prime Minister of India Jawaharlal Nehru followed a slightly different line in his opposition to marrying corporate interests to the press. He felt that private advertising posed a danger to the project of building a socialist society. Nehru was suspicious of advertising for its power to influence the masses and inculcate in them a wrongful desire for consumerism. '"Advertising", he once told the Indian Society of Advertisers, "is essentially a thing to induce consumption, to make people buy things they do not want"' (Nehru; cf. Jeffrey 2000: 55; see also 51–57). Indira Gandhi was no less critical of advertising and clearly favoured state regulation. She saw state management as superior to private ownership in the media business and came down heavily on news organisations during the Emergency when she imposed censorship (Raghavan 1994: 147–64). No postcolonial government actually pushed through a law that would have destroyed the plurality of ownership in the Indian newspaper market. Yet they did create a culture of political appeasement. Party finances played a significant role in seducing newspapers to collaborate with the government. The justification was an ethos that saw politics and journalism as occupying twin roles in the project of enlightenment and modernising. The practice was more prosaic, essentially producing excessive closeness between the press and politics (Peterson 1996: 22–69; see also Jeffrey 2000: 55-56).

What was the rule before 1991 was discarded in post-liberalisation development. Today, large regional and national newspapers have no need for political financing. The brisk growth of the advertising industry – which reached the giddy heights of over thirty per cent growth per year – has supplied a more attractive source of income (Jeffrey 2000: 58; Mazzarella 2003c: 12–15; Rajagopal 1998: 18–21). Capital investment in the press from private advertising continues to grow in spite of the stiff competition newspapers face from electronic media. While television and the internet have continuously increased their share of the overall advertising market, the absolute income that the news business generates from the corporate sector is still growing. To increase their attractiveness to private advertisers, newspapers have adopted a number of pro-industry measures. Advertiser-friendly reporting includes infomercials as well as the promotion of feel-good journalism. In a bid to attract more readers, a price war was instigated. Slashing prices and aggressive marketing have rapidly increased circulation. Newspaper companies began to target more systematically the prosperous urban middle classes, because delivering affluent readers to advertisers fetches a higher price. A means to this end are an appealing format, high-quality colour printing and modern design (Sahay 2006).

The commercialisation of news operations has enormous consequences for content, across the spectrum of news media. Thussu (2007a, 2007b) analyses the transformation of Indian television news after the introduction of private channels. He identifies five tendencies of 'Murdochisation' promoted by Star News, which influence the whole news landscape. These are: (1) the celebration of the free market and the highlighting of news from the corporate world at the expense of reports about (economic interventions by) government agencies; (2) extensive coverage of celebrities, especially from the Indian film business in Bollywood; (3) more reporting about cricket, the most popular sport in India; (4) a narrow focus on metropolitan news and concerns of urban people, especially from the middle classes, as well as the use of drama and sensation; and (5) the almost complete absence of international news and a simultaneous emphasis on the cultural and spatially proximate.

All these developments find their equivalent in the press. The *Times of India* is the recognised leader of the shift towards popular journalism (Sahay 2006). The Vice-President of Bennet, Coleman & Co Ltd, the owner of the *Times of India*, leaves no doubts about what drives his management philosophy:

News or information is no longer the logic for buying newspapers... The question what will make people buy and read the newspaper is getting more and more challenging. You have to entertain them, constantly... I tell my journalist friends that these days each headline is looked at for entertainment. And what's wrong in it? When businesses and political sentiments are down why not offer feel-good journalism? In a happy mood you consume more. And that's what every advertiser wants. (Joseph 2004: 167; cf. Das 1999: 58)

The consequences of commercialisation are obvious in the everyday business of reporting in Lucknow. Journalists working for the English-language market[1] describe how they are relentlessly pushed towards advertiser-friendly writing. Infotainment is a key technique to this end.

The term infotainment was coined in the 1980s and has a range of connotations. It is used to refer to entertaining ways of presenting information or media products that mix entertainment and information. It is also a catchword thrown in whenever the discussion turns to new developments in news-making and it is a technical term that describes computer programs for interactive learning or playing (Wittwen 1995: 15–26). Journalists in Lucknow use infotainment in a rather unspecific way to signify a bundle of new influences on their work. There is a fundamental thematic reorientation with newspapers now heavily reporting on the culture industry, consumer goods, the media, business, education and health. These themes are covered in an ever-growing number of supplements that prove to be extremely popular with readers and advertisers. The *Times of India* and *Hindustan Times* provide several supplements every day. Hindi newspapers are catching up slowly. During my research, *Dainik Jagaran* had one daily supplement with city news (*Sahar Apna Sahar*, City my City). It was distinct from the English-language counterpart which focused more on tourism, traditional entertainment and high culture. However, times are changing. Three years later there is an additional, more commercially oriented insert.

In the past three months or so along with *Sahar Apna Sahar* [City my City] the paper [*Dainik Jagaran*] has started another pull out for at least four days a week: *Jagran City* which tries to cover the elite people who speak Hindi with a lot of English. The approach is different with accent on life style, fashion presented in a mixed language as you can make out by the use of the word 'city', a sort of 'page three', culture, to counter the *Times of India*'s *Lucknow Times*. (Email correspondence, Journalist, 15 January 2005)

The introduction of new themes is paralleled by new writing styles. Soft news and creative writing are encouraged and rewarded.

As might be expected, the attitudes of journalists towards these trends are complex. While some hail infotainment as a new form of social criticism, others reject it as sensationalism. The reactions are set within a discursive space in which news-making is perceived alternately as 'fact finding' or 'creative invention'. On the one hand, 'objectivity' and 'completeness' rate highly as ideals in journalistic writing. Employers demand from their reporters that they do not 'miss news', refrain from personal involvement, and do not comment but rather give straightforward reports of what they observed. On the other hand, constructivist theories have had an enduring impact on reporters' perceptions. Those who have gone through a formal education in mass communication learn that everything has the potential to become news and that writing is a process of inventing meaning. Superficially this contradiction is avoided by declaring 'fact reporting' and 'creative writing' (or 'hard' and 'soft' news, 'news' and 'features') to be different things, each having its own place in the newspaper.

However, the distinction does not solve the problem. In actual practice the two perspectives cannot be kept separate, since they offer two radically different understandings of the nature of texts and thus compete as grounding ideologies of the news discourse. Thus, it is hardly surprising that the issue creates friction between different groups of journalists. Opposing the shift towards selling 'soft stories' as news, one of the senior journalists with the *Times of India* remarked:

> A new brand of journalism has developed which I call 'enterprising journalism'. This means to create something to have a story. You make things readable and sellable, though the content is minimal. There is also the practice of going around at random asking everyone what he has to say on a current issue. This is not news. It is a means to fill the pages. What is needed instead are pieces full of information content, organised in a logical way and reaching a logical conclusion. (Journalist, *Times of India*, 14 February 2000)

However, what appears to some as a decline in 'fact finding' and the invention of random sensations is for others an acknowledgement of the 'perspectivity' of news, which allows journalists and companies consciously to define their goals. Guided by the idea that the publication of news is creative invention, the selection of articles is not informed by notions of 'completeness' but determined by images of what might interest the reader and what serves the company's policies.

Adopting new themes and styles does not necessarily mean giving up the idea that newspapers should be informative and critical. For example, this is the opinion of a journalist who works in a features section of the *Times of India* called the *Lucknow Times*:

> *Lucknow Times* is a supplement to the newspaper because it is supposed to be different than the paper. It might talk about the same things, but it does so in a different way: reader-friendly language, upbeat, pointing at the beauty of life instead of just talking about the negative side […]. Of course the instruction from the head office in Delhi is that it should be light and easy, but we do try to go deep and also tackle serious issues, but in a reader-friendly way. It is not so much a question of what you write but how you write. (Journalist, *Lucknow Times*, 7 May 2002)

Here the journalist is seen as a creative agent, who is experimenting with language in order to convey information. The journalist becomes a writer in his own right. This is recognised also in the increasing use of by-lines in the English-language press. By giving more credit to authors, reporters move from acting as conduits to being recognised as individuals who make a difference. What is pushed by the English-language press is registered with disgust in the Hindi press, still more attuned to a writing philosophy that sees journalists as gate keepers who produce objective reports.

> We give a by-line only for very special exclusive stories. See how *Times of India* is doing it. That is vulgar! They even give a by-line for a press conference. I don't think this is an appropriate approach at all. (News Editor, *Dainik Jagaran*, 9 February 2000)

What the news editor from *Dainik Jagaran* does not appreciate is the encouragement English-language journalists are given to produce unusual twists, especially when covering routine events. 'Look behind the scenes of a press conference, spell out why and when it was organised and what it was designed to accomplish. We need to uncover the rules of the political game.' This instruction, given by the *Times of India* editor during a morning meeting, was reiterated in many different forms during the daily routines at the English-language press. Journalists savoured the new freedom in political writing. Newer journalists no longer subscribe to a professional ethos that sees the press as acting in tandem with the state and are much less inclined to promote and justify the movements of the political class.

However, more freedom in political news-making has its disadvantages. Journalists resent what they experience as increasing pressure from private advertisers and they take it for granted that the introduction of new forms of news-making is motivated solely by financial calculations, a strategy to make newspapers more sellable and thus increase revenue from advertising. When writing up my material, I wrote an email to a journalist friend in Lucknow, communicating my conclusion that I saw innovative potential for new forms of subversive news-making as a result of changes in newspaper financing. I received an answer that strongly resisted my rather optimistic interpretation:

> Dear Ursula, […]. As far as my experience in journalism goes I am of the perception that every business house running a newspaper is driven by its definite agenda regarding the primary motive/objective of a newspaper. In the *Times of India* the primary objective is not so much promoting journalism as a means to highlight the truth and thereby ferment change in the society as to rake [in] *moolah.* This has led the paper to vest unnatural powers in the hands of advertisers, so much so that in Lucknow it has led to a clash of egos between the journalist community and the marketing department. If a report (irrespective of the fact that it stands for the truth) threatens the interest of the business community it is spiked. […] As far as imbuing the newspaper with a new perspective by the way of viewing it through the advertiser's eyes goes, well I can say not all advertisers are cerebral enough to look beyond their vested interest towards making the newspaper a more readable and informative product. As long as their particular area of interest is attended to they seldom whimper a change. (Email correspondence, journalist, *Times of India,* 22 July 2002)

This letter mirrors the experiences of other reporters, who feel that newspaper companies do not promote critical analysis or social engagement. Regular work in the news room consolidates this opinion and proves how much consumer ideology penetrates everyday decision-making. The following comment was made by the editor of the *Times of India,* who explained to me the considerations governing front-page decisions:

> I am told not to put stories of prisons on the first page. No one wants to read them. Although people do want to read them! But the *management wants only feel-good things.* Readers should not be upset, because then the ads do not go down well. (Editor, *Times of India,* 5 April 2002)

The context for this comment is a significant change in management structure at the *Times of India.* While in the past the editorial team worked independently, today the editor is subordinate to the general manager. The latter orchestrates the cooperation of all sections (editorial, advertisement, production and distribution) informed by the paramount goals of maximising profit. There are daily meetings between the management and the editor and significant, direct interference in editorial content.

The production of a financially viable product is a combined effort of management and editorial. Managers tend to play down the significance of editorial content, since only advertising earns money. To the dismay of journalists, their work is treated as secondary in the contemporary business environment. Yet it is the editorial team that has to put into practice what the management defines as advertisement-friendly content, while keeping in mind that the newspaper should also appeal to readers. Management imposes infotainment as a promising option. The popular catchword of a business culture needs to be translated into practice by the writing profession. It is this *doing* of infotainment that I will focus on.

Through selected case studies I will demonstrate new leader narratives that emerge from the structural and ideological transformations of the publishing business. My debate begins with an example of critical reporting about a private industry that was brought under control very quickly through pressure from the criticised company. Similar disparaging articles about political leaders could not be prevented by the politicians. The discrepancy between the powers of advertisers and politicians produces a paradigmatic shift in the way the political is conceived. Politics is losing its glamour. The critical re-imagination of politics acts as a counter force to the chumminess acted out in the shared arena of political news-making.

Who Dares to Criticise Sahara?

To celebrate the fiftieth anniversary of the Indian constitution, the leader of the pan-Indian industrial conglomerate, Sahara organised a week-long festival at the company's large park-like resort (Sahara City) in Lucknow. A great number of politicians, religious leaders and artists were flown to Lucknow at great expense to meet, perform and consume. The public was excluded from this 'India Festival'. Journalists were saddled with the task of popularising the event through daily reports on the sensational events and important visitors. To facilitate reporting, the organisation's general manager Subrata Roy Sahara held a press conference on 27 February 2000, midway through the festival.

Diverging from the normal press conference procedure, Subrata Roy called not just one representative from each news outlet, but invited all reporters in Lucknow personally to the meeting as well as to an exclusive lunch. The press conference certainly did not promise any revealing statements. It was quite an honour for the reporting profession and was much appreciated. Two hundred press representatives accepted, heeding the invitation's message: 'Needless to reiterate your participation is a Must. If you fail to attend, I will be forced to construe that you have no emotional attachment with the Sahara Parivar [Sahara Family]' (Invitation Letter from Sahara). For most Hindi reporters, attendance was an opportunity to celebrate and enjoy a world of glamour and rub shoulders with the rich and powerful. I asked whether I could come along. The brief hesitation – whether I could enter without invitation – soon made way for an enthusiastic announcement that they would do anything to get me inside. For here was a chance to show off to a Westerner and prove that India could indeed be thrilling and glamorous. English-language journalists seemed less dazzled. While they also came in great numbers, most maintained a cynical tone when speaking about the event.

We left the office at 11:30 A.M. and drove to Sahara City. At the entrance gate we were showered with rose petals and greeted with bright, slightly staged smiles from women dressed in smart Western office attire. The same beauties ushered us into company-owned shuttles to take us on a sight-seeing tour through Sahara City which ended at a large conference building. We entered a hall decorated for a press conference. There were embellished tables, on which welcome presents had been laid: a writing pad, a large colourful coffee table-like book narrating the history of the company, two expensive ballpoint pens and a bottle of mineral water. The gifts were practical enough to pass as part of the press conference routine, yet their expensive look gave the event an edge over similar meetings. The press conference started with a long, emotionally charged lecture by Subrata Roy Sahara who elaborated on his outlook that Sahara was not an anonymous company but a family working jointly and harmoniously for the prosperity of India and the well-being of its citizens. The 'India Festival' was to be seen in this light, as a patriotic festival of Indians, who express their love for their country by engaging in joyous celebration at the golden jubilee of the constitution.

The journalists were appalled by the exaggerated emotionality of the presentation. Yet they listened patiently for almost one hour, before they interrupted their host and started showering him with critical questions. He was asked why he wasted such excessive amounts of money on this festival instead of investing in social betterment. Reporters demanded justification for excluding the public from this so-called 'India Festival'.

Why not call it the 'Sahara Festival', when all it does is showcase the company and its director? Subrata Roy Sahara had to defend his involvement in the media business. Why call his newspaper *Sahara*, making a direct connection with the company? Why create another television channel that will be no different from all the others? He was accused of cheating and bribing, and was grilled about his dispute with the tax department and his conflict with former Chief Minister Kalyan Singh.

In spite of the hostile atmosphere, Subrata Roy Sahara remained calm, trying hard to present himself as a visionary. Only occasionally did he lose patience and scoffed at the journalists for their negative and ever suspicious attitude. He expressed a desire for better journalism and more positive reporting, including about his company. The journalists reacted immediately and asked why he did not invest in the education of journalists if he was so unhappy about the condition of the profession. After about two hours the press conference came to an end and everyone proceeded to an exquisite lunch. On their way back reporters strolled through an exhibition of company products without much interest before they left the site and returned to their offices.

All the newspapers covered the event the next day in a routine fashion. Writing the reports, journalists executed the well-learned exercise of reproducing the positive and promotional self-image the leader presented. Reporters followed the line of compliance also adopted when politicians make themselves accessible to journalists. They reiterated Subrata Roy Sahara's statements and turned the host into the far-sighted leader he wanted to be. There was no hint of the aggressive tone present during the press conference and the vigour with which Subrata Roy Sahara had to defend his image. Texts mused over a joyful 'India Festival' celebrated by a patriotic company, delivering to India prosperity via consumer products, media engagement and public welfare schemes. The text from *Pioneer* demonstrates the style:

'Bharat Parva emotional homage to motherland'
Bharat Parva [India Festival], a six-day-long cultural festival, is being celebrated at the sprawling Sahara City to mark the golden jubilee celebrations of the country's Independence.

'*Bharat Parva*' for Sahara India chief Subrata Roy is the emotional homage to the motherland. Such festivals will inculcate feelings of 'Indianness' amongst countrymen, Mr Roy believes. [...]

Elaborating further the concept of *Bharat Parva*, Managing Worker and Chairman of the Sahara India, Subrata Roy, felt that *Bharat Parva* would establish emotional bond amongst all Indians which would in turn motivate all to perform their duties towards the nation. He added that the country's interest was above the interest of any '*Majhab*' (religion).

Speaking on his future plans the ever-enthusiastic Mr Roy said besides adopting villages and creating models, he would launch a TV news and entertainment channel on March 13 and another channel exclusively for cinema and entertainment on April 19.

He said a large number of people from far and near participated in the Festival celebrations and wished others would also hold such programs to engender nationalist feeling. 'Such events helped to promote the feelings of nationalism,' he observed. Defending the lavish celebrations, Mr Roy said that glamour added with intellect developed perception. 'If such functions have to be popularised some amount of glamour was a must in the beginning,' Mr Roy said adding that he did it because it gave him a sense of satisfaction '*Santushti*'. He said one did not look for logic to derive pleasure. [...]

Explaining the ongoing projects, Mr Roy said they were constructing 40,000 houses of which 14,000 would be in Lucknow itself. Moreover, he said there was a provision of 30 to 40 per cent discount on these houses for war widows and handicapped persons. He went on to say that they were discussing with other entrepreneurs about financial assistance to the victims of other wars in the past on the pattern of the relief provided for the families of the victims of Kargil.

In reply to a question, he said it was unfortunate that the government did not extend the cooperation desired as a result of which many good schemes such as 350-bed Trauma Hospital and Amusement Park planned for Lucknow could not materialise.

To another question, he explained how the Income Tax department were [sic!] harassing him and compelled him to retaliate. He categorically ruled out having nurtured any thought of entering politics. (*Pioneer*, 28 January 2000).

The article makes no mention of the negotiated nature of the news. All critical elements dominating the press conference were censored in a bid to portray a shining festival. The similarities between this and other articles are striking:

The start of Sahara TV Channel with an 'India Festival'
The launch of the new TV channel by Sahara India on 13 March will be preceded by an auspicious beginning with the 'India Festival' programme which is being filmed currently in the Sahara City. The information regarding this intention was given by Mr. Subrata Roy, the manager and chairman of Sahara India, at a press conference here.

Mr. Roy explained that the 'India Festival' which was inaugurated at the juncture of the silver jubilee celebrations of the Republic Day, is a symbol for Sahara India Family's emotional expression of unity of the nation and self happiness. This event will be broadcast to the entire nation through the new TV channel which will be launched in March. He also announced that a second TV channel will be started on 19 April 2000. This channel will be totally adapted for entertainment purposes. Not only will this channel be devoid of programmes containing violence and sex but also differ in many respects from various other channels too. Mr. Roy also said that a film is being made on the India Festival which began three days back. This film is being produced by Trans World International (T.W.I). He said that the villages will also be apprised of the idea of the India Festival which is being celebrated in the Sahara City. He also said that Sahara India has undertaken the service and support of villages, the poor and resource poor people since years, as a result of which the works at all the unsupported orphanages and women protection homes is under progress. Mr. Roy also said that Sahara Family will be taking up the responsibility of the developmental work of some villages and these will then be presented as the ideal villages. He said that Sahara India is building 40,000 houses in forty cities for low income and middle income people. Ten percent from these houses will be reserved for handicapped people and war widows.

He said that because of the former chief minister Kalyan Singh, the 350 beds most modern hospital could not be built in Lucknow since the former chief minister did not give permission to build it and instead sanctioned the plan for someone else. He said in a similar manner their plans to build entertainment parks and to take over the buses plying in the city were blocked. In spite of the fact that both these were loss filled ventures, the Sahara Family had decided to undertake them for the good of the citizens.

He claimed that although practically all political parties had recommended him to file his papers for Rajya Sabha [Upper House] elections, he had declined the offers. Mr. Roy said that he has no interest in active politics. He also claimed that till today he had never taken help from any political person. He said that sometimes people spread false rumours about Sahara. In this context the income tax issue is mostly brought up. About this we declare as a challenge that no person or officer in the country can prove the accusations about the income tax scandals. Two years back when an officer of the income tax department had tried unnecessarily to trouble him, he had got the entire truth published in the newspaper. The result of this was that the officer got transferred and till today no one has dared to lift a finger at Sahara regarding the income tax issue. The reason for this is that we believe in dealing fair. The money we collect from the public is absolutely secure. 80% of the collected amount is put into nationalised banks and only 20% of the amount is invested. The profit on this latter amount is then also spent in several steps. 35% is put into Net Owned fund and 25% is spent on social work. On being asked the question that even after reaching maturity the money of the investors are not returned, Mr. Roy said that this was only a rumour spread to make mischief. He said that the amount invested in the Net Owned Fund is very much more than the number of investors and therefore the question of not being able to return the money of the investors does not arise at all. (*Dainik Jagaran*, 27 January 2000, my translation)

In both articles Subrata Roy Sahara is celebrated as a benevolent player in society who deserves positive coverage for his vibrant engagement, his innovative enterprises and the splendid India Festival. There is a high congruence in themes and the order in which they are presented. The table below shows that all journalists 'intuitively' consented on the news value of various items, writing their texts in the typical pyramid style starting with the most important item and sorting the rest in order of decreasing importance (e.g. Keeble 1994).

The only information that journalists considered news was the imminent launching of the Sahara TV channel. They had insisted that Subrata Roy Sahara specified a date, so that they could at least pay lip service to what they considered their main duty, to break news. All other information was redundant. Even the festival itself could no longer pass as 'news', since it had started four days before the press conference. In line with the assumption that press people must always know first, reporters had complained bitterly about Sahara's timing. They should have been called on the first day of the festival. Yet in spite of their dismay, reporters were tame. They promoted the festival and the host. Only three articles mentioned towards the end the allegation raised by the tax department; and even here it was Roy who had the last word on this issue.

There was one text that did not fall in line and refused to play the game of 'gift and return gift'. The *Times of India* published two articles on the back page of the main newspaper reserved for 'cultural news'. The first article, on 28 January 2000, said little about the press conference. Rather, it delved more generally into the character of Sahara City and the programme of the 'India Festival'. The report on the press conference followed a day later. It embedded Subrata Roy Sahara's statements in a narration of context:

Table 5.1. Press coverage of the press conference at the Sahara 'India Festival' of 28 January 2000.

HINDI-LANGUAGE PRESS			ENGLISH-LANGUAGE PRESS	
Dainik Jagaran	*Sahara*	*Aj*	*Pioneer*	*Hindustan Times*
			Description of 'India Festival'	
Start of Sahara TV channel	Start of Sahara TV channel		Start of Sahara TV channel	Start of Sahara TV channel
Description of 'India Festival'	Description of 'India Festival'	Description of 'India Festival'	Description of 'India Festival'	
			Launch of new consumer products	
Social engagement of Sahara company	Social engagement of Sahara company	Social engagement of Sahara company	Social engagement of Sahara company	Social engagement of Sahara company
Roy has no interest in active politics	Roy has no interest in active politics			
Comment on Roy's quarrel with the tax department			Comment on Roy's quarrel with the tax department	Comment on Roy's quarrel with the tax department
Financial position of Sahara	Financial position of Sahara			Financial position of Sahara
	Roy's request: journalists should write positively			
		'India Festival' Program announcement		

A midsummer nights's dream or as you like it!
Nobody does anything for the others. On the contrary everyone does
everything for the self. They do it for either material or spiritual gain and
they do it to avoid material or spiritual loss. That is why nobody ever
makes any sacrifice for others.

These sentences, highlighted by the publisher, seem to be the cornerstone
of the author's philosophy. And the author of the tome, 'Shanti… Sukh…
Santushti' [Peace… Happiness… Satisfaction], which looks like a copy of
the Bible makes it obvious that he fancies himself as a philosopher. Plato's
'Philosopher King' may or may not have left any imprint but Subrata Roy
'Sahara' leaves no opportunity to air his philosophy on virtually everything
under the sun. At a press conference on Thursday, he once again
launched on an exposition of 'Anand' [joy] or pleasure. His 'anand',
however, is no hedonistic voyage, he claimed, even though some pressmen
thought he was indulging in a vulgar display of wealth.

Even as belligerent journalists labelled Sahara's ongoing 'India Festival'
as a mindless waste of money and resources, Roy spoke of the joy of
celebration and of giving into the spirit of gay abandon. Journalists as a
group are difficult customers at the best of times. And Roy's sermon on
Sahara did nothing to douse their hostility. He was questioned at the
purpose behind the show, on the politics of the show and on the money
he had squandered. Mr Roy was patience personified. 'In a wedding',
said he in well modulated and deep throated voice, 'the expenditure can
never really be determined. And here I am celebrating the day when
Indian Constitution came into force. How can I really define monetary
parameters for this joyous occasion. The details of expenditure will be
available only after the festival comes to an end', he explained.

Journalists smirked and giggled while some of them asked, somewhat rudely,
if the money could have been put to better use. Journalists seemed to suggest
that they did not really need a lesson on seeking pleasure. Roy remained
unfazed. 'We have specific budgets for social and welfare activities'. […]
Why call it a Bharat Parva [India Festival] when all that it was showcasing
was Sahara and Saharashri [Mr. Sahara], was the snide question that was
hurled at him next. The man seemed to have rehearsed his reply. 'Artists
from all over the country have gathered under one roof and the
subsequent mingling of cultural fragrances is surely reason enough to
call it a festival of India', he added.

What was the nature of his difference with former chief minister Kalyan
Singh, jeered a newsman while another reporter wondered how he
managed to get government officials transferred at the drop of a hat. Others

reminded him of his hobnobbing with politicians [...]. Roy brushed them off like water shaking from a duck's back. With a perpetual smile plastered on his face, he acted the perfect host, not losing his cool, patiently explaining that none of the charges against him had ever been proved [...]. 'The man is a fraud', fumed a reporter while another protested, 'Ha! why doesn't he spend all his money on the welfare of the poor... see, he has an obsession with films; everything is so "filmi" about him... his "shahar" [resort], his guests, his show...', while a fourth one reminded the group that Roy had indeed created employment for several hundred thousand people. 'You cannot say the same thing about the government', he scoffed. The final word may not have been spoken yet. The debate on the enigma that is Subrata Roy 'Sahara', meanwhile, continues unabated. Will the real Subrata Roy please stand up? (*Times of India*, 29 January 2000)

The approach in this article differs fundamentally from all others. Here context is the main focus. The article introduces a number of different speakers and hence is able to capture the conflict-laden atmosphere at the press conference. Subrata Roy Sahara's explanations are contrasted with the critical questions and comments of the journalists. There is also a vivid description of the bodily habitus of the speaker that in the article appears as a well-trained theatrical performance designed to impress the audience. Subrata Roy Sahara is systematically deconstructed through a text that communicates less about what he said, but more about how and why he said it.

The attention of the reader is diverted from the glamour. The meticulous description of the sleaziness of the event is coupled with a probing of the power relations at work during the press conference and in a society that enshrines great inequality. Subrata Roy Sahara appears as the status quo personified and society as a system of domination and subordination, in which a privileged few are in command. However, the journalist does not pass a judgement, admitting that there is no simple solution to the social predicaments of a divided society. The 'enigma that is Subrata Roy "Sahara" [...] continues', as does discussion about what is morally right in a society characterised by great social and economic differences.

Subrata Roy Sahara did not take the article well. He was infuriated and strongly objected to this portrait that offended his idea of decent reporting – after he had explicitly requested journalists to adopt a positive attitude. It was impossible to miss his subsequent intervention as accounts rapidly circulated among journalists. After hearing about Sahara's reaction, I sought confirmation from the residential editor of the *Times of India*. He explained that Subrata Roy Sahara rang the head office in Bombay, who in turn informed him, the residential editor at Lucknow, about the distressed

director. Sahara punished the *Times of India* by withdrawing its
advertisements from all editions of the newspaper country-wide.

In spite of this extreme reaction, the editorial team in Lucknow did
not relent. Maria, the author of the article, enjoyed the backing of her
editor. He calculated that financially the company was sound enough to
absorb this loss[2] and estimated that the management would allow some
time to elapse, and once the incident was forgotten would send
representatives to re-establish cordial relations with the company and
re-invite investment. However, the newspaper did change its approach
to the Sahara Festival. Two more stories appeared marvelling about the
beauty of Sahara City (*Times of India*, 31 January 2000 and 1 February
2000). Two days after Maria's satirical text, romantic pictures of Sahara
City dominated the back page. Everyone interpreted these picture
stories as an effort to douse Subrata Roy Sahara's anger.

This turn of events is hardly surprising, considering the rapid
commercialisation of Indian news-making. The business interests of
advertisers enjoy high priority. The punishment of the *Times of India*
reinforced the power structures that had produced the 'silent
agreement' among the majority to keep criticism at bay. If reporters
needed a reminder, the intervention was a clear signal to the
community that there are limits to what can be written about the very
powerful. What surprised me more than the interference of Sahara was
the way in which press people gloated about the punitive action.
Journalists felt genuinely that Subrata Roy Sahara's reaction was
justified as a means of punishing the 'negative attitude' of the *Times of
India*. I had expected that reporters would admire Maria for attacking
the 'giant' and secretly congratulate her for the analytical piece. My
intuition was wrong. While many press people agreed with her analysis,
they considered it a personal opinion and hence biased. Journalists
were indebted to their generous host and felt that he deserved positive
publicity for putting on this grandiose show, even if it was a
promotional event. They had been given a perfect opportunity to
highlight the enumerable achievements of Sahara, which was after all
an extremely successful company which contributed substantially to
India's prosperity. Journalists did not forget the controversies
surrounding Sahara – as the question-and-answer session proved – yet
they had no reason to raise them at that moment. There was no new
scandal and hence no cause to be critical. Maria had disregarded this
'common sense' approach. She transgressed a boundary by allowing
outsiders to get a glimpse of internal power negotiations. It was a
breach of good conduct in a field where reciprocity is a cherished value.
Making a scandal out of Maria's article in journalistic circles was a way

to heal a social situation that threatened to disrupt the spirit of cooperation between journalists, informants and financiers.

The gossip castigating Maria proves how deep the transformation has gone. The consumer-friendliness of newspapers is not solely a result of the direct pressure from advertisers. It is part of a transformation producing new role models for journalists as well as a consequence of the growing hegemony of market ideologies. Traditionally politics used to be the main and most respected domain of reporting and certainly the most suitable for striking 'deals'. Today the supplements offer an alternative career path. They command respect due to their enormous commercial success but also because writing about life-style is removed from the sordid business of politics. Some journalists expressed relief that they no longer have to face the redundant self-presentation of narcissistic leaders or spend their days researching political intrigues. Journalists know about the pressures extended by the corporate world on news-making. Yet, they also have a high regard for the achievements of private enterprises and value the products they offer. Journalists are fascinated by the dazzling world of luxury and stardom and partake in the positive evaluation of consumerism typical of the upwardly mobile middle classes.

The Sahara show was a perfect place to observe the positive appraisal of affluence. In fact, my attention was drawn to the event because I noticed the unusual excitement gripping journalists at the prospect of communicating with one of the richest Indians, being invited to his place and offered lunch by him. When I went to the office of *Dainik Jagaran* on 27 January 2000 I was unaware of the Sahara programme. I had prepared myself for another routine day with politicians. As soon as I entered the press room I sensed that something special was going on. The atmosphere was laden with expectation and excitement. Everyone talked about Sahara City, about which there were many rumours but little first-hand knowledge. No one had ever set foot in this fortress, which was reserved for the meetings of the very powerful and rich. Suddenly there was a chance to enjoy a lavish lunch at the most elitist place in the city, invited by the man who has it all – money, power and influence.

Their expectations were not disappointed. Journalists were impressed by the sight and relished the most deluxe Indian cuisine (one of the sweet dishes was even flown in from Calcutta). After this uplifting experience, journalists could not reconcile themselves with the 'negative attitude' of Maria towards a host who had offered the most fantastic service. What the team from the *Times of India* described as 'garish' or a 'vulgar display of wealth' was for most others an impressive show of affluence. Subrata Roy Sahara appeared as the perfect role model and an incarnation of the stereotypical 'American Dream'. The book distributed during the press conference dramatically presents the narrative of a self-made man. On the page entitled *Our Beginning* there is a photograph of an old scooter and a table with two chairs, indicating the humble beginnings. Underneath the picture are some details from the company's first year, in 1978: 'Capital 2000 Rs.; Place: Gorakhpur; Establishment: One small room, with two chairs and a table'. These details are contrasted with information about the current size of the company on another page.

Sahra India Pariwar

Table 5.2. Information about the company Sahara, quoted from *Sahara Indian Pariwar,* a coffee table-like book distributed during the press conference.

1978	1999
Started from Gorakhpur with 3 workers	All India presence with over 6 *lac*[3] workers
15 dependants' livelihood	Over 30 *lac* dependants' livelihood
42 depositors	Over 2.5 *crore*[4] depositors (1 out of every 40 Indians)
Assets – Rs. 2000 only	Assets – Over Rs. 9,600 *crore*
1 establishment	1342 establishments
No Trade Union	No Trade Union
No Malik [owner]	No Malik

Subrata Roy Sahara's achievement stood in stark contrast to the common image of politicians. The respect politicians attract because of their affluence is often mixed with the suspicion (or knowledge) that their prosperity results from corruption. Politicians are portrayed as shrewd personalities who profit from the financial flows that pass through the institutions they head. While there were speculations about Subrata Roy Sahara's corrupt practices, he nevertheless was considered to have earned his money.

What we encounter here is an evaluative attitude that sees more glamour and benevolence in the private economy. When contrasted with the idealised images of managers, politicians appear much less impressive and their actions more questionable. Changes in the Indian economy have produced new heroes. Their images are forged in collaboration with journalists who are pressurised to write in favour of industry and are also personally impressed by the fantastic achievements of 'real' professionals. This has significant consequences for the political discourse. The larger-than-life images of the new role models diminish politicians and may reduce them to a subordinate position. The image of the impressive leader propagated through the newspaper is contested. Next to leader-centred articles there are subversive texts deriding the pomposity and inadequacy of the political show.

When I was writing up my conclusions from the Sahara show, an article was brought to my attention that impressively demonstrates the culture of devaluing politics through contrast. It was published in the Sunday edition of the *Hindustan Times* (Delhi),[5] a portrait of twenty men represented as the most attractive in India and everything a woman could want 'in a single package'. To qualify, a man had to be 'well-read, well-travelled, a man of power and some wealth, sophisticated, self-assured, intelligent, articulate and experienced' – and 'good-looking' (*Hindustan Times*, 4 April 2004). The selection suggests that not many politicians have these combined qualities. Only three politicians made it to the hit-list,[6] celebrated for their fresh and innovative style of politics. The article suggests that in the new India respect is not found foremost in politics, and certainly not the 'old' kind of politics, but is generated in many other professions, ones that contribute prosperity, knowledge, security and national enthusiasm, like sportsmen, medical doctors, managers, artists and journalists. These are the men the nation (and women) can be proud of, look up to and follow.[7]

In the following section I turn to those political men and women whose performances lack allure. Their handling of affairs is critiqued for being inefficient, corrupt or outright criminal. My first example is an article that was very critical of the chief minister and, unlike the Sahara piece, was extremely well received among both politicians and journalists. It provides a starting point for my discussion of an emerging writing style that makes politicians vulnerable to ridicule. With politicians having lost their financial dominance over the printing business, they have less power over their images. Following the regime of infotainment, newspapers deploy fresh styles and shift thematic orientations towards the popular. The upshot is the production of new perspectives and the forging of criteria for evaluating performances generated from outside politics. It is an investment in a new form of political criticism that is married to the celebration of liberalism.

Who Believes in Ram Prakash Gupta?

The text I now introduce shared Maria's critical tone. Again a reporter from the *Times of India* hit the news by writing acidly about a powerful man, this time the chief minister of Uttar Pradesh, Ram Prakash Gupta. The article was extremely successful and had a remarkable career in the world of news-making. Annu, the author of this text, coined the phrase 'the forgetful chief minister' and managed to set an agenda that haunted Ram Prakash Gupta during a sensitive period of his chief ministership.

The text formed part of pre-election reporting. It was published on 24 February 2000, communicating the BJP's decision that the chief minister would not contest the imminent by-election, during which vacant posts in the state assembly and the national parliament were to be filled. This announcement came as a surprise. Most political observers were convinced that the BJP would seize this opportunity to make the leader of the government a regular member of the legislature. As I have mentioned ealier, Ram Prakash Gupta was 'new' in politics. After an absence of twenty years, he was introduced as a surprise candidate in November 1999 to replace Kalyan Singh as chief minister.[8] He was selected for office even though he was no longer a member of parliament. This is possible under the constitution for a limited period. If Gupta were to keep the office, he needed to be elected to either house of parliament within six months of taking office. Scheduled three months after his swearing in, the by-elections would have been an ideal time to prove Gupta's credibility before the electorate. However, the BJP decided otherwise.

All newspapers disseminated the fact that, against all expectations, the chief minister would not contest the February elections. Annu was the only person who deviated from the routine style of press conference reporting. She wrote up the news in a text debating the inability of the aged chief minister to live up to expectations. The reporter shared the common perception that the BJP abstained from fielding Gupta because he was too unpopular. Annu's article spells out the reasons for why this might be so:

Forget me not, Mr Chief Minister
LUCKNOW: The 76-year-old chief minister of UP has a habit of forgetting things. The other day he asked his minister of state, 'Who are you?' The minister was taken aback, but replied politely that he was Shivendra Singh, Minister of State attached to the chief minister. If you are Shivendra Singh, then who is that man with curly hair, asked the chief minister referring to Rangnath Mishra, another minister of state!

This habit of CM [Chief Minister] has become a topic of discussion in political and bureaucratic circles. Bureaucrats recount with glee the encounter between the Union Power Minister PR Kumaramangalam and the chief minister. Mr Gupta, who has a habit of telling everyone that he was deputy CM in 1967 [sic!] told the Union minister: [...] 'Were you in union cabinet when I was deputy CM.' It took a few minutes for Mr Kumaramangalam to realise what the CM was saying. He corrected him saying: 'Mukhyamantriji [Mr. Chief Minister], you are talking about my father.'

The legislators have begun taking advantage of Chief Minister's memory slip. A MLC [Member of Legislative Council] said it is better to meet the CM, introduce oneself and get the work done the same day. If you take a chance then there is all possibility that the CM would ask next time 'Who are you!' A joke going around the BJP office is that the CM has refused to contest by-elections because before the polling day he would forget from which seat he is contesting elections.

Caught in this strange situation, Mr Gupta has been declared persona non grata by the BJP. Senior leaders are not even ready to discuss about the CM and his prospect of contesting elections. 'Please talk about something else', said a senior BJP leader [...]

By now the scenario is clear that the chief minister will not contest election in the coming by-assembly polls. (*Times of India*, 24 January 2000)

Like Maria, the author of this article gave a new context to routine information. The text discards the pyramid style employed by all others. Annu did not treat the announcement of the non-candidature as the main peg. To her it was subordinate information, a consequence that followed from the forgetfulness of the aged leader. In an essayistic style, she speculates about internal political debates, suggesting that the failure to nominate Gupta could be either part of a strategy to get rid of an inefficient chief minister or a calculated move coupled with a plan to find a safer way of securing a seat in parliament for the unpopular leader, for example, through nomination to the upper house.

The reception of the article was incredible. Gupta became a laughing stock among journalists and politicians alike. The positive assessment of the article began in the offices of the *Times of India* itself. The residential editors in Lucknow and Delhi were delighted and the article was seen to be of national importance, since it criticised the head of the most influential state. Thus, the article was printed twice. First it appeared on the front page of the Delhi edition (23 January 2000) and the next day again on page one in the Lucknow *Times of India* (24 January 2000). It was subsequently and endlessly recycled in debates between leaders and journalists and quoted in the newspapers. Dialogues followed the style of re-circulating statements and decisions in leader-centred interviews described in the last chapter. Leaders absorbed the popular phrase – 'the forgetful chief minister' – and used it as a peg to formulate their own criticism of the government.

The BSP leader and former chief minister of Uttar Pradesh, Mayawati, echoed Annu's text in a private interview. She commented on the highly controversial statement that Ram Prakash Gupta had made in favour of the Ram Temple in Ayodhya: 'Poor Mr. Gupta, he always forgets everything, even that he was told not to disclose the true opinion of the BJP on Ayodhya' (interview, 2 February 2000). The statement was published the next day.[9] The Lok Dal leader, Chaudri Ajit Singh, commented on Gupta's forgetfulness in a different context. He criticised the size of the state government in Uttar Pradesh. With a cabinet of almost a hundred ministers it had become ungovernable, he stated. This was demonstrated most clearly by the inability of the leader to recognise his own ministers: 'The chief minister was not able to recognise ministers owing to the large size of his ministry' (*Hindustan Times*, 30 January 2000). Annu reported from a press conference in Delhi during which a female journalist asked the chief minister about his forgetfulness and requested him to identify the officials who accompanied him (*Times of India*, 31 January 2000). Almost a month later the minister of state for animal husbandry, Prem Prakash Singh demanded the removal of the chief minister. He complained that under the current regime the government had become completely inefficient and that work in many ministries was at a standstill. He phrased his negative comments with reference to the now well-known phrase: 'Anything may happen if a forgetful person like him [the CM] is allowed to remain in office by the BJP leadership. Is it not strange that he does not even recognise his cabinet colleagues?' (*Pioneer*, 24 February 2000; see also *Sahara*, 24 and 25 February 2000).

The press cashed in on the popular phrase even when not directly quoting politicians. In a background article about the state of affairs in the Lucknow government, the state correspondent of the *Times of India* added to earlier criticism: 'UP Chief Minister Ram Prakash Gupta emerges not only as "forgetful" but also a pale shadow of a "lost man", leaving his party men disappointed and dejected on many accounts' (*Times of India*, 26 February 2004). Ram Prakash Gupta's 'fame' also spread outside Lucknow when the popular weekly national magazine *Outlook* took up the theme:

He's a relic among politicians and suffers from frequent 'memory loss'. UP chief minister Ram Prakah Gupta, also deputy CM in 1968, recently turned to his own private secretary and asked him, 'Who are you? What do you want from me?' And a few days later, he stunned union power minister R. Kumaramangalam with the poster. 'Were you in the Union cabinet when I was deputy CM?' The CM was, of course, referring to Kumaramangalam Sr. Ministers in the state cabinet are now so paranoid about the CM's forgetfulness that they don't risk leaving any work for another day. After identifying themselves, they just ask the CM to sign on the dotted line and scoot. (*Outlook*, 14 February 2000)

Ram Prakash Gupta was confronted directly with his weakness. The chief reporter from *Dainik Jagaran*, a newspaper normally known for its friendliness towards the BJP, goaded the chief minister into a personal interview with the statement: 'You are remembered for not making timely decisions or if you do make them you do not take action and then you quickly forget' (*Dainik Jagaran*, 16 February 2000, my translation). The chief minister contradicted the reporter and claimed that his government was one of the most efficient. He gave the example of his successful fight against the electricity strike, the restoration of electricity to the people and the rise in the price of sugar cane to benefit the farmers.

Another interview appeared in the online edition of the *Times of India* more than six months after Annu had invented the phrase:

Question: One hears stories from Lucknow that the CM cannot remember things, that you suffer from forgetfulness.

R.P. Gupta: I take that as a compliment. There is no issue that can be used against me. So new stories are being churned out every day. It shows there are no serious charges against me.

(*Times of India*, online edition 10 August 2000)

Annu successfully coined a phrase and – what is even more interesting – set an agenda. The phrase 'the forgetful chief minister' became a trigger for people to come out openly against Ram Prakash Gupta. The point was pursued not only by opposition leaders, but – as the quotation from Prem Prakash Singh proves – also by members of the government itself (see also a statement by BJP General Secretary Sanghpriya Gautam in *Sahara*, 22 February 2000). Public criticism of the highest man in the state appeared to be safe, because it played on an already commonly accepted 'truth'. The constant repetition of the same phrase constructed a continuity between several otherwise unconnected issues that now appeared to emanate from one single problem, namely the inability of Ram Prakash Gupta to lead an efficient government. Whenever there was criticism of the state BJP, hints of the senility of the chief minister came to the surface, whether the debate focused on the BJP agenda on Ayodhya, the way in which the party dealt with protests against the making of the film *Water* in Varanasi, the fear of the increasing power of Hindu nationalist organisations like the RSS, the handling of the energy strike, the inefficiency of the political apparatus or the unsatisfactory management of the coalition.

Criticism of Gupta was, of course, also countered by other statements challenging suggestions that the chief minister might be removed.[10] Several BJP heavyweights came out publicly to defend the leader of the state and reassure the public that he would serve a full term in office, for example, Urban Development Minister Lalji Tandon[11] and BJP Vice-President Jana Krishnamurthi.[12] Yet the hearsay did not die down. Just like politicians, journalists used the atmosphere to add more criticism about the government. Annu realised her own success and wrote a sequel that showed the inability of the BJP leadership to maintain party discipline:

BJP squeezed between forgetful CM and arrogant president
Lucknow. Caught between a forgetful chief minister and an arrogant state president the state unit of the BJP finds itself in a quandary. Over 100 days in power the CM, Ram Prakash Gupta, is yet to get familiar with his MLAs. On the other hand, the party's state president Om Prakash Singh is finding it hard to stamp a seal of authority on party workers.

Almost a fortnight ago, BJP workers clashed in full view of the state president in Aligarh. Charges and counter-charges were openly traded on the issue of the formation of a committee. Mr Singh, however, remained a mute spectator and was taken out of the meeting hall when the situation went out of control.

His rhetoric of regimentation of party cadres again fell flat when, in a state-level meeting of the Intellectual Cell […] in Meerut, a senior leader called the BJP government a conglomeration of goons. He said half of the ministers were 'criminals'. Although he apologised for his speech later, the message had been sent loud and clear till then.

Mr Singh is still not ready to believe that indiscipline has set in the BJP. 'I know, what is happening in the state, who is doing this and under whose instruction,' he said adding that the BJP was a 'disciplined organisation' and action would be taken against all those trying to act against the norms of the party.

Another rhetoric! At least half a dozen BJP MLAs had shared the platform with the president of the Rashtriya Kranti Party (RKP) Kalyan Singh in different rallies held in the state. Still, the BJP is finding it hard to take action against them. Instead, the BJP general secretary, Ramapati Ram Tripathi said, these MLAs are still part and parcel of the BJP. [...] 'They had shared platform due to old friendship'. In the floor of the House these legislators obey the party whip, he said. (*Times of India*, 13 February 2000).

In the article three separate incidents are tied into one coherent narrative, namely a fight over a committee, accusations against ministers for criminal activities and Kalyan Singh's efforts to try and hurt the BJP by wooing its members for his newly founded party (RKP). All episodes took place in different locations and were embedded in different local dynamics, and none of them directly involved the chief minister. Yet, in the article they all appear like the symptoms of a single problem, namely indiscipline in the party as a direct outcome of the top leaders' inability to run the government and the party organs efficiently. The headline makes this argument strongly by constructing an image of a party that is falling apart because it is being 'squeezed' between two individuals who are unsuited to their posts (Ram Prakash Gupta and Om Prakash Singh).

Other 'exclusive' articles critical of the BJP top leadership followed. Most of these were written by senior journalists, who proved their capacity to turn gossip into personal career advantage. On 22 February 2000 Virendre Sengar of *Amar Ujala* reported from Delhi on Sangh Priya Gautam's accusations against Gupta as well as on a range of other positive and negative opinions about the leader's performance. Tavishi Srivastava of *Pioneer* explained that no one had reason to celebrate Gutpa's hundredth day in office and that the chief minister explicitly forbade a feast from being held (*Pioneer*, 22 February 2000). Two days later she covered the chief minister's concern regarding the imminent *panchayat* (local council) elections and the budget session (*Pioneer*, 24 February 2000). Sunita Aron wrote an article dwelling at length on Gupta's inability to cope with the work load, asserting that he does not clear pending files and that, if he does, it is at the special request of ministers and he issues contradictory orders (*Hindustan Times*, 25 February 2000). Arvind Singh Bisht continued the publishing marathon with a comment on Gupta's inability to instil discipline in the cabinet and on his indecisiveness, which resulted in many cases left pending. The article quotes speculations about plans to recruit Gupta for the post of Governor of Harayana and thereby save the BJP in UP from further embarrassment (*Times of India*, 26 February 2000).

Bisht's article came out on the same day that the results of the by-elections were published. They were positive for the BJP, which led to contradictory reporting by the *Times of India*. While Bisht continued to criticise the chief minister, another article on the front page declared: 'By-poll results in a shot in the arm for CM' (26 February 2000). Although the chief minister had not participated in the by-elections, he became the key. The scene for such an interpretation had already been set a day earlier, when several newspapers declared – quoting internal talk in the ruling party – the by-elections to be a 'referendum on RP Gupta's (non-)performance!' (*Hindustan Times*, 25 April 2000; see also *Hindustan Times*, 22 February 2000[13] and *Sahara*, 25 February 2000). The *Times of India* article interpreted the election results as follows:

> The BJP never looked confident in this by-election. This may be the reason why CM Ram Prakash Gupta preferred not to contest the elections. Much before the by-election results were declared murmurs had begun in the highest echelons of the party to replace Gupta. But, the victory of the BJP in the bypolls has come as a shot in the arm for the septuagenarian CM. 'The people who were talking about CM's non-performance could not shut their mouth,' said BJP spokesman Shayamnandan Singh. (*Times of India*, 26 February 2000)

Another article in *Sahara* reported the strength that Gupta had drawn from the elections. It was written by Rakesh Arya quoting the Urban Development Minister Lalji Tandon, who claimed that the positive result would make Gupta's seat secure (*Sahara*, 26 February 2000).

Lalji Tandon was proved right at least as far as the time immediately following the election was concerned. The controversy surrounding Gupta started to die slowly and the Chief Minister stayed in office for another eight months, until 10 October 2000.[14] I left the field in May 2000 and was unable to follow the press during the period of Gupta's removal. However, the issue here is not one of BJP politics. Reporting about Gupta caught my attention because of the way it came into being. Annu attracted interest for her attack on a powerful man, because she considered in detail possible reasons for a decision that was otherwise kept low key by embarrassed leaders as well as by surprised journalists. She dragged out what BJP leaders wished to conceal. She was not sanctioned and her article was not considered inappropriate. Quite the opposite happened; the author was congratulated for her witty piece and the phrase of 'the forgetful CM' became a standard formula repeatedly exploited to ridicule the government.

There is nothing new in the fact that the press can effectively destroy the authority of a man or woman in power through negative publicity, even to the point of forcing their resignation. It is a typical dynamic that follows the 'discovery' of a person's involvement in a scandalous affair, the losing of an election, or the implementation of an unpopular political measure. However, in this case nothing of that kind had happened. There was no obvious event that justified the heightened attention that the press gave to the Chief Minister. The article *was* the event. It appeared at a time when Gupta had not even been in office for a hundred days, a typical time-line for commencing a public assessment of a leader's performance. With her peremptory evaluation Annu led a fontal attack which did not focus on political issues but rather on leadership style. Her secret was the witty approach. She offered the narration of 'funny' incidents and jokes from political circles, which were sure to catch attention. Annu realised (to perfection) the new style of news-making that is both entertaining and informative.

One could dismiss the article as a piece of gossip, a contribution to dumbing down the standard of news writing, proving true all those apocalyptic voices lamenting the tabloidisation of the public sphere following commercialisation (Blumler 1997; Blumler and Gurevitch 1995). One could accuse Annu – or more generally the *Times of India* – of exchanging serious political debate for a cheap effect. In the typical style of celebrity news, Annu relied on rumours and malicious gossip to produce an entertaining and pejorative profile of a major leader. However, the judgement appears pre-mature, when some of the alternatives are considered. The editor of the *Times of India* declared the need to revolutionise political reporting by breaking through the journalist–politician nexus. He opposed much of the work produced by senior journalists socialised into the profession when newspapers were more or less the mouthpiece of the government. In turn, he promoted all those who managed to keep a distance from the political field and who demonstrated an analytical approach. This move is not trivial considering the flourishing exchange economy between journalists and politicians described in the last chapter. Editors in the English-language press in Lucknow were reluctant to accept reports that reiterated the opinions of leaders. They called for context. 'It is not sufficient to write what leaders have said. We need to know how they said it, when, to whom and why' was a typical instruction (editor, *Times of India*, 25 January 2005). Annu added depth to routine news by debating political strategies that may have informed (the unusual) decision.

Coverage of the forgetful chief minister was not a one-day-wonder, but rather part of a trend. Polemic deconstructions of political performances are printed next to the stylised images of strong, determined and benevolent leaders. The new perspectives are an integral part to a changed business culture. Routine news poses a problem for newspapers that want to be original and for ambitious journalists who wish to progress in an increasingly competitive market. The desire to be different can turn the least spectacular events into news-worthy articles. Journalists can exploit the financial security of their paper to offer political analysis which is unpopular with leaders yet difficult to suppress, as the following two examples demonstrate.

Attacking Fierce Men

In the middle of February, Deepak from the *Times of India* decided to write on the by-election campaign in the district of Kannauj, although he had not travelled to the constituency himself. He was reacting to an ongoing debate about the contest that, in his view, had grown out of all proportion because of the excessive amount of energy and money that leaders had invested into the prestigious competition between the son of SP leader Mulayam Singh Yadav and BSP heavyweight 'Dumpy'. He was horrified by narratives from the 'battlefield'[15] and the brutality of the language used. Hence, he decided that it was time to write an article exposing the nature of the campaign.

Deepak called several colleagues from various newspapers to collect quotations made by politicians on the stages in Kannauj. Based on his interviews with colleagues, he wrote a text that dwelt on the language of leaders and what it indicated about the attitude of politicians towards their electorate. On 15 February 2000 the front page of the *Times of India* read 'Politicians in Kannauj speak like villains'. In a pink box three statements appeared, one from each of the main contestants for the post of MP in Kannauj. The sentences were printed in (the) original Hindi.[16]

'*If anyone dares to glare at my workers, I will gouge his eyes out, and if anyone dares to raise his hands on them, I will get their arms chopped off.*' (LCP President Naresh Aggarwal)

'*There have been only two powerful goondas [thugs] in the whole country – Sanjay Gandhi and myself. From where has this third goonda, Mulayam Singh Yadav, come from?*' (BS candidate Akbar Ahamad 'Dumpy')

'*If anything goes wrong here, then this place will be strewn with dead bodies.*' (SP chief Mulayam Singh Yadav, *Times of India*, 15 February 2000)

The article analysed these and further statements. Deepak compared the election phrases with dialogues from c-grade Hindi films and criticised the bad taste of the campaigns. The gist of his argument was not only that contestants' performances appeared too 'filmy', but that by portraying themselves as villains, politicians were morally ambiguous if not evil. The brutal language was an indication of the way in which power is attained and exercised. Deepak's article was a hit. Colleagues from all newspapers congratulated him for his courage in coming out against powerful men like Mulayam Singh Yadav and 'Dumpy'. Deepak had expressed a common sentiment about the increasing criminalisation of politics.

Mulayam Singh Yadav was not happy. He nurtured a deep resentment against the English-language press and reacted instantly. He issued a disclaimer, stating that he had never made the proclamation attributed to him in the text. The *Times of India* published his statement but did not change the line of reporting. Mulayam's intervention was replicated in an article that also quoted the energy minister as saying that Mulayam was 'threatening "mass killings" if anything went wrong [in the Kannauj election]' (*Times of India*, 16 February 2000). The article, printed on page three, was announced on the front page underneath another text about Mulayam Singh Yadav. The front page news was classified 'Run-up to Kannauj bypolls' and reported on Mulayam's election strategy regarding Brahmins.

Mulayam extends olive branch to Brahmins
'Mulayam Singh Yadav has apologised to us', said a smug Om Prakash Tiwari (name changed), who claimed to have been one of the 120 prominent Brahmins in the area who were invited to a closed-door meeting on Sunday with the Samajwadi Party president. […] Mulayam Singh, he recalled, claimed that it was the BJP which has projected him as a 'villain' but he was not such a bad man after all […] 'I am not this type of a man. But, if you still feel that way I ask to be forgiven', he recalled Mulayam Singh as saying. (*Times of India*, 16 February 2000)

The remaining nine paragraphs interpret this apology as a means to woo Brahmin votes for the SP, the context being that there was no BJP candidate in the constituency who could normally be expected to be the first choice of Brahmins. The general tone of the article is neutral. Yet, it reinforces the image of Mulayam as villain, which he himself plays up to as part of his appeasement strategy. The latter is reported by a '*smug*' Brahmin who wants to remain anonymous, demonstrating that to expose Mulayam is dangerous. This personalised account makes a mockery of the leader–centred reporting introduced in the last chapter. The leader remains in the centre, but his authority is systematically undermined through polemic language, the juxtaposing of contradictory statements or the exposure of shrewd manoeuvres. One more example, this time from a text exposing Mayawati's wasteful spending of state resources, will consolidate the argument.

What's amiss amidst the Swiss
Chief Minister Mayawati's five-nation tour is all about the powers-that-B. B as in Bureaucrats, BSP, *Behnji* [sister, title typically used for Mayawati], her *Baiya* [brother], *Bhabhi* [sister-in-law], and her *Bhatijis* [brother's children]. For apart from her principal secretary PL Punia, Director of Information Rohit Nandan, Commissioner of Industrial Development Shashank Shekhar Singh, UP-SIDC MD Rajeev Kumar and a host of other senior bureaucrats, also accompanying the CM is her brother Siddhartha, his wife and two daughters. While the chief minister will have a 'nice' time visiting Uncle Sam's land after a brief stopover in London and Toronto, it's her Switzerland sojourn that is being talked about back home. For no one in the *sarkar* [government] seems to know what business – official or unofficial – the CM and her entourage have in Switzerland. And so, some have been quick to point that while scenic beauty and NRIs may both be found there, say 'Swiss' and the first word you associate with it is either chocolates or – heaven forbid – banks! (*Lucknow Times*, 28 May 2003)

The article continues with further details about the trip and the inability of Mayawati's staff to explain its purpose. The implications are clear: Mayawati wastes public money, indulges in corruption and reigns like an empress with a team that is not informed of her moves and intentions.

It was in view of such publicity that Mayawati complained about the negative attitude of the press towards her. Her complaints are in line with laments from the SPs, who regularly grumble about the anti low-class and low-caste attitude of the English-language press. The recurrent expressions of helplessness by politicians and their inability to get their public image under control stand in stark contrast to the powerful interference of Subrata Roy Sahara, who needed only one day to force the *Times of India* back on track. The trend is clear. While newspapers offer little critical analysis of the private economy, they regularly scrutinise politicians. This is not to say that there is no political interference at all or that political pressure is always ineffective. The last chapter showed how politicians woo reporters.[17] However, following post-1991 developments politics has lost inherited privileges and hence its structural advantage. Today politicians struggle much more to manipulate coverage. A personalised style used to promote individual leaders is used equally to deconstruct them.

By critiquing political heavyweights journalists accomplish more than the deconstruction of individuals. They attack a fundament of Indian society. The hierarchically organised social system traditionally pays great respect to its leaders and reveres seniority. The hero worshipping of political figures is highly pronounced with respect to founding fathers like Mahatma Gandhi, Jawaharlal Nehru or Dr B.R. Ambedkar but applies also to much more controversial figures like Indira Gandhi. Every party, region, city and caste has its heroes. They are sculpted in statues placed at roundabouts or in parks. Their photographs are printed on huge posters. Cardboard figures are a popular medium used during election campaigns or when announcing leaders' visits. Attacking these over-size images of 'great' leaders, journalists challenge the basis of leader worship. They take what could have been admiration for seniority and turn it into senility. What could have been awe for the economic power of politicians becomes a trigger for seeking out corruption. Criticism of leaders is not without precedence. Public performances – like the Ram Lila, the Ganapati Festival – have always been known as formats for subverting the powerful, and there is a history of cartoons and critical literature. However, there has been a change in scale. The dismantling of top leaders here is not confined to the anti-structure (Turner 1974) of festivals or the arts, but is part of a daily discourse disseminated by an elite institution. The political anti-hero is a staple in the contemporary English-language press.

The visibility of these images is increased when they are formulated in an entertaining, personalised style. They stand out against routine news, which is written in factual language, following the classical pyramid style and quoting politicians at length. They also provide a contrast to the slick texts praising consumer goods and corporate engagement. These contrasts are significant. Routine news and shiny advertisements constitute the background for recognising and constructing difference. To show this contrast I will debate routine news in the following section and demonstrate the creative input of infotainment that makes a difference in political reporting. I then move on to debate the structural conditions that turn the economy into a benevolent player. This section is the linkage between my examples and a more general theoretical debate about infotainment.

Against the Boredom of Routine Coverage

The enthusiasm with which a new generation of journalists embrace infotainment is tied to the boredom that daily routine can produce. As I have demonstrated in the last chapter, many political journalists spend their day labouring in the field. There are countless redundant press conferences during which a predictable amount of comments are disseminated. Breaking news in such an environment is hard. Personal interviews with top leaders are a highlight and often inspire engaging personal portraits. Yet, more often than not journalists find themselves reiterating leaders' statements.

Coverage is predictable and synchronised. The Sahara press conference is a case in point. All journalists produced a particular selection of quotations in almost exactly the same order, following a shared sense of what is more and what is less important. They also knew what to leave out. All newspapers erased the homage the director paid to the family ideal; it was too ideological and did not fit the framework of the 'India Festival'. There was also no reference to the lengthy debate about Subrata Roy Sahara's lack of engagement for quality journalism. This information was filtered out as non-official communication. The strategic interplay between journalists and informants is not thought fit for publication. The case demonstrates the well-established finding that news-making is a structured process which reproduces and naturalises the viewpoint of established institutions and people in power (van Dijk 1988; Donahue et al. 1995; Hartley 1982; Fishman 1980; Glasgow Media Study Group 1976, 1980, 1993). Synchronicity flows from common notions of reality as well as negotiations in the field.

Van Dijk (1988) explains that during their daily activity, journalists recursively update news models and news schemata, which produce a collectively shared basis for assessing news-worthiness. News schemata help reporters to select events for coverage, while news models guide perceptions to make news-writing efficient. Daily routines and deadlines define the framework for collecting news, while 'news event schemata', 'news actor schemata' and 'news situation schemata' channel the selection of topics. In this way, only particular kinds of events, actions, actors, locations and time segments come to journalists' attention and are dealt with. Once selected, observations are integrated into the narrative order of stereotypical model situations, which have been abstracted from the practice. Models are used to select the relevant information and fill in the missing parts (see also van Dijk 1988: 110–14; Golding and Elliott 1979; Hartley 1982: 63–86; Merten et al. 1994: 237–46; Sigal 1973: 181; Tuchman 1978).

Models and schemata are updated and matched to events through constant debate. Agreement about good pegs and an appropriate narrative flow have three obvious sources.

(1) Journalists exchange information and keep each other informed about what is 'new'. In a competitive market where all newspapers feel the need to follow the 'pack',[18] journalists rely on each others' help for complementing coverage. Sharing information ensures that all newspapers cover the same events in the same way.

(2) Confusion is reduced by negotiating perspectives dialogically after an event. A pragmatic approach saves journalists from any embarrassment that may arise from divergent coverage (Pedelty 1995: 124; Tuchman 1978: 72–81; Schlesinger 1978). While not all journalists talk about all events all the time, regular meetings at press conferences, dinners or in the press club serve to recursively align personal perceptions and shared standards.

(3) Finally, there is the disciplining influence of daily reading. Reporters consume their colleagues' product on a daily basis. News companies also monitor how they scored in the market by comparing their coverage with that of all other newspapers in the city (also across the language divide). Information that was missed is covered the next day.

The similarity in approach and the depth of agreement about what is news is particularly apparent when performances fail. While any activity may be classified exciting, it does not become news if a majority of reporters see no news-value. The boycott of the director-general was such a case. A meeting organised by the ex-Admiral Bhagwat experienced a similar fate. The host failed miserably when trying to win over the press for his social ideals. He fixed a meeting with the press on 15 February 2000 to debate his political plans. There was an air of anticipation and the hope of some front-page news because of the recent controversy surrounding Bhagwat. In 1999 the BJP-dominated national government had raised corruption charges against the leader, retiring him prematurely from his post as admiral and discharging him dishonourably from the army. Reactions in the political world were strong. Most critics of the BJP believed that the case had been manufactured in order to get rid of an uncomfortable political enemy. Jayalalita, the head of the AIADMK party[19] and a member of the BJP-led coalition government, shared this opinion and withdrew her support, leading to the fall of the central government and forcing the national government to announce fresh elections. Given this background, it was not surprising that representatives from all the major newspapers attended. Journalists expected an important announcement, for example that the ex-Admiral intended to join active politics to fight the BJP. However, the patience of reporters was tested by a lengthy speech lamenting the dire social situation in the country and the need for selfless commitment to the poor. But where was the news?

None of this information was worthy of a headline. What made it worse was that Bhagwat seemed to be deliberately subverting the interpretative framework proposed by journalists. He ignored the impatience of his audience and the provocative questions about his personal history, political enemies and plans for the future. The following dialogue is a case in point:

Reporter 1:	During the last elections, you campaigned for one party!
Bhagwat:	I did not campaign for *one* party. I stood for *all* secular constellations.
Reporter 2:	Will you join politics?
Bhagwat:	First ask what is politics? It is everything: service to the country!
Reporter 3:	*We* mean *active* politics?
Bhagwat:	That is the problem. Politics is always narrowed down to electoral politics. But I want to work for the development of the country. You should join me. Why is this question of the election always uppermost in people's minds?
Reporter 4:	But if you do not join politics, how do you want to improve the situation in the country?
Bhagwat:	Active politics is far from my mind. Everyone should participate!

(Press conference with Bhagwat on 15 February 2000, my translation)

Journalists kept insisting and almost begged Bhagwat to give them some news after they had listened for over two hours. However, Bhagwat persisted in avoiding definite or polarising statements. He made it clear that he had no desire to be the subject of controversial headlines again. All he wanted was to start a dialogue between socially committed individuals and fight for a just society. His performance failed to impress the audience. Reporters fumed about the fact that they had wasted their time and refused to fall in line with Bhagwat. In their reports, they almost unanimously stripped the meeting of its main theme, namely social work.[20] Instead they focused on Bhagwat's attacks on the state government. This was against the explicit will of the host, who had emphasised several times that he had not come to raise his

Table 5.3. Summary of the content of reports from the press meeting with Bhagwat, 16 February 2000.

HINDI-LANGUAGE PRESS			ENGLISH-LANGUAGE PRESS	
Dainik Jagaran	*Sahara*	*Amar Ujala*	*Times of India*	*Hindustan Times*
Complaints against the government: On defence policies		Complaints against the government: On Kargil		
History of his removal from office; His bitterness; Will not enter active politics		Will not enter active politics		
Complaints against the chief minister, home minister, defence minister: On constitution committee; Hinduisation of politics	Complaints against the government: On Kargil, constitution committee, RSS	Complaints against the chief minister: On international politics, hidden agenda of the BJP	Complaints against the chief minister: On RSS, Kashmir politics	
			Complaints against home minister: On Pakistan politics	
Complaints against the government: On army management, Kargil	Complaints against defence policies	Complaints against the chief minister: On army management	Complaints against the defence minister: On RSS, Kashmir politics (Kargil)	
	Will not enter active politics			
	Wants to work for the poor			State does not work for the poor
		Denounces crime and corruption in politics		Denounces crime and corruption in politics
		Complaints against the government, the chief minister: On Hinduisation of politics		Complaints against the government, the chief minister: On constitution committee, Hinduisation of politics

finger against specific individuals. Disregarding this comment, journalists portrayed him as a bitter enemy of the government critiquing the Prime Minister, Atal Behari Vajpayee, the Union Home Minister, Ram Advani, and the Defence Minister, George Fernandes.

The similarity of reports flows from a collectively forged negative evaluation of the performance. During the press conference journalists updated their criteria of selection and interactivity, establishing that only an explicit statement that the speaker wanted to enter active politics would make the event worthwhile. Debates continued at lunch afterwards. Reporters assured each other that the meeting was a hoax and stretched their memory to recall whom Bhagwat had attacked personally. Only such quotations were able to satisfy their desire for drama. Since Bhagwat was not a leader and did not intend to become one, there was little news-worthiness in his sober speech. He was like a tiger without teeth, and hence, became reduced to a retired officer attacking men in power.

The articles stood in stark contrast to the numerous reports from all the other boring press conferences, including that at Sahara. While most journalists were impressed by the sparkling Sahara City, they certainly thought that the press conference was a bore. Yet, Subratra Roy Sahara got away with it, as did most major leaders. Journalists repeatedly describe the powerful as engaged personalities acting as benevolent forces in society. While Sahara could enforce such a view through financial interference, leaders depend on the more contingent exchange economy of personal favours and sympathy. While personalities may be pitched differently, there is a common structural condition that feeds all press conference reports. Journalism is an activity of reporting others' reports of social commotion. Reporters evaluate statements according to the status of the speaker and sort them with regard to criteria of significance, novelty and drama. They follow a set of common criteria which is updated through personal communication and mutual reading of papers.

It is this routine against which individual articles stand out. Journalists debated the case of the forgetful chief minister and the analytical piece about Sahara because they broke the routine and the boredom. It is this impact journalists hope for. Ambitious personalities wish to be recognised as individuals in a profession that demands a high degree of conformity. A career is made when a person can demonstrate the necessary compliance *and* ability to develop a creative approach. In chapter two I described how English-language news have relaxed the beat system significantly and created flat hierarchies. These structural changes are thought to encourage journalists to take charge of their own work and become creative individuals. They can accomplish this task by appropriating infotainment as a tool for cutting through routine reporting. It allows journalists to share their observations and their analysis, which they gain as privileged observers of society. They break news through fresh analysis rather than by quoting (exclusively) authorities' observations and opinions. Re-contextualisation of information through non-routine framing dramatically alters the way in which information is presented. Diverting from routine coverage produces alternative avenues for thinking through the social. It is this potential that is lacking in the predetermined rejection of popular formats.

Yet, there is no reason for a naïve celebration of a new freedom delivered by infotainment. Liberties are curtailed by power structures in the field. Creative writing must be adjusted to advertisers' desires. Hence, critical analysis excludes most generally leaders in the corporate world as well as political parties and ideologies supported by private industry. Furthermore advertisers prefer feel-good journalism. Appreciation for advertisement is accelerated when readers are in a happy mood, so the number of stories about prisons, social inequalities or rural poverty is kept down. It also explains the different trajectories of the articles on Sahara and Gupta.

Maria's article was rejected as biased and castigated for displaying an unjustified negative attitude towards the host. Maria certainly did not accept this judgement. She did not invent her story but, like all the others, wrote it up as her recollection of experiences. In fact, she felt that she had come much closer to the 'truth', since her article also transported the feeling of hostility to Subrata Roy Sahara that had prevailed during the meeting. However, Maria failed because her interpretation was collectively rejected by journalists and attacked by Sahara. In total contrast to this reception dynamic, the Gupta article shamed reporters. They felt they should have dug deeper to get to the core of the story. No one considered Annu's article biased or informed by a negative attitude towards the chief minister. Annu realised her success by measuring the speed by which her perspective became an accepted 'truth'. Her no less subjective article became an important piece of journalistic work, uncovering the hidden structures of political power.

The discrepancy in the evaluation of strong men and strong women does not only follow economic pressure. I already mentioned the admiration of journalists for consumerism and the new elites. The positive representation of magnates is party to the transformation of social consciousness in the post-developmental period (Mazzarella 2003c). Growing economic potency nurtures dreams of a new India removed from the classical images of poverty, caste discrimination and rural economy. Indians take pride in belonging to a country considered to be a 'tiger state', welcomed as an upcoming market and feared as a economic competitor.[21] Everyday journalists in India produce powerful images of a dynamic, young and competitive India. There is veneration for the new Indian female, who is admired for her international success. Images of the new beauties are perpetually circulated through all mass media and influence body styles and fashions (Munshi 2001, 2004; Sangari 2003). Bollywood actors and actresses enjoy a wide following. They are given much media hype (Dwyer 2001; Juluri 2003), celebrated in clubs (Dickey 1993a, 2001; Osella and Osella 2004), and wooed by political parties (Dickey 1993b; Hardgrave and Neidhart 1975). There are also the heroes from private industry who invest heavily in carefully crafted advertisements (Mazzarella 2003c) and who seduce editors to promote their interests through infomercials and product placement.

These images from the new India are mediated by calculated public relation campaigns, designed by professionals with the aim to impress. This is not to say that they are controlled in every aspect of their production and reception. In-depth studies of public relation officers (Hess 1984; Manning 2001; Scammell 1995; Schudson 2003) and advertisement agencies (Malefyt and Moeran 2003; Mazzarella 2003c; Moeran 1996) inform us about the intricacies of these businesses. However, the activity invested in the media presence of the new stars stands in stark contrast to the everyday reality of political reporting. Public relations are still rarely exploited by the Indian political class. To date there are few mediating personnel and no 'spin' culture. Journalists directly confer with leaders and are the prime mediators of political information. Furthermore, professional ethics drives critical appraisal of politics. A whole fleet of people investigate political actions and produce daily proof of the shrewdness of leaders. There is no comparable coverage in newspapers about the private industry. While the economic section of newspapers covers market development, there is little debate of business practices. When the residential editor of the *Times of India* suggested to the management that one should investigate the trading practices of Sahara, he was sternly rejected. Power constellations precluded such a project.

However, the structural absence of critical perspectives on private industry should not diminish the accomplishments of political reporters. Reporters repeatedly resist the seduction in exchange relations. They counter-balance uncritical engagement with leaders and regularly craft texts about deleterious political manoeuvres. Such writing is facilitated by the input journalists receive in a commercialised, competitive press institution. In the case presented here the reporters have used typical features of infotainment, such as dramatisation, personalisation of news and the portrayal of politics as a game, to formulate a critique of the political status quo. Certainly, infotainment does not promote critical analysis per se. However, it does demand experimentation with narrative styles. It forces journalists to move beyond the routinised journalistic gaze.

My line of reasoning diverts significantly from the typical tendency to consider infotainment a nuisance or even a curse. My argument is thrown into sharp relief when compared to Doris Graber's (1994) study in the U.S. which is considerably milder in its judgement of commercialisation. Doris Graber asked leading news personnel to develop fifteen story-lines into a routine news item and a dramatised story. The author found that the dramatic stories were more compelling and generally did not lose out on information content. News directors clearly preferred dramatic framing because of its greater audience appeal but also because they resent being used by politicians for the repetitive coverage of ritualised events with no substance. An interviewee commented thus:

> What I try to do is find ways to get around the straightforward aspect of it. Because the straightforward is just so predictable, and it is so boring, and again, it is so diffuse. There is no density, there is no richness to any of it... It is empty and devoid of any content. (Graber 1994: 502)

The above quotation suggests that applying a non-routine frame may add depth. This possibility does not interest Graber. Her concern is whether dramatisation leads to loss of information and she concludes that while dramatisation diverts attention from crucial content, it simultaneously serves to create interest and involvement. In turn, the editor considers the dramatic depiction as drawing attention to the particular aspects he wants to communicate as well as to the news item as such. This latter attitude also prevailed among those journalists who appreciated the shifts, and who considered the stylistic freedom as a means to intensify their message. Writing practices in Lucknow drew my attention to the way in which reporters used essayistic writing as a means of subverting standard perceptions. It is with this in mind that I conceive the need for a shift in the infotainment debate.

Infotainment Revisited

I have written about infotainment as a practice rather than as a text, ideology or managerial approach alone. 'Doing infotainment' is a field for experimentation set within a particular power matrix. Infotainment is a drive to appease the corporate sector and to improve the marketability of newspapers by making stories compelling; however, it is not a coherent perspective. It is not the hegemony of one ideology, but a polymorphic field that contributes towards reorienting consciousness in a consumer oriented society. To capture this moment and consider its multiple consequences, the analysis of the market-driven reorientation of the news business needs to move beyond the lament of dumbing down. This position is reminiscent of the attack against popular culture put forward by the Frankfurter School and ignores the contribution of cultural studies writing.

The Frankfurt School (Marcuse 1964; Horkheimer and Adorno 1998 [1944]) had formulated a fundamental critique of media-generated popular culture in the 1950s. In a Marxist tradition, it castigated mass media products as an instrument exploited by the elite to subdue the critical spirit of common people, diverting attention from social issues through shallow entertainment.[22] The critique was formulated in a spirit of resistance emerging from the memory of the traumatic experience of dictatorship and war during Hitler's regime. A critical, alert and educated population was considered a necessary bastion against inequalities and injustice promoted by self-serving elites. This position has been critiqued for overstating the ability of the seemingly unified elite to manipulate media output through rational intervention. It also misses the ambiguity of texts and the multiplicity of reading contexts. In a nutshell, Marxist critiques of popular culture have overstated the unity of texts and removed the reflection on media from actual practices of production and appropriation (Goodall 1995; Kellner 2003; Tulloch 2000).

In spite of an extensive and sophisticated scholarly debate about popular culture, the polemically overstated negative evaluation of popular culture has not disappeared, but resurfaces in debates about contemporary media developments. An example is Neil Postman's book, *Amuse Ourselves to Death* (1985). His book laments the trivialisation of the public sphere through television, which imposes a culture of entertainment. Brantlinger (1985) analyses the scholarly descriptions in which the production of dramatic visual entertainment for the masses is seen as triumphing over meaningful experience. Criticism has also been directed at news media in the infotainment age, and gained strength in the late 1990s when the effects of political decisions to progressively privatise the media – especially in Europe – became apparent. Scholars observe a process of Americanisation, also dubbed tabloidisation, that significantly impacts on the political process (Blumler 1992; Gavin 2007; Patterson 2000). The spectacle has replaced serious political debate. The audiences are addressed as consumers instead of as citizens (Sparks and Tulloch 2000).

At times the demonising of private media is mixed with nostalgia for the (lost) benefits of the public broadcasting system. Commercialisation is the sell-out of the public service ethos of journalism (Curran 2002; Tracey 1998), which is idealised in the Habermasian sense as an area for interest-free deliberations produced by the public for the public. Yet, there is also acknowledgement of the deficits of public broadcasting. These are illustrated in the demands for more social responsibility, inclusiveness and transparency in state-managed television as a platform for quality reporting and public education (Jakubowicz 2007).

Infotainment is identified as a major force driving the sell-out of serious information. It diverts the attention of the masses from 'real' political issues, narcotising them through soft stories and spectacle. Unlike most other studies, which focus mostly on Western news media, Thussu (2007b: 151-55) has attempted a broader global perspective. He believes that the global proliferation of infotainment promoted by media moguls – foremost the Murdoch empire – has serious political consequences. Feel-good journalism is a deceitful influence which diverts attention from the inequalities of the neo-liberal order. 'False consciousness' eliminates resistance to an unjust dominance of the new hyper-rich global elite. Infotainment is an instrument of neo-liberal imperialism in its attempt at global dominance.

> The globalisation of neo-liberal ideology and the near global reach and circulating of televised infotainment has provided neo-liberal imperialism with a powerful opportunity to communicate directly with the world's populace, as more and more global infotainment conglomerates are localising their content to reach beyond the 'Westernised' elites. (Thussu 2007b: 154)

Localisation here is conceptualised as a top-down movement, the process of transferring a core ideology (originating from the West) into a vernacular medium. The argument echoes the debate of global 'culture synchronisation' (Hamelink 1983: 3). Champions of this position have diagnosed a flattening out of cultural diversity through the continuing spread of Western ideologies, commodities and technologies.[23] In this theory of media imperialism, the U.S. has been identified as the main exporter of media products, exercising pressure on local economies to adapt to the 'dominant' model (Boyd-Barrett 1977; Smythe 1981; Schiller 1976).[24] It re-emerges in more recent works on the Anglo-Saxon media nexus (Tunstall and Machin 1999).

Against this argument stands a vast number of empirical studies detailing processes of cultural diversification through the re-appropriation of global influences in local contexts, as part of what could be called the 'glocalisation' debate (Appadurai 1990). Cultural studies and media anthropology scholars have depicted the multi-directional processes of reinterpretation of globally available media products through the lenses of the local (Askew and Wilk 2002; Curran and Morley 2005; Ginsburg, Abu-Ludghod and Larkin 2002; Peterson 2003; Pink 2006; Spitulnik 1993). Thussu is aware of this position. He takes note of recent debates about the persistence of cultural diversity and the equivocal nature of infotainment (p. 162-70). However, the summary of more positive studies on infotainment bears no connection to the overall thesis that the global spread of infotainment promotes a 'false global "feel good" factor' (p. 9). The Indian case study in particular treats local culture as a vessel appropriated by the Murdoch empire in order to spread its influence while disguising the colonising impetus of the expansion (Thussu 2007a; 2007b).

My aim is not to rekindle the homogenisation versus diversification debate.[25] Rather, I offer an argument about how a local media product and its adaptation of global developments informs cultural transformation and feeds back into the recursive re-imagination of what it means to participate in the new (global) order. In this chapter I have shown that infotainment enables journalists to critique a particular political order, at the cost of collaborating with another. Journalists confront the ostentation of political rituals and the inefficiency of leaders. It is an attack directed at specific individuals and more generally at a political culture feeding on leader-worship. Highlighting this moment of resistance and subversion does not fail to recognise the blind spots created by a media entrenched in market dealings. However, it refuses to fall in line with views marking out a unidirectional process of dismantling sophisticated political culture.

The argument about an ongoing demise of quality in political debate in the contemporary media age is informed by the value-laden bifurcation between the 'high' political acts of rational argumentation and 'low' forms of popular politics. The concern is that the high art of rational debate suffers from the commercialisation of media. The financial dominance of the corporate world has lead to the substitution of entertainment for information. Corner and Pels (2003: 4) have called this the 'disabling perspective':

> In this […] view, the media are seen as variously undermining the practice of democracy or, at least, of having a strong propensity to do so. They perform their subversive function through such routes as the substitution of entertainment for knowledge, the closing off of true diversity, the pursuit of an agenda determined primarily by market factors and their susceptibility to control by government and corporate agencies. (Corner and Pels 2003: 4)

Corner and Pels go on to argue that the disabling view comes across in two forms. In one version media representations are believed to be controlled by political interests. In the other politics is seen to be governed by media imperatives. Either way, there is misrecognition of the interconnectedness of the two domains. Politics, like all cultural action, is fashioned by its media of expression. Following this performative approach, Corner and Pels demand enquiries into mediated political culture at the conjunction of political processes and media activities (p. 5). This approach mirrors Couldry's (2004) plea for an examination of the way in which media-related practices anchor other social practices, however, without assuming a primacy of media as dominant agents.

Such an approach acknowledges the historical and cultural relativity of political practices and ideologies. It avoids the pedagogical gestures of well-meaning scholars and journalists who declare the universal validity of a particular modernistic ideal forged in the West, as a supreme standard for 'rational' politics. There are few studies that challenge this model. Exceptions are Zaller (2003) and Baum (2005). Their studies break with an elitist view by providing an analysis of the relation between infotainment and popular politics.

Zaller (2003) propounds voters' limited capacity as an argument against perpetuating the ideal of the informed citizen, a person constantly monitoring political processes to make an informed choice. America saw the emergence of this value in the late nineteenth century, when it replaced blatant partisanship among voters and newspapers (Schudson 1998). The demand to continuously scrutinise a wide range of complex political processes exceeds the capacity and interest of most people, especially in today's information age. Hence Zaller sketches a novel news-making formula which transforms news from being a 'police patrol' to a 'burglar alarm' (p. 100):[26]

> The many citizens who, by the evidence, dislike politics should not be led by reporters on wide-ranging patrols of political terrain. Rather, they should be alerted to problems requiring attention and otherwise left to private concerns. [...] Journalists should routinely seek to cover non-emergency but important issues by means of coverage that is intensely focussed, dramatic, and entertaining and that affords the parties and responsible interest groups, especially political parties, ample opportunity for expression of opposing views. Reporters may use simulated drama to engage public attention when the real thing is absent. (Zaller 2003: 121, 122)

Zaller explicitly welcomes infotainment as a means to draw attention. It is not an obstruction to serious political debate, but a method to allow less politically interested citizens to be drawn into important debates. The argument is supported by empirical evidence presented by Baum (2005). Through campaigns for the U.S. presidential election in entertainment shows, less politically engaged viewers were brought into the reach of political activities, fostering participation and influencing their voting behaviour.

Infotainment is a new format for political debate. Its non-compliance with the ideal of composed rational debate challenges the assumptions of liberal news ideologies. It absorbs the post-modern notion of the 'constructedness' of social discourses. The new political and economic constellations allow for the emergence of new perspectives. These new perspectives are not neutral or innocent. They contribute to the updating of power relations under changing conditions. In India commercialisation has liberated the press from structural domination by the government and hence has opened avenues for the diversification of political viewpoints. It has brought grassroots politics into the local pages and has strengthened the position of journalists in leader–reporter negotiations. Simultaneously it has put at risk the celebrity status of politicians, who now compete with glamorous personalities from private industry and the media. Admired for their international status, their cosmopolitan outlook and potency, these new idols – promoted through infotainment – generate new images of a successful citizen. Citizens continue to eschew political participation in leader-centred universes. Yet they also desire to participate in a world of fashion and life-style promoted by the new celebrities. Some reporters – disenchanted by or disinterested in politics – embrace the alternative career path of covering culture and consumer goods, rather than racing after political leaders.

There is a synergy between advertisements and editorial that is sought after by commercial investors and lamented by opponents of a consumer society. Juxtaposing critical political analysis with bright infomercials seduces readers towards a more positive evaluation of consumerism. The editorial (in tandem with the advertisement) defines an alternative social position in the nation of the consumer citizen (Baudrillard 1988; Scammell 2003). The newspaper produces persuasive arguments in favour of this new position, superseding the politically engaged citizens, who seem to belong to the past. The contrast between these two idealised postures is thrown into sharp relief in Mazzarella's study (2003c), in which contemporary advertising for KamaSutra condoms is compared with an earlier campaign for condom use disseminated by the governmental department for family planning. The government adverts used the device of an enlightened elite's pedagogical message to citizens to serve the nation by using a condom and prevent pregnancy and overpopulation. In contrast, the KamaSutra commercials are designed to seduce individuals, asserting that condoms enhance sexual pleasure. The consumer is addressed as a mature subject, replacing the dutiful citizen focused on national progress.

The ideal of the mature consumer subject is at the root of contemporary news production. Political interest is no longer taken for granted or considered a social duty. The citizen subject is seduced to consume political information. The trade-off in this reorientation is collaboration with an emerging global regime of truth that devalues state institutions and celebrates the market. The new perspectives are oblivious of or even hostile towards those who are excluded from participation in a consumer society. Hence, there is no reason to celebrate this development. However, nostalgia for the olden days is hardly a satisfactory starting point for critical theory. There is sufficient evidence for the shortcomings of political debate in state-sponsored media. A polemic bifurcation which idealises the past as embracing relational debate and contemporary news discourse as mere sensationalist misses the complexities of these developments. I have identified daring articles which are critical of leaders as a crack in the mirror. Their contribution towards a critical consciousness needs to be taken seriously, even if they address 'only' the wastefulness, corruption and brutality of the political class.

Notes

1. While English-language newspapers in India have introduced this new trend, Hindi-medium newspapers are following suit with more and more supplements devoted to 'traditional culture', tourism, show business, consumer goods (Neyazi 2008).
2. The residential editor had anticipated the possibility of this reaction. He felt that the advantage of working in a large and profitable enterprise like the *Times of India* was that he did not have to worry too much about losing even a major customer, who, in fact, contributed only a small part of the overall advertising revenue.

    Schudson observes a similar attitude in the media business in the U.S. He looks at the freedom of the press from a commercial angle: 'There is a paradox here: the desire for profit makes a news operation vulnerable to influence by advertisers, but the more profitable a news outlet is, the more it is able to withstand such pressure' (Schudson 2003: 126).
3. One *lac* denotes the number 100,000.
4. One *crore* denotes the number 10,000,000.

5. I am grateful to Dipankar Gupta for drawing my attention to this article.

6. Jairam Ramesh (Congress), Saleem Sherwani (Samajvadi Party) and Sitaram Yechury (Communist Party of India [Marxist]).

7. Rankings like this have become a regular feature, especially in the weekly magazines like *Outlook* and *India Today*. Similarly, in the case I quoted here, there is a conspicuous absence of politicians in these lists.

8. Ram Prakash Gupta's term as chief minister lasted from 9 November 1999 to 27 October 2000. Before that he had been an MLA for three terms in the 1960s and 1970s and held the office of deputy chief minister in 1968.
   'Taking exception to the UP CM's recent comments that the government would do anything to prevent any move to construct the Ram Temple at Ayodhya, Ms Mayawati said half in jest, "It's not the CM's fault as I am told that he is a forgetful man... probably he has been privy to the discussions amongst BJP leaders about the temple construction and couldn't help blurting out the hidden agenda in public"' (*Times of India*, 3 February 2000).

9. See, for example, *Hindustan Times*, 14 February 2000; *Sahara*, 14 February 2000; *Dainik Jagaran*, 15 February 2000; *Times of India*, 15 February 2000; *Dainik Jagaran*, 16 February 2000; *Dainik Jagaran*, 18 February 2000; *Sahara*, 22 February 2000; and *Pioneer*, 2 March 2000.

10. *Aj*, 18 February 2000; *Times of India*, 19 February 2000; and *Pioneer*, 24 February 2000.

11. *Dainik Jagaran*, 22 February 2000; *Hindustan Times*, 22 February 2000; and *Sahara*, 22 February 2000.

12. This article on the by-elections illustrates the situation in Kannauj during the campaign. Although it does not refer directly to the chief minister, he appears as a gimmick in the headline: 'Kannuaj [sic!] by-poll brings BJP-BSP closer to stabilise RP Gupta?'

13. Later he was made Governor of Madhya Pradesh. He died in 2004.

14. For a description of the situation, see, for example, Mohit Dubey, *Times of India*, 5 February 2000; Deepak Gidwani, *Hindustan Times*, 8 February 2000; Ursula Rao, *Times of India*, 15 February 2000.

15. The quotations were printed in roman script. The translations were provided in the main text.

16. There are also more drastic examples of government sanction. A case in point is the state-sponsored prosecution of the Tehelka.com journalists who uncovered a defence scandal. Mazzarella's analysis of this operation reveals that its offensiveness was not a sole corollary to the corrupt practices that were unravelled. Rather, the operation made palpable the contradictions of the Indian political order, and hence contributed to what I am describing in this chapter: the weakening appeal of political ideologies, which dominated the public arenas in the pre-market period (Mazzarella 2006).

17. Whether in Hindi or English-language newspapers, it was part of the daily routine to instruct reporters to catch up on stories that had been omitted and write a continuation on themes they had missed. *Dainik Jagaran* and *Hindustan* made the system watertight. Every day a freelancer had to compare the different newspapers systematically. In this process equivalent articles were crossed out, exposing in the end those areas in which one's own newspaper had outdone the others and where they lagged behind. In cases of major differences, feedback was instant.

18. *Anna's Dravida Munnetra Kazhagam* (Federation for the Advancement of the Dravidians).The party is a regional party from Tamil Nadu.

19. Only the text in *Hindustan Times* was different. Here the reporter adopted Bhagwat's perspective as the main theme and peg for the headline and communicated Bhagwat's desire to change the social environment in India.

20. India and other successful countries at the threshold of development stand in contrast to the 'orientalised' image of Africa, in a state of economic and political disintegration. With regard to the postcolonial character of Africa, Mbembe (2001) described the continent's transition from a first phase of optimistic, though rather ineffective and extremely violent, nation-building to a phase where states fragment and the African economy has been largely disconnected from the official markets and has increasingly become part of an international parallel economy. In a similar vein Ferguson observes that subalterns in Africa have lost their belief in modernity as a vision for a better future, a goal that is in reach, and towards which everyone is striving collectively. Modernity in post-1980s Africa has becomes a marker associated only with the powerful and rich (and particularly the West). No longer a common social cause, development then becomes the project of individuals, families and clans searching for ways to participate in the world of the privileged, through migration, conspicuous consumption, symbolic action, etc.

21. See also the influential book by Guy Debord (1994 [1967]) which analyses the culture of the spectacular as an instrument of diversion and de-politicisation.

22. Against the idea that the world is becoming more homogenous, 'cultural synchronisation' signifies the persistence of culture differences at the symbolic level. Divergent traditions turn into mere signifiers of difference that mask underlying structural similarities.

23. A fundamental critique and revision of this concept is formulated by Boyd-Barrett (1998).

24. Rantanen (2005) offers an excellent summary of this debate by media scholars.

25. Zaller takes his cue from McCubbins and Schwartz (1984).

Conclusions

Regionalisation and Commercialising

News as culture is a study of news-making as politics and of politics. My discussion interrogated the intersection between journalists' activities and the media-related actions of publicity-seeking citizens, politicians and corporations, at a historical juncture, where commercialising is transforming the press.   Newspapers have inherited from modernisation discourses the idea of an objective press, whose aim is to educate and inform the citizens. This ideal is recast in an environment that has begun to devalue politics and depoliticise public culture. Journalists readily express their disillusionment with the political class in their writing, while becoming servants of a 'new master', the corporate sector. In the course of adjusting to corporate interests, the reader is re-imagined. Newspapers address mature citizens as political activists (who want to be heard) and as consumers (who wish to be seduced). The effect is a paradox: contemporary news writing strengthens political leadership traditions while simultaneously undermining them.

I began with an analysis of how big-men politics is extended into the news writing domain. Local citizens rephrase in a media context a cultural model for the public display of importance. Aspiring leaders and aggrieved citizens alike take advantage of the open-door policy of vernacular newspapers to disseminate their demands, desires and activities. As an authorising medium, the newspaper authenticates their voices and qualifies them as being worthy of public attention. In rare cases, announcements in the media can replace activities in the public arena. However, more often than not, public performances and media activities are amalgamated. While in an ideal construction, the public sphere (idealised as an arena for rational debate) and the public arena (as practice of showcasing individuals) occupy distinct positions in public culture, in practice they overlap, producing debates that are tied to the recognition of (leading) individuals and their struggles for power. Journalists have their own stake in these politicised dynamics. Citizens reach out to the media through a hierarchical network of 'reporters' who embrace a political culture of trading favours for loyalty. Brokership in media-related networks mimics political traditions of eminence, while creating alternative avenues for public articulation.

The logic of patronage also constitutes a governing principle in the domain of political reporting. Breaking news, accumulating fame and trading favours are activities that flow from the ability of journalists to speak to leaders, or more precisely to have the means to inveigle leaders to listen. News is an object of trade that governs exchange relations between leaders and journalists. In leader-centred articles, journalists create powerful images of political personalities. They personalise achievements and interpret political progress as an effect of the intervention of visionary individuals. In return they are singled out for special treatment by the political class. Journalists' closeness to the governing elite translates into personal advantages and a powerful position in networks of patronage. Such activity subverts the idea of the press and politics as separate entities. The ability of journalists to mediate public concerns is tied to the network logic that extends into all spheres of social life. While the publication of grievances and the denouncing of corruption in a mass medium may or may not bring the desired change, personal intervention is highly effective.

I have clarified the logic of patronage relations as a cultural matrix directing media activities. I do not claim that this is the only governing principle that determines all actions and representations. The press also embraces other cultural models. Journalists in India – like everywhere else – are a highly organised group of professionals following global standards of news-making that produce a predictable set of typical stories (Ståhlberg 2002). Journalists act as political watchdogs (Sahay 2006) and embrace managerial decisions to produce drama and entertainment (Thussu 2007a, 2007b). My elaboration on the significance of news networks fills a gap in a scholarly discourse that overemphasises the separateness of the professional culture of news workers and tends to engage with texts rather than social practice. I have bridged the gap between production and reception, text and context by outlining continuities produced through network logics and embodied in concrete connection between readers, writers and informants. As possible nodal points in a network society, journalists participate in creating and producing incentives for recreating patronage relations. They create an alternative avenue for becoming known and respected, while also feeding into the political process of making, identifying and unmaking leaders.

The conditions under which this takes places are heavily influenced by market changes. Regionalisation is concomitant with commercialisation. The compulsion to increase circulation and the growth in advertising for down-market sectors (Rajagopal 1998) has contributed significantly to the expansion of the vernacular press, which has not only become more profitable but has also increased in quality, thus reaching a level where vernacular journalists can compete with English-language products (Jeffrey 2000; Ninan 2007). This has strengthened regional political parties. Several studies show that the triumph of the Hindi press has given vernacular elites a voice and an instrument of power (Pande 2006; Rajagopal 2001). Extending this argument, I have demonstrated that Hindi-language journalists maintain contacts with political actors at all levels of society. They communicate not only with regional elites but also work their way through hierarchies of leaders proclaiming importance. Hence, they not only disseminate the ideologies of dominant vernacular elites, but contribute towards shaping these elites and influencing local power struggles over posts and positions.

Yet, the same political class that is promoted through the localisation of news-making is also undermined by market developments. The growing independence from political money,[1] the drive to entertain and seduce the reader, and the hero-worshipping of the economic elite propagate an alterative model for upward mobility. The 'new heroes' are admired for their financial success, their cosmopolitan personalities and their sober images. Their coverage flows from PR activities and paid advertisements rather than negotiation in media networks. Hence, images of the corporate sector differ significantly from those of political actors. Economic leaders do not suffer the same amount of negative publicity that is routinely part of political reporting. The latter is informed by the notion of the press as the Fourth Estate and the deep familiarity of journalists with the political universe. Reporters' work is far removed from the corporate sector. They rarely convene with the economic elite. Meetings with advertising customers are the domain of the management who push through the agenda of maximising profit through feel-good journalism and advertorials. There is always the suspicion that economic barons are no less corrupt, but there is no resulting investigation, since critiquing the corporate sector has no currency in the contemporary publication business. Simultaneously, a history of deep political patronage – a recent and potent memory – and an overdose of political insider knowledge make it easy to give in to the seduction of capital, amidst suspicion and disgust. Journalists embrace market ideologies out of economic compulsion and/or because they offer an alternative to the suffocating experiences in a bureaucratic raj. The 'new' journalism addresses the consumer citizen along with the network citizen and the voting citizens.

The newspaper discourse speaks with three different voices. Political news and leader–centrism still play a significant role and are assigned a central place in the newspapers. However, the political finds itself in the company of Bollywood stars and consumer 'information'. They ensure not only the financial success of the publication but are thought to be the main attraction to readers. Finally, network society acquires a new format through the regionalisation of the press. It is eagerly sought by those who have little hope of any gain from commercialisation and who experience new forms of exploitation in the liberalised market.

Multiple Voices in a Competitive Market

The representations of a consumer-orientated, prosperous India appear in stark contrast to the proliferation of publicly voiced local worries over employment, the infrastructure and hygiene. The disparity is thrown into sharp relief in a comparison between local and national newspapers. National dailies lead the move towards sleek representations of benevolent consumer society, while local newspapers exploit the desire of citizens for news from their own environment. The latter often struggle financially in a media market undergoing centralisation. The difference between local and national newspapers follows to a certain extent the language divide. Yet, a clear distinction becomes increasingly difficult. The regionalisation of the English-language press and the growing significance and profitability of major regional vernacular newspapers have accelerated competition. This leads to policy decisions that bridge the gap between the 'two publics'. What I perceived in the early years of the new millennium as nascent competition in the 'middle ground' appears to have stiffened in the meantime (Ninan 2007; Neyazi 2008).

In my sample the adjustment of the English-language press to the new challenge of the vernacular newspapers was played out in strategies for localisation. An example was the way in which *Hindustan Times* cashed in on the local credentials of its Hindi sister publication

(*Hindustan*) during programmes such as *At Your Doorstep*. I also observed the successful struggle of the editor of the *Times of India,* Lucknow to get permission to fill two more pages of the main newspaper with local coverage. He saw this as an essential measure to avert the movement of readers away from the English-language press. In turn, the Hindi press is becoming glossier. The most recent data is from Ninan (2007). She describes the dramatic adjustments the Hindi press has made in the last ten years. Major regional players have adopted the measure that made the *Times of India* a market leader and upgraded their products, turning newspapers into advertiser-friendly, glossy products, with a multiplicity of supplements and a depoliticised content. Some have even begun to embrace the hybrid 'Hinglish' to cater to young people from the growing urban middle classes and compete with the English-language products. Hindi dailies poach top employees from English-language newspapers to speed up the transformation towards commercialisation.

In the competitive battle, the encouragement of participation is one means to bind readers to newspapers. English-language publications draw the reader into the discourse by inviting popular debate, by conducting regular surveys and covering public life in the city. The tone is mostly positive and in line with the drive towards infotainment. Local people find their place in the news pages as achievers and 'heroes of everyday life'.[2] Hindi newspapers copy this strategy in the proliferation of city supplements. At the same time they continue to push into the hinterlands; they increase their circulation by diversifying their product, offering specialised pages for sub-districts and small towns. More and more voices are drawn into the public domain (Ninan 2007).[3]

The growing number of publications, the competition and the drive to appeal to local readers leads to the multiplication of viewpoints. The specific character of newspapers turns them into a prime medium for their absorption and the juxtaposition of this multiplicity. They are popular, highly permeable and have a wide reach. The unique openness of newspapers to non-media professionals encourages participation. People invest hope and ambitions into the newspaper. The publication of contradictory viewpoints creates an image of India as made up of innumerable sub-cultures and interest groups. Newspapers create the public as a cacophonic bundle of voices. The diversity is appreciated by consumers, as Peterson (1996: 300–24; forthcoming) demonstrates. Urban readers are conscious of the variable character of different newspapers and thus subscribe, if they can, to several in order to keep in touch with numerous social discourses and to satisfy various desires. Newspapers are classified according to language, status and information value. They are bought by the individual, family or business for political news, the advertisements, reading pleasure, or to keep up with local gossip, to follow a family tradition or demonstrate status and so on.

Newspapers do more than represent diversity. The unprivileged, in particular, push their voices into the public domain for empowerment. Gupta (1995) observed in the early 1990s that detailed narrations in newspapers provide pedagogical tales for the majority of the poor. They are provided with an endless stream of stories about bureaucratic neglect, political arrogance and the daily struggle for basic amenities. I have elaborated on the activities that shape these tales. Citizens take advantage of the opportunity of media relations. Hence, newspapers act not only as a screen for projecting power structures, but as a medium for exerting pressure and overcoming the limitations of ones social status. The seriousness of the newspaper, the authority of the written word and the closeness of journalists to powerful personalities all embody hope for solutions. By investing in media networks and negotiating for the publication of grievances, people turn private struggles into 'public scandals'. Contrary to neo-liberal ideologies that see the responsible individual as a prime agent for success and liberation, citizens denounce systemic ills as reasons for their misery. They demand attention from powerful people and publicly claim that the solution to their problem lies with them. While I emphasised that few problems get solved through publication, the amassing of voices demanding governmental intervention is a significant ideological force. It keeps alive the memory that there are many people who do not participate in the new glossy world. It also aligns public consciousness with the socialist past and the idea that the state is responsible for the care of its citizens.

I emphasise this point but do not deny that newspapers entice readers to believe in the benevolence of the market and promote the glamour of consumerism. Newspapers hail economic success, bow to the corporate sector through advertorials and feel-good journalism, and offer little in terms of a critique of market ideology. Yet, the democratisation of access, as a concomitant of localisation and commercialisation, has opened new avenues for self-representation. The little voices speak of hardship, conflict and despair. This finding stands in contrast to other accounts of the way in which the media reinvented itself in liberalised India (Butcher 2003; Thussu 2007a).

Consider the example of music programmes described by Vamsee Juluri (2003). The hosts of these shows perpetually glamorise India and ridicule the working class. They forge new, modern, young identities by locating the nation in an idealised space of exotic metaphors. These images are communicated in programmes that invite participation and draw in the viewer to identify with stereotypical 'oriental' images. '[T]elevision lends new dimensions to the notion of being represented. Audiences claim a sense of representation also in the modern, imagined, self-relativising term of being represented as the public and the nation in a global context' (Juluri 2003: 24). The exotic beauty of India is brought to the fore at a time where social relations are undergoing massive changes, tearing apart traditional family structures. They provide a new centre for the construction of identities that do not clash with the need to re-work relationships under circumstances of economic globalisation. India is thus securely frozen in essentialised metaphors of 'elephants, soothsayers, princes', giving citizens the feeling that they are still rooted in a rich tradition, even while social life is radically changing around them (Juluri 2003: 24–27).[4]

Mazzarella (2003a, 2003b) identifies a similar trend in the advertisement industry, whereby professionals negotiate with clients for new, positive representations of locality. The demand for glamorous images of the local follows on from market liberalisation that has plunged Indian business into competition with foreign corporations. Indian clients want advertisements that promote their company as traditional, warm and close to the people. At the same time they wish their goods to be promoted as fashionable, modern and reliable, attributes normally attached only to foreign products. The outcomes are clichés that set India in metaphors of modernity and tradition while removing every reference to the messiness of local lives.

> The globalisation of brands was touted precisely on the basis that it would liberate both producers and consumers from the constraints of locality. In an equal field, all market players could now compete on the same terms. Of course, on an economic level the claim was preposterous. But much of its appeal, I think, lay in its promise to liberate identity from history. Globalisation represented [...] the promise of finally transcending second-class citizenship status in the global ecumene. As such, it was the latest instalment of a sequence of rhetorical gifts made in the name of universalism: bourgeois citizenship, nationalism, developmentalism. (Mazzarella 2003c: 205)

These nebulous images are also the substance of newspaper advertisements. They are promoted in the editorial part that informs about life-styles, celebrities and consumer goods. Yet, unlike the examples described by Mazzarella and Juluri, newspapers do not gloss over the contradictions that emerge from globalisation, rather they embody them. Local coverage and little voices disprove the glossy images of a shining India. They do not transcend everyday life, but indulge in it to excess. The proliferation of the local is not the traditional 'other' of the new India. It is an expression of the life reality of the majority of people. Ironically the dissemination of local hardship itself is a result of the new market dynamics that have turned local complaints and political aspirations into a commodity, sold with a profit by the newspaper to the locality.

News as Culture

Looking at news as social practice, I propose a shift in the way journalism is studied. In order to understand the social significance of news, we need to analyse how it is rooted in the social processes that form them and turn them into valuable assets. We also need to move beyond institutions as a framework for the study of journalistic practices. I have identified two approaches to news-making dynamics. One set of studies investigates the impact of organisational structures on news output. People working in the news room are seen to apply a set of predefined principles that direct their attention and serve as guidelines for selecting and presenting news. Alternatively, we encounter studies about power negotiations among members of elite institutions. Legislators, administrators and police officers struggle with journalists to produce representations that are to the advantage of the respective institutions or individuals.

News-making in these studies appears like a hide-and-seek-game involving mostly elites in battles over issues and spin. My study offers data that supports this conclusion. However, the desire of (professional) elites to disseminate 'information' alone cannot account for the dynamic of the news discourse. News is a trade object in a network society. It is a currency in relations and as such is an effective social force. The affiliation to an elite institution and the article as material object are matters of status. They are used to substantiate claims to power, authority and entitlements and to manipulate relations. At different levels of society the use-value is cast in different terms. News is exploited in material struggles, power conflicts and for economic growth. Outcomes are not easily measurable, but this hardly affects the aspirations and hopes invested in publicity.

When I agree with Jeffrey (2000) that India is experiencing a newspaper revolution, I mean not only that more people access newspapers and are better informed about political processes – at the regional level too – but also that more people float the currency of news and participate in recasting the market that is India. The ongoing transformation of the publishing business widens the scope for establishing manipulative relations with news. The transformation to the market system surfaces not only in the ideological recasting of the public sphere. It engages people in a competitive battle over public recognition through mass media. There exists no absolute boundary between producer and consumer. While professional structures and structural inequalities perpetuate in practice distinctions between readers and writers, journalists and informants, paid advertisement and editorial coverage, these distinctions are fraught with ambivalence. In reading the newspaper, consumers are drawn into the realm of publicity. People turn publicity into an instrument for empowerment when they lobby their cases before reporters, manipulate coverage or pay for publicity.

Viewing news as a culture produces a fine-grained appreciation of a range of influences that shape public culture. It avoids the monumental rhetoric of the top-down approach that captures contemporary development in the fashionable phrases of murdochisation or tabloidisation. Here news production is treated as flowing unmediated from the dominance of global elites or from the hegemony of market ideology. A local study in turn produces evidence of the concrete marketplace in which global developments are turned into social tools. With this statement I am not placing myself on the opposite side of a dichotomous debate swaying between the local and the global. I have not studied local resistance to global influences, or culturally tainted appropriations of a global flow. I have rather reclaimed the local as the place in which the transnational is played out as a process of recasting lives. People produce and consume substances that are made meaningful in relations and for social positioning. The cultural is replayed and recursively updated in a process of pushing for and consuming change.

Notes

1. Some of the smaller news companies catering to local markets, regions and villages still depend today on political financing. The aggressive expansion of regional vernacular newspapers has made their survival more difficult and investment by political leaders is crucial for survival (Ninan 2007).
2. Perfect examples are the issues of *Hindustan Times* that followed the occasion of International Women's Day, which covered 'women of the city

202 | News as Culture

excelling in various fields' (*Hindustan Times*, 8 March 2002; see also all subsequent days till 14 March 2002). The sequence introduced women who have left behind a solely domestic life and who now contribute to public welfare as professionals or voluntary social workers. As a result of the new tradition of feel-good journalism, these articles are justified as providing role models. However, they are also a way of dealing with the potentially disruptive theme of woman's precarious situation in society in a way that does not upset readers, or more importantly, advertisers.

3. The growth of the local news market does not serve everyone. Ninan observes a new bifurcation that disadvantages people who act at the state level. Today the tendency for local newspapers is to communicate exhaustively about the immediate local environment and to give the larger Indian picture. Yet, less space is devoted to news from the state and the region. The connecting regional picture is in danger of disappearing (Ninan 2007).

4. Mankekar (2000 [1999]) follows a different argument. Her study engages with viewing practices that make sense of the various representations in television. Debating ideological positions and individual fates, viewers reflect on national ideals as well as private fears.

References

Abu-Lughod, Lila. 1995. 'The Objects of Soap Opera: Egyptian Television and the Cultural Politics of Modernity', in Daniel Miller (ed.), *Worlds Apart.* London: Routledge, pp. 190–210.

Agnihotri, R.A. 1998. *Film Stars in Indian Politics.* Delhi: Commonwealth Publisher.

Alasuutari, Pertti (ed.). 1999. *Rethinking the Media Audience.* London: Sage.

Alvarez, Robert R. 1995. 'The Mexican-US Border: The Making of an Anthropology of Borderlands', *Annual Review of Anthropology* 24: 447–70.

Andersen, Walter K. and Shridhar D. Damle. 1987. *The Brotherhood in Saffron: The Rashtriya Swayamsevak Sangh and Hindu Revivalism.* Boulder, Co: Westview Press.

Ang, Ien. 1996. *Living Room Wars. Rethinking Media Audiences for a Postmodern World.* London: Routledge.

Appadurai, Arjun (ed.). 1986. *The Social Life of Things. Commodities in Cultural Perspectives.* Cambridge: Cambridge University Press.

———. 1990. 'Disjuncture and Difference in the Global Cultural Economy', *Public Culture* 2(2): 1–24.

Askew, Kelly. 2002. 'Introduction', in Kelly Askew and Richard R. Wilk (eds), *The Anthropology of Media. A Reader.* Oxford: Blackwell, pp. 1–13.

Austin, J.L. 1990 [1962]. *How to Do Things with Words.* Oxford: Oxford University Press.

Barnett, Steven. 1997. 'New Media, Old Problems', *European Journal of Commmunication* 12: 193–218.

Barth, Frederik (ed.). 1969. *Ethnic Groups and Boundaries. The Social Organisation of Cultural Difference.* Boston: Little Brown.

Basu, Tapan, Pradip Datta, Sumit Sarkar, Tanika Sarkar, and Sambuddha Sen (eds). 1993. *Khaki Shorts and Saffron Flags.* Delhi: Orient Longman.

Bathla, Sonia. 1998. *Women, Democracy and the Media. Cultural and Political Representations in the Indian Press.* Delhi: Sage.

Baudrillard, Jean. 1988. 'Consumer Society', in *Selected Writings.* Cambridge:

Polity Press.

Baum, Matthew. 2005. 'Talking the Vote. Why Presidential Candidates hit the Talk Sow Circuit', *American Journal of Political Sciences* 49: 213–34.

Belz, Johannes. 2005. *Mahar, Buddhist and Dalit. Religious Conversion and Socio-Political Emancipation.* Delhi: Manohar.

Berger, Guy. 2000. 'Grave New World? Democratic Journalism Enters the Global Twenty-first Century', *Journalism Studies* 1(1): 81–99.

Bhandari, Romesh. 1998. *As I Saw It.* Delhi: Har-Anand.

Binsbergen, Wim van. 2005. ‚Commodification: Things, agency, and identities: Introduction', in Wim van Binsbergen and Peter Geschiere (eds), *Commodification. Things, Agency, and Identities.* Münster: Lit, pp. 9–51.

Bird, Elizabeth S. 2003. *The Audience in Everyday Life. Living in a Media World.* London: Routledge.

Blumler, Jay G. 1992. *Television and the Public Interest.* London: Sage.

——. 1997. 'Origins of the Crisis of Communications for Citizenship', *Political Communication* 14(4): 395–404.

——. and M. Gurevitch 1995. *The Crisis of Public Communication.* London: Routledge.

Boorstin, Daniel. 1962. *The Image. A Guide to Pseudo-Events in America.* New York: Harper and Row.

Bourdieu, Pierre. 1990. *Was heißt Sprechen? Die Ökonomie des sprachlichen Tausches.* Wien: Braumüller.

——. 1998 [1996]. *On Television and Journalism.* London: Pluto.

Boyd-Barrett, Oliver. 1977. 'Media Imperialism. Towards an International Framework for the Analysis of Media Systems', in James Curran, Michael Gurevitch and John Wollacot (eds.), *Mass Communication and Society.* London: Arnold, pp. 116–35.

——. 1998. 'Media Imperialism Reformulated', in Daya Krishan Thussu (ed.), *Electronic Empires.* London: Arnold.

Brantlinger, Patrick. 1985. *Bread & Circuses. Theories of Mass Culture as Social Decay.* London: Cornell University Press.

Brass, Paul R. 1965. *Factional Politics in an Indian State. The Congress Party in Uttar Pradesh.* Berkeley: University of California Press.

——. 1968. 'Uttar Pradesh', in Myron Weiner (ed.), *State Politics in India.* Princeton: Princeton University Press.

——. 1983. *Caste, Faction and Party in Indian Politics. Vol.I: Faction and Party.* Delhi: Chanakya Publication.

——. 1998. *Theft of an Idol. Text and Context in the Representation of Collective Violence.* Calcutta: Seagull.

Brosius, Christiane. 2005. *Empowering Visions. An Ethnography of Hindutva Nationalism and New Media Technologies (1989–1993).* London: Anthem.

Butcher, Melissa. 2003. *Transnational Television, Cultural Identity and Change. When STAR Came to India.* Delhi: Sage.

Butler, Judith. 1997. *Excitable Speech. A Politics of the Performative.* New York: Routledge.

Calhoun, Craig. (ed.). 1992. *Habermas and the Public.* Cambridge: MIT Press.

Cashman, R. 1970. 'The Political Recruitment of God Ganapati', *Indian Economic and Social History* 7: 347–73.

Chakravarty, Jaya. 2002. *Women in Journalism. Volume II: Media for Women's Development.* Delhi: Sarup & Sons.

Clifford, James. 1997. *Routes. Travel and Translation in the Late Twentieth Century.* Cambridge: Harvard University Press.

Coleman, S. and P. Collins (eds). 2006. *Locating the Field. Space, Place and Context in Anthropology.* Oxford: Berg.

Couldry, N. 2004. 'Theorising Media as Practice', *Social Semiotics* 14(2): 115–32.

Corner, John and Dick Pels (eds). 2003. *Media and the Restyling of Politics. Consumerism, celebrity and Cynicism.* London: Sage.

Curran, James. 2002. *Media and Power.* London: Routledge.

——. and David Morley. 2005. *Media and Cultural Theory.* London: Routledge.

Dahlgren, Peter and Colin Sparks (eds). 1991. *Communication and Citizenship. Journalism and the Public Sphere in the New Media Age.* London: Routledge.

——. 1995. *Television and the Public Sphere.* London: Sage.

Das, B. 1999. 'The paper chase', *Gentleman*, pp. 57–61.

Das, Veena. 1995. 'On Soap Opera. What Kind of Anthropological Object is It?', in Daniel Miller (ed.), *Worlds Apart.* London: Routledge, pp. 169–89.

Davis, Richard H. 1996. 'The Iconography of Rama's Chariot', in David Ludden (ed.), *Making India Hindu.* Delhi: Oxford University Press, pp. 27–54.

Debord, Guy. 1994 [1967]. *The Society of the Spectacle.* New York: Zone Books.

Derrida, Jaques. 1988 [1972]. 'Signatur, Ereignis, Kontext', in *Randgänge der Philosophie.* Vienna: Passagen Verlag, pp. 291–314.

Dickey, Sara. 1993a. *Cinema and the Urban Poor in South India.* Cambridge: Cambridge University Press.

——. 1993b. 'The Politics of Adulation. Cinema and the Production of Politicians in South India', *The Journal of Asian Studies* 52(2): 340–72.

——. 2001. 'Opposing Faces: Film Star Fan Clubs and the Construction of Class Identities in South India', in Rachel Dwyer and Christopher Pinney (eds), *Pleasure and the Nation.* Delhi: Oxford University Press, pp. 212–46.

Dirks, Nicholas. 1987. *The Hollow Crown. Ethnohistory of an Indian Kingdom.* Cambridge, Cambridge University Press.

Donnan, Hastings and Thomas M. Wilson (eds). 1999. *Borders: Frontiers of Identity, Nation and State.* Oxford: Berg.

Donohue, George A., Phillip J. Tichenor, Clarice N. Olien. 1995. 'A Guard Dog Perspective on the Role of Media', *Journal of Communication* 45(2): 115–32.

Doron, Assa and Ursula Rao (eds). 2009. 'From the Edge of Power. The Cultural Politics of Disadvantage in South Asia', *Asian Studies Review* 33(4).

Dracklé, Dorle. 1999. 'Medienethnologie: Eine Option auf die Zukunft', in Waltraud Kokot and Dorle Dracklé (eds), *Wozu Ethnologie? Festschrift für Hans Fischer.* Berlin: Reimer, pp. 261–90.

Dwyer, Rachel and Christopher Pinney (eds). 2001. *Pleasure and the Nation. The History, Politics, and Consumption of Public Culture in India.* New Delhi: Oxford University Press.

Eckert, Julia. 2003. *The Charisma of Direct Action. Power, Politics, and the Shiv Sena.* Delhi: Oxford University Press.

Eckman, Alyysa and Thomas Lindlof. 2003. 'Negotiating the Gray Lines: An Ethnographic Case Study of Organizational Conflict between Advertorials and News', *Journalism Studies* 4(1): 65–77.

Edwards, David and David Cromwell. 2005. *Guardians of Power. The Myth of the Liberal Media.* Media Lens.

Elst, Koenraad. 2003. *Ayodhya: The Finale: Science versus Secularism in the Excavations Debate.* Delhi: Voice of India.

Engineer, Asghar Ali (ed.). 1990. *Babri-Masjid Ramjanambhoomi Controversy.* Delhi: Ajanta Publishing.

Epstein, Edward Jay. 1973. *News from Nowhere. Television and the News.* New York: Random House.

Ericson, Richard V., Patricia M. Baranek and Janet B.C. Chan. 1989. *Negotiating Control. A Study of News Sources.* Toronto: University of Toronto Press.

Eschmann, Anncharlott, Herman Kulke and Gaya Charan Tripathi (eds). 1978. *The Cult of Jagannath and the Regional Tradition of Orissa.* Delhi: Manohar.

Fishman, Mark. 1980. *Manufacturing the News.* Austin: University of Texas Press.

Fiske, John. 1994. 'Audiencing. Cultural Practice and Cultural Studies', in Norman K. Denzing and Yvonna S. Lincoln (eds), *Handbook of Qualitative Research.* London: Thousand Oaks, pp. 189–98.

Franklin, Bob and David Murphy (eds). 1998. *Making the Local News. Local Journalism in Context.* London: Routledge.

Fraser, N. 1992. 'Rethinking the Public Sphere', in Craig Calhoun (ed.), *Habermas and the Public Sphere.* Cambridge, Mass: MIT Press.

Freitag, Sandria B. 1989. *Collective Action and Community. Public Arenas and the Emergence of Communalism in North India.* Berkeley: California University Press.

Fuller, Jack. 1996. *News Values. Ideas for an Information Age.* Chicago: University of Chicago Press.

Gamson, Joshua. 1994. *Claims to Fame: Celebrity in Contemporary America.* University of California Press.

Gans, Herbert J. 1979. *Deciding What's News. A Study of CBS Evening News, NBC Nightly News, Newsweek, and Time.* New York: Pantheon Books.

Garfinkel, Harold. 2002 [1971]. *Ethnomethodology's program. Working out Durkheim's Aphorism.* Lanham: Rowman & Littlefield Publishers.

Gavin, Neil T. 2007. *Press and Television in British Politics. Media, Money, and Mediated Democracy.* New York: Palgrave Macmillan.

Geertz, Clifford. 1999 [1973]. 'Religion as a Cultural System', in *The Interpretation of Culture.* New York: Basic Books.

Geiber, W. 1956. 'Across the Desk. A Study of 16 Television Editors', *Journalism Quarterly* 33: 423–32.

Gell, Alfred. 1998. *Art and Agency. Towards a New Anthropological Theory.* Somerset: Midsomer Norton.

Gillespie, Marie. 1995. *Television, Ethnicity and Cultural Change.* London:

Routledge.

Ginsburg, Faye. 1994. 'Culture/Media. A (mild) Polemic', *Anthropology Today* 10(2): 5–15.

——. 1996. 'Indigenous Media. Faustian Contract or Global Village?', *Cultural Anthropology* 6: 92–111.

——. 1999. 'Shooting Back: From Ethnographic Film to Indigenous Production/Ethnograpy of Media', in T. Miller and R. Stam (eds), *A Companion to Film Theory*. Malden, Mass: Blackwell, pp. 295–322.

——. Lila Abu-Ludghod and Brian Larkin (eds). 2002. *Media Worlds. Anthropology on New Terrain*. Berkeley: University of California Press.

Glasgow University Media Group. 1976. *Bad News*. London: Routledge.

——. 1980. *More Bad News*. London: Routledge.

——. 1993. *Getting the Message: News, Truth and Power*. London: Routledge.

Godelier, Maurice. 1986. *The Making of Great Men. Male Domination and Power Among the New Guinea Baruya*. Cambridge: Cambridge University Press.

——. and Marilyin Strathern (eds). 1991. *Big Men and Great Men. Personifications of Power in Melanesia*. Cambridge: Cambridge University Press.

Goffman, Erving. 1955. 'On Face-Work. An Analysis of Ritual Elements in Social Interaction', *Psychiatry* 18(3): 213–31.

Goldenberg, E. 1975. *Making the Papers*. Lexington, MA.: D.C. Heath.

Golding, Peter and Philip Elliott. 1979. *Making the News*. London: Longman.

Goodall, Peter. 1995. *High Culture, Popular Culture. The Long Debate*. St Leonards, N.S.W.: Allen & Unwin.

Goyal, Desh Raj. 1979. *Rashtriya Swayamsewak Sangh*. Delhi: Rādhā Krishna [Prakashan].

Graber, Doris A. 1994. 'The Infotainment Quotient in Routine Television News. A Director's Perspective', *Discourse & Society* 5(4): 483–508.

Graff, Violette (ed.). 1999 [1997]. *Lucknow. Memories of a City*. Delhi: Oxford University Press.

——. Narayani Gupta and Mushirul Hasan. 1999 [1997]. 'Introduction', in Violette Graff (ed.), *Lucknow. Memories of a City*. Delhi: Oxford University Press, pp. 1–31.

Gripsrud, Jostin. 1999. *Understanding Media Culture*. London: Arnold.

Guha, Ranajit. 1996. 'The Small Voice of History', in Shahid Amin and Dipesh Chakrabarty (eds), *Subaltern Studies IX. Writings on South Asian History and Society*. Delhi: Oxford University Press, pp. 1–12.

Gupta, Akhil. 1995. 'Blurred Boundaries: The Discourse of Corruption, the Culture of Politics, and the Imagined State', *American Ethnologist* 22(2): 375–402.

Gupta, Akhil and James Ferguson (eds). 1997. *Anthropological Locations. Boundaries and Grounds of a Field Science*. Berkeley: University of California Press.

Habermas, Jürgen. 1992 [1962]. *The Structural Transformation of the Public Sphere. An Enquiry into a Category of Bourgeois Society*. Cambridge: Polity Press.

Hall, Stuart. 1992a [1980]. 'Introduction to Media Studies at the Centre', in Centre for Contemporary Cultural Studies (ed.), *Culture, Media, Language*.

London: Routledge, pp. 117–21.

———. 1992b [1980]. 'Encoding/Decoding', in Centre for Contemporary Cultural Studies (ed.). *Culture, Media, Language*. London: Routledge, pp. 128–38.

———. Chas Critcher, Tony Jefferson, John Clarke and Brian Roberts. 1978. *Policing the Crisis. Mugging, the State, and Law and Order*. New York: Palgrave Macmillan.

Hamelink, C.J. 1983. *Cultural Autonomy in Global Communications*. New York: Longman.

Handelman, Don. 1998 [1990]. *Models and Mirrors. Towards an Anthropology of Public Events*. Oxford: Berghahn.

Hannerz, Ulf. 1998a. 'Of Correspondents and Collages', *Anthropological Journal on European Cultures* 7: 91–109.

———. 1998b. 'Other Transnationals. Perspectives Gained from Studying Sideways', *Paideuma* 44: 109–23.

———. 2002. 'Among the Foreign Correspondents: Reflections on Anthropological Styles and Audiences', *Ethnos* 67(1): 57–74.

Hansen, Thomas Blom and Christophe Jaffrelot, (eds.). 1998. *The BJP and the Compulsions of Politics in India*. New Delhi, Oxford University Press.

Hardgrave, R.L.J. and A.C. Neidhart. 1975. 'Films and Political Consciousness in Tamil Nadu', *Economic and Political Weekly* 10(1/2): 27–35.

Hartley, John. 1982. *Understanding News*. London: Methuen.

———. 1996. *Popular Reality. Journalism, Modernity, Popular Culture*. London: Arnold.

Hartung, Jan-Peter. 2004. *Ayodhya 1992–2003. The Assertion of Cultural and Religious Hegemony*. Delhi: Media House.

Hasan, Mushirul. 1988. 'Indian Muslims since Independence', *Third World Quarterly* 10: 818–42.

Hasty, Jennifer. 2005. *The Press and Political Culture in Ghana*. Bloomington: Indiana University Press.

———. 2005. 'Sympathetic Magic? Contagious Corruption. Sociality, Democracy, and the Press in Ghana', *Public Culture* 17(3): 339–69.

Hertz, Rosanna and Jonathan B. Imber (eds). 1995. *Studying Elites Using Qualitative Methods*. Thousand Oaks, California: Sage.

Hess, Stephen. 1984. *The Government/Press Connection*. Washington: Brookings Institution Press.

Horkheimer, Max and Theodor W. Adorno. 1998 [1944]. 'Kulturindustrie, Aufklärung als Massenbetrug', in *Dialektik der Aufklärung*. Frankfurt: Fischer.

Hörning, Karl Heinz and Julia Reuter. 2006. 'Praktizierte Kultur. Das Stille Wissen der Geschlechter', in Ursula Rao (ed.), *Kulturelle VerWandlungen*. Frankfurt: Peter Lang, pp. 51–72.

Horster, Detlef. 1997. *Niklas Luhmann*. Munich: Beck.

Huntington, Samuel P. 1998 [1997]. *The Clash of Civilizations and the Remaking of World Order*. London: Touchstone.

Imhof, Kurt and Peter Schulz (eds). 1996. *Politisches Raisonnement in der Informationsgesellschaft*. Zürich: Seismo.

Iyengar, A. Seshadri. 2001. *Role of Press and Indian Freedom Struggle*. New Delhi:

A.P.H. Publisher.

Jaffrelot, Christoph. 1996. *The Hindu Nationalist Movement and Indian Politics 1925 to the 1990s. Strategies of Identity-Building, Implantation and Mobilisation.* Delhi: Viking.

——. 2003. *India's Silent Revolution. The Rise of the Lower Castes in Indian Politics.* Delhi: Permanent Black.

Jakubowicz, Karol. 2007. 'Public Service Broadcasting. A Pawn on an Ideological Chessboard', in E. D. Bens (ed.), *Media between Culture and Commerce.* Bristol: Intellect, pp. 115–50.

Jeffrey, Robin. 1993. 'Indian-Language Newspapers and Why They Grow', *Economic and Political Weekly* 28(38): 2004–11.

——. 2000. *India's Newspaper Revolution: Capitalism, Politics and the Indian Language Press 1977–1999.* Delhi: Oxford University Press.

Jensen, K.B. 1986. *Making Sense of the News.* Aarhus: Aarhus University Press.

Johnson, Pauline. 2006. *Habermas. Rescuing the Public Sphere.* London: Routledge.

Joseph, Ammu and Kalpana Sharma (eds). 1994. *Whose News? The Media and Women's Issues.* Delhi: Sage.

——. 2000. *Women in Journalism. Making News.* Delhi: The Media Foundation/Konark.

——. 2004. 'The Gender (Dis)advantage in Indian Print Media', in Marjan de Bruin and Karen Ross (eds), *Gender and Newsroom Cultures. Identities at Work.* Cresskill, New Jersey: Hampton Press, pp. 163–80.

Juluri, Vamsee. 2003. *Becoming a Global Audience. Longing and Belonging in Indian Music Television.* New York: Peter Lang.

Kakar, Sudhir. 1971. 'The Theme of Authority in Social Relations in India', *The Journal of Social Psychology* 84: 93–101.

——. 1991 [1981]. *The Inner World. A Psycho-Analytic Study of Childhood and Society in India.* Delhi: Oxford University Press.

Kaniss, Phyllis. 1991. *Making Local News.* Chicago: University of Chicago Press.

Kapferer, Bruce. 1988. *Legends of People, Myths of State. Violence, Intolerance and Political Culture in Sri Lanka and Australia.* Washington: Smithsonian.

Kaur, Raminder. 2001. 'Rethinking the Public Sphere. The Ganpati Festival and Media Competitions in Mumbai', *South Asia Research* 21(1): 23–50.

——. 2003. *Performative Politics and the Cultures of Hinduism. Public Uses of Religion in Western India.* Delhi: Permanent Black.

Keeble, Richard. 1994. *The Newspapers Handbook.* London: Routledge.

Kellner, Douglas M. 2003. *Media Spectacle.* London: Routledge.

Kohli-Khandekar, Vanita. 2006 [2003]. *The Indian Media Business.* Delhi: Response Books.

Krishna, Gopal. 1972. 'Muslim Politics', *Seminar* 153: 18–21.

Landau, Paul S. and Deborah D. Kaspin (eds). 2002. *Images and Empires. Visuality in Colonial and Postcolonial Africa.* Berkeley: University of California Press.

Lang, K. and G. Lang. 1953. 'The Unique Perspective of Television and its Effects. A Pilot Study', *American Sociological Review* 18(1): 3–12.

Lee, Minu and Chong Heup Cho. 1990. 'Women Watching Together: An Ethnographic Study of Korean Soap Opera Fans in the US', *Cultural Studies* 4(1): 30–44.

Liebes, Tamar and Elihu Katz. 1988. *The Export of Meaning. Cross-Cultural Readings of Dallas.* Oxford: Polity Press.

Llewellyn-Jones, Rosie. 1985. *A Fatal Friendship: The Nawabs, the British and the City of Lucknow.* Delhi: Oxford University Press.

——. 2000. *Engaging Scoundrels. True Tales of Old Lucknow.* Delhi: Oxford University Press.

Lotter, Stefanie. 2005. 'Diebstahl als Sabotage ritueller Effizienz', in Ursula Rao (ed.), *Kulturelle VerWandlungen.* Frankfurt: Peter Lang, pp. 285–303.

Luhmann, Niklas. 2000 [1996]. *The Reality of Mass Media.* Stanford, California: Stanford University Press.

——. 2002 [1984]. *Soziale Systeme. Grundriß einer allgemeinen Theorie.* Frankfurt a.M.: Suhrkamp.

Malefyt, Timothy Dewaal und Brian Moeran (eds). 2003. *Advertising Cultures.* Oxford: Berg.

Mandelbaum, David G. 1989 [1970]. *Society in India.* Bombay: Popular Prakashan.

Mankekar, Purnima. 2000 [1999]. *Screening Culture, Viewing Politics. Television, Womanhood and Nation in Modern India.* Delhi: Oxford University Press.

Manning, Paul. 2001. *News and News Sources. A Critical Introduction.* London: Sage.

Manuel, Peter. 1993. *Cassette Culture. Popular Music and Technology in North India.* Chicago: University of Chicago Press.

Marcinkowski, Frank. 1993. *Publizistik als autopoietisches System. Politik und Massenmedien. Eine systemtheoretische Analyse.* Opladen: Westdeutscher Verlag.

Marcus, George E. 1995. 'Ethnography in/of the World System. The Emergence of Multi-Sited Ethnography', *Annual Review of Anthropology* 24: 95–117.

——. 2006. 'Reflexivity Unbound: Shifting Styles of Critical Self-awareness from the Malinowskian Scene of Fieldwork and Writing to the Emergence of Multi-Sited Ethnography', in Ursula Rao and John Hutnyk (eds), *Celebrating Transgression.* Oxford: Berghahn, pp. 13–22.

Marcuse, Herbert. 1964. *One-Dimensional Man.* Boston: Beacon Press.

Marx, Karl. 1976 [1867]. *Capital, Volume I.* London; Penguin.

Maturana, Humberto R. and Francisco J. Varela. 1980. *Autopoiesis and Cognition. The Realization of the Living.* Dordrecht: Reidel.

Mauss, Marcel. 1996 [1950]. *Die Gabe. Form und Funktion des Austauschs in archaischen Gesellschaften.* Frankfurt: Suhrkamp.

Mazumdar, Aurobindo. 1993. *Indian Press and Freedom Struggle (1937–42).* London: Sangam Books.

Mazzarella, William. 2003a. 'Critical Publicity / Public Criticism: Reflections on Fieldwork in the Bombay Ad World', in Timothy Dewaal Malefyt and Brian Moeran (eds), *Advertising Cultures.* Oxford: Berg, pp. 55–74.

——. 2003b. '"Very Bombay": Contending with the Global in an Indian Advertising Agency', *Cultural Anthropology* 18(1): 33–71.

——. 2003c. *Shovelling Smoke. Advertising and Globalization in Contemporary India.* Durham: Duke University Press.

——. 2004. 'Culture, Globalization, Mediation', *Annual Review of Anthropology* 33: 345–67.

——. 2006 'Internet X-Ray: E-Governance, Transparency, and the Politics of Immediation in India.' *Public Culture* 18(3): 473–505.

Mbembe, Achille. 2001. *On the Postcolony.* Berkeley: University of California Press.

McCubbins, M. and T. Schwartz. 1984. 'Congressional Oversight Overlooked. Police Patrols vs. Fire Alarms', *American Journal of Political Sciences*: 165–79.

McNair, Brian. 2006. *Cultural Chaos. Journalism, News and Power in a Globalised World.* London: Routledge.

Merten, Klaus, Siegfried J. Schmidt and Siegfried Weischenberg (eds). 1994. *Die Wirklichkeit der Medien.* Opladen: Westdeutscher Verlag.

Miller, Daniel and Don Slater. 2001. *The Internet. An Ethnographic Approach.* Oxford: Berg.

Mines, Mattison. 1996. *Public Faces, Private Voices. Community and Individuality in South India.* Delhi: Oxford University Press.

Moeran, Brian. 1996. *A Japanese Advertising Agency. An Anthropology of Media and Markets.* Honolulu: University of Hawai'i Press.

Molotoch, Harvey and Marilyn Lester. 1974. 'News as Purposive Behavior: On the Strategic Use of Routine Events, Accidents, and Scandals', *American Sociological Review* 39(1): 101–12.

Munshi, Shoma (ed.). 2001. *Images of the 'Modern Woman' in Asia. Global Media, Local Meanings.* Richmond: Curzon Press.

——. 2004. 'A Perfect 10 – "modern and Indian": Representations of the Body in Beauty Pageants and the Visual Media in Contemporary India', in James H. Mills and Satadru Sen (eds), *Confronting the Body.* London: Anthem, pp. 162–81.

Murdock, Graham. 1982. 'Large Corporations and the Control of the Communications', in Timothy Dewaal Malefyt and Brian Moeran (eds), *Culture, Society and the Media.* London: Methuen, pp. 118–54.

Nader, Laura. 1999 [1969]. 'Up the Anthropologist – Perspectives Gained from Studying Up', in Timothy Dewaal Malefyt and Brian Moeran (eds), *Reinventing Anthropology.* Ann Arbor: University of Michigan Press, pp. 284–311.

Nandy, Ashis, Shikha Trivedy, Shail Mayaram and Achyut Yagnik. 1995. *Creating a Nationality. The Ramjanmabhumi Movement and Fear of the Self.* Delhi: Oxford University Press.

Natarajan, J. 1955. *History of Indian Journalism. Part II of the Report of the Press Commission.* Delhi: Ministry of Information and Broadcasting, Government of India.

Natrajan, S. 1962. *A History of the Press in India.* London: Asia Publishing House.

Nayar, Baldev Raj. 2001. *Globalization and Nationalism: The Changing Balance in India`s Economic Policy, 1950–2000.* Delhi: Sage.

Neyazi, T. 2008. 'Cultural Imperialism or Indigenous modernity: Hindi Newspapers in Globalizing India', conference paper presented at the 17th Biennial Conference of the Asian Studies Association of Australia, Melbourne, 1 March 2008.

Ninan, Sevanti. 2007. *Headlines from the Heartland*. Delhi: Sage.

Noam, Eli. 2004. Will Internet TV be American. *Internet Television*, eds. Darcy Gernbar, Jo Froebel, Eli Noam. Mahwah, JJ, Lawrence Erlbaum.

Oldenburg, Veena Talwar. 1984. *The Making of Colonial Lucknow 1856–1877*. Princeton: Princeton University Press.

Omvedt, Gail. 2006. *Dalit Visions. The Anti-Caste Movement and the Construction of an Indian Identity*. Delhi: Orient Longman.

——. 1990. 'Hinduism and Politics', *Economic and Political Weekly* 25: 724-729.

Osella, Caroline and Filippo Osella. 2003. 'Young Malayali Men and their Movie Heroes', in Radhika Chopra, Caroline Osella and Filippo Osella (eds), *South Asian Masculinities. Context of Change, Sites of Continuity*. Delhi: Kali for Women, pp. 224–63.

Padhy, K.S. 1994. *The Muzzled Press. Introspect and Retrospect*. Delhi: Kanishka Publishers Distributors.

Page, David and William Crawley. 2001. *Satellites over South Asia. Broadcasting Culture and the Public Interest*. Delhi: Sage.

Pande, M. 2006. 'English for the Elite. Hindi for the Power Elite', in Uday Sahay. (ed.), *Making News*. Delhi: Oxford University Press, pp. 60–66.

Parathasarathy, R. 1989. *Journalism in India. From the Earliest Times to the Present Day*. New Delhi: Sterling Publishers.

Patterson, T.E. 2000. *How Soft News and Critical Journalism are Shrinking the News Audiences and Weakening Democracy*. Cambridge, MA: Shorenstein Center for Press, Politics, and Public Policy, Kennedy School of Government, Harvard University.

Pedelty, Mark. 1995. *War Stories. The Culture of Foreign Correspondents*. London: Routledge.

Peterson, Mark Allen. 1996. *Writing the Indian Story. Press, Politics and Symbolic Power in India*. Unpublished dissertation thesis, Brown University, Providence.

——. 2003. *Anthropology and Mass Communication. Media and Myth in the New Millennium*. New York: Berghahn.

——. forthcoming. 'But it is my Habit', in John Postill and Birgit Bräuchler (eds), *Theorising Media and Practices*. Oxford: Berghahn.

Pinney, Christopher. 1997. *Camera Indica. The Social Life of Indian Photographs*. London: Reaktion Books.

——. 2004. *Photos of the Gods. The Printed Image and Political Struggle in India*. New Delhi: Oxford University Press.

Postill, J. and Birgit Bäuchler (eds). forthcoming. *Theorising Media and Practice*. Oxford: Berghahn.

Postman, Neil. 1985. *Amusing Ourselves to Death. Public Discourse in the Age of Show Business*. New York: Viking.

Pink, Sarah. 2006. *The Future of Visual Anthropology*. London: Routledge.

Price, Pamela G. 1989. 'Kingly Models in Indian Political Behavior', *Asian Survey* 29(6): 559–72.

Raghavan, G.N.S. 1994. *The Press in India. A New History*. Delhi: Gyan Publishing House.

Raheja, Gloria Goodwin. 1988. *The Poison in the Gift. Ritual, Prestation, and the*

Dominant Caste in a North Indian Village. Chicago: Chicago University Press.

Rajagopal, Arvind. 1994. 'Ram Janmabhoomi, Consumer Identity and Image-Based Politics', *Economic and Political Weekly* 29: 1659–68.

——. 1998. 'Advertising, Politics and the Sentimental Education of the Indian Consumer', *Visual Anthropology Review* 14(2): 14–31.

——. 2001. *Politics after Television. Hindu Nationalism and the Changing of Indian Public.* Cambridge: Cambridge University Press.

Rantanen, Terhi. 2005. *The Media and Globalization.* London: Sage.

Rao, Ursula. 2002. 'Assessing the Past in Search for a Future: The Changing of Caste and the Writing of Caste History in Contemporary Urban India', in *A Place in the World. New Local Historiographies from Africa and South Asia.* Leiden: Brill, pp. 347–66.

——. 2003. *Negotiating the Divine. Temple Religion and Temple Politics in Contemporary Urban India.* Delhi: Manohar.

——. 2005. 'Ritualpolitik. Die (nicht-) Emergenz von sozialer und politischer Autorität durch ritualisierte Performanz', in Erika Fischer-Lichte, Christian Horn, Sandra Umathum and Matthias Warstat (eds), *Diskurse des Theatralen.* Tübingen: Francke, pp. 193–209.

——. 2006. 'News from the Field. The Experience of Transgression and the Transformation of Knowledge during Research in an Expert-Site', in Ursula Rao and John Hutnyk (eds), *Celebrating Transgression.* Oxford: Berghahn, pp. 23–37.

——. 2009a.. 'Ritual as Politics', in *Man in India.*

——. 2009b. 'Empowerment through local news-making. Studying the media-public interface in India', in Elizabeth Bird (ed.), *Anthropology of News.* Indiana: Indiana University Press.

——. 2010. 'Embedded/Embedding Media Practices and Cultural Production', in John Postill and Birgit Bräuchler (eds), *Theorising Media and Practice.* Oxford: Berghahn, pp. 147-168.

Robbins, Bruce (ed.). 1993. *Phantom Public Sphere.* Minneapolis: University of Minnesota Press.

Roshco, Bernard. 1975. *Newsmaking.* Chicago: University of Chicago Press.

Rösler, Michael and Tobias Wendl (eds). 1999. *Frontiers and Borderlands. Anthropological Perspectives.* Frankfurt a. M.: Peter Lang.

Rothschild, Joseph. 1981. *Ethnopolitics. A Conceptual Framework.* New York: Columbia University Press.

Ruhrmann, George. 1994. 'Ereignis, Nachricht und Rezipient', in Klaus Merten, Siegfried J. Schmidt and Siegfried Weischenberg (eds), *Die Wirklichkeit der Medien.* Opladen: Westdeutscher Verlag, pp. 237–56.

Sahay, Uday (ed.). 2006. *Making News. Handbook of the Media in Contemporary India.* Delhi: Oxford University Press.

Sahlins, Marshall. 1963. 'Poor Man, Rich Man, Big-Man, Chief: Political Types in Melanesia and Polynesia', *Comparative Studies in Society and History* 5(3): 285–303.

——. 1987. *Islands of History.* London: Tavistock.

Saltzman, Devyani. 2005. *Shooting Water*. Toronto: Key Porter Books.

Sangari, Kumkum. 2003. 'New Patriotism: Beauty and the Bomb', in Indira Chandrasekhar and Peter C. Seel (eds), *body.city. Siting Contemporary Culture in India*. Berlin: Tulika Books, pp. 199–217.

Sarkaria, R.S. 1995. *A Guide to Journalistic Ethics*. Delhi: Press Council of India.

Scammell, Margaret. 1995. *Designer Politics. How Elections Are Won*. Basingstroke: Macmillan.

———. 2003. 'Citizen Consumers: Towards a New Marketing of Politics?', in John Corner and Dick Pels (eds), *Media and the Restyling of Politics*. London: Sage, pp. 117–36.

Schieffelin, Edward L. 1998. 'Problematizing Performance', in Felicita Hughes-Freeland (ed.), *Ritual, Performance, Media*. London: Routledge, pp. 194–207.

Schiller, H. 1976. *Communications and Cultural Dominations*. New York: Sharpe.

Schlesinger, Philip. 1978. *Putting 'Reality' Together. BBC News*. London: Constable.

Schmidt, Siegfried J. 1993. *Kognitive Autonomie und soziale Organisation. Konstruktivistische Bemerkungen zum Zusammenhang von Kognition, Kommunikation, Medien und Kultur*. Frankfurt: Suhrkamp.

Schneider, Maria-Luise. 1997. *Der Shell-Boykott als neue Form symbolischer Politik*. Arbeitspapier Nr. 1/97, Rhein-Ruhr-Institut für Sozialforschung und Politikberatung e.V.

Schnepel, Burkhard. 2006. 'Jagannath: Eine ostindische Gottheit im Spannungsfeld politisch-ritueller Machtkämpfe', in Ursula Rao (ed.), *Kulturelle VerWandlungen*. Frankfurt: Peter Lang, pp. 259–84.

Schudson, Michael. 1998. *The Good Citizen*. New York: Free Press.

———. 2003. *The Sociology of News*. New York: W.W. Norton & Company.

Sengupta, Shuddhabrata. 1999. 'Vision Mixing: Marriage, Video-Film and the Video-walla's Image of Life', in Christiane Brosius and Melissa Butcher (eds), *Image Journeys*. Delhi: Sage, pp. 277–307.

Shah, Ghanshyam. 2001. *Dalit Identity and Politics*. Thousand Oaks, CA: Sage.

Sharar, Abdul Halim. 1975. *Lucknow: Last Phase of an Oriental Culture*. London: Paul Elek.

Shore, Cris. 2000. *Building Europe. The Cultural Politics of European Integration*. London: Routledge.

———. and Stephen Nugent (eds). 2002. *Elite Cultures. Anthropological Perspectives*. London: Routledge.

Sigal, Leon V. 1973. *Reporters and Officials. The Organization and Politics of Newsmaking*. Lexington, Mass.: D.C. Heath and Company.

Sparks, Colin and John Tulloch (eds). 2000. *Tabloid Tales. Global Debates over Media Standards*. Lanham, Md: Rowman and Littlefield.

Spitulnik, Debra. 1993. 'Anthropology and Mass Media', *Annual Review of Anthropology* 22: 293–315.

Ståhlberg, Per. 2002. *Lucknow Daily. How a Hindi Newspaper Constructs Society*. Stockholm: Almqvist and Wiksell.

Stein, Burton (ed.). 1978. *South Indian Temples. An Analytical Reconsideration*. Delhi: Vikas.

Tharyan, Punnoose. 1999. *Good News, Bad News. Little Known Facts about Well-Known Editors.* New Delhi: Paul's Press.

Thussu, Daya Krishan. 2007a. 'The "Murchochization" of News? The Case of Star TV in India', *Media, Culture and Society* 29(4): 593–611.

——. 2007b. *News as Entertainment. The Rise of Global Infotainment.* London: Sage.

Tiffen, Rodney. 1989. *News and Power.* Sydney: Allen and Unwin.

Tracey, Michael. 1998. *The Decline and Fall of Public Service Broadcasting.* Oxford: Oxford University Press.

Tuchman, Gaye. 1978. *Making News. A Study in the Construction of Reality.* New York: The Free Press.

Tulloch, John. 2000. *Watching Television Audiences: Cultural Theories and Methods.* Oxford: Oxford University Press.

Tunstall, Jeremy and David Machin. 1999. *The Anglo-American Media Connection.* New York: Oxford University Press.

Turner, Terence. 1992. 'Defiant Images. The Kayapo Appropriation of Video', *Anthropology Today* 8(6): 5–16.

Turner, Victor. 1974. *The Ritual Process. Structure and Anti-Structure.* Harmondsworth: Penguin.

van der Veer, Peter. 1997. *Gods on Earth. Religious Experience and Identity in Ayodhya.* Delhi: Oxford University Press.

van Dijk, Teun A. 1988. *News as Discourse.* Hillsdale, NJ: Lawrence Erlbaum Associates.

Warner, Michael. 2002a. *Publics and Counterpublics.* London: MIT Press.

——. 2002b. 'Publics and Counterpublics', *Public Culture* 14(1): 49–90.

Watson, James. 2003 [1998]. *Media Communication. An Introduction to Theory and Process.* New York: Palgrave MacMillan.

Weber, Stefan. 1995. *Nachrichtenkonstruktion im Boulevardmedium.* Vienna: Passagen Verlag.

Weiner, Myton. 1957. *Party Politics in India. The Development of a Multi-Party System.* Princeton: Princeton University Press.

Wittwen, Andreas. 1995. *Infotainment. Fernsehnachrichten zwischen Information und Unterhaltung.* Bern: Peter Lang.

Yadava, J.S. 1991. 'Press System in India', *Media Asia: An Asian Mass Communication Quarterly* 18(3): 132–42.

Zaller, John. 2003. 'A New Standard of News Quality. Burglar Alarms for the Monitorial Citizen', *Political Communication* 20(2): 109–30.

Index

A

advertisement, 5–7, 25, 33, 35, 42, 88, 139, 145, 151, 160, 175, 181–82, 188, 195, 198–99, 201

advertisement revenue, 5–6, 150, 189n

advertiser, 2, 7, 17, 39, 41, 85, 145–47, 150–51, 160–61, 181, 189n, 197, 202n

advertorials, 195, 198

agency, 9, 12, 48, 79, 82, 92, 127, 131, 136

  media, 9

  news 16, 93–95

Akhilesh Yadav, 100, 104, 110, 118–20, 123, 125

Anthropology, 4, 8–9, 13, 18n, 88n, 94, 141n, 186

Appadurai, Arjun, 94, 187

audience, 10, 40, 45, 85, 107, 109, 114, 116, 123, 128, 133, 159, 178, 183–84, 199

  see also reader

Austin, J.L., 73

authentic, 7, 13

authenticate, 65, 79, 193

authority

  in the cultural domain, 48

  through hierarchy, 73

  in news company , 26, 32–33, 39, 44n, 108

  of the newspaper, 76, 198

  in politics, 168, 170, 174, 200

  as representative of state, 51, 53, 67

Ayodhya conflict, 7, 18n, 56–57, 89n, 111–12, 122, 166, 168, 190n

B

beat, 18n, 27, 30, 34, 51, 100, 105, 109

beat system, 11, 18n, 21, 34, 46, 79, 136, 180

bias, in the media, 76, 136

  towards authorised speakers, 11

  towards local news, 23

  political bias, 46, 52, 102, 106, 140n, 160, 181

  towards upper class, 7, 85, 107

'big men', 64–65, 87n, 107, 139, 193

Bird, Elizabeth, 10, 12

BJP (*Bharatiya Janta Party*),

  anti-BJP statements and activities, 113–14, 123, 164–72, 179

  and the Ayodhya controversy, 111–12, 141n, 190n

  and relations to journalists, 98, 125

  and state politics, 22, 95, 98, 125, 139n, 140n, 141n, 164–72, 173, 177–79, 190n

  and *Water* controversy, 50–53, 55, 86n, 87n, 89n

border
  between media reception and
    political activism, 54
  between politics and journalism,
    92–93, 117, 124, 127, 130–31,
    135–39
  between social fields, 14, 141n
Bourdieu, Pierre, 12, 16, 73–74, 76,
  88n, 92, 127, 132–34, 136
broker, journalists as, 46, 65–73, 79,
  118, 194
BSP (*Bahujan Samaj Party*), 95, 103,
  105–107, 113, 125, 126, 166, 172,
  174, 190n

C
capital
  cultural, 65
  economic, 84, 134, 162, 196
  social, 85, 121
  symbolic, 73–74, 76
capitalism
  and the press, 145–47
caste, 5, 11, 89, 100, 116, 138, 175,
  181
  inter-caste competition, 105, 126,
    175
  intra-caste fight and newspapers,
    45, 48, 58–65, 78, 87n
  and leadership, 53
  Scheduled Caste, 46, 53, 87n
  as vote bank, 122, 140n, 141n
  see also Khatik caste; OBC; Yadav
    caste
censorship, 5, 28, 134, 145
citizen, 152, 155, 189, 193
  citizens' rights ,76, 88n, 198
  consumer, 184, 188–89,196
  informed, 187–88, 193, 196, 199
  and local politics 2, 6, 8, 16–17,
    38, 40, 45–50, 57, 64–65, 69,
    72, 75, 79, 85, 135, 193–94, 198
  and political action, 2–4, 40, 76,
    79–83, 110, 115 , 135, 196
city editor, 26–37, 43n, 47

class, 5, 9, 53, 100
  caste and, 54, 68
  division and newspapers, 69
  lower class to lower middle-class,
    1, 54, 174, 198
  upper-middle class to upper class,
    7, 86, 105, 126, 146, 161, 197
  see also OBC
commercial interest, 5, 188, 189n
commercialisation, 3, 6–7, 17, 21,
  38–39, 41, 139, 143–47, 160, 171,
  182–88, 193, 195–98
conduit
  newspapers as political conduits,
    109, 135, 149
consumerism, 145, 161, 181, 188, 198
corruption
  and journalism, 76, 79, 117, 118,
    121, 124
  political, 65, 79, 162, 174, 179, 189
  press provides protection against,
    75, 128, 175, 177, 194
criticism, 143
  absence of, 198
  of the media, 184
  in news companies, 28–31, 43,
    123–24
  political, 6, 17,129, 143–44, 163,
    166–68, 175, 182, 186
  prevention of, 160
  social, 75, 148
critique, see *criticism*
Cultural Studies, 4, 8, 18n, 184–85

D
Dahlgren, Peter, 82, 88n
developmentalism, 199
distinction, social, 18n, 38, 54, 121
Durkheim, Emil, 129

E
editor, 1, 2, 24–25, 26–38, 42n, 43n,
  44n, 46, 56, 65, 72, 104–106, 119,
  120–22, 123–24, 149–51, 159–60,
  165, 171, 182–3,189n, 197

see also city editor; news editor
electronic media, 4, 83,146
empowerment, 45–46, 55, 65, 72–74,
    85, 105 198, 201
ethnography, 13, 18n, 87n
evaluation
    of the industry and consumerism
        by the press, 144, 161, 181, 188
    of journalists at work, 15, 31, 96,
        121
    of politics by the press, 112, 144,
        171, 180, 181
    press and, 80, 107

F
family, company as, 26–33
feel-good journalism, 6, 147, 150,
    181, 185, 195, 198, 202n
festivals, 53, 59, 60, 63, 81, 88n
fetish, 2–3, 93
fieldwork, 1, 3, 8, 13–15, 35, 41, 70,
    78, 95
Frankfurter School, 184,
front-page, 23, 25, 68, 77–78, 95–96
    121, 150, 166, 170, 172–73, 177

G
Gandhi, Indira, 5, 18n, 145, 175
Gandhi, Mahatma, 54, 145, 175
gate-keeper, journalists as, 10, 149
Gell, Alfred, 94
gift, in journalism, 85, 94, 94, 124,
    152, 156
globalisation, 3, 5, 185, 199–200
Gupta, Akhil, 13, 40, 79, 89n, 198

H
Habermas, Jürgen, 74, 82–84, 88n,
    185
habitus, 101, 128, 133–34, 159
Hall, Stuart, 18n, 85
Hannerz, Ulf, 15
Hasty, Jenifer, 73, 94, 136, 138
hero
    of everyday life, 197

journalists as, 79, 117
    leaders as, 6, 54, 121, 175
    new heroes, 17, 143, 163, 182, 195
hierarchy
    Hindu family, 32, 19n
    among journalists, 24, 25–39, 130
    political, 53–54, 64, 85–86, 91,
        107, 135
    social, 6, 14, 17, 64–65, 73, 125
Hindu Fundamentalism, *see* Hindu
    nationalism
Hindu nationalism, 48–53, 55–56, 64,
    77–78, 87n, 111–12, 114, 122, 138,
    168
Hindu nationalist politics & BJP,
    113–14, 179
Hindu Temple, 59–65, 87n
Huntington, Samuel P., 52

I
identity, 3, 116–17, 199
infomercial, 7, 17, 146, 182, 188
informant, *see* sources
infotainment, 17, 41, 143–44, 148,
    151, 163, 175–76, 180–89, 197

J
Jeffrey, Robin, 4–7, 43n, 46, 88n,
    145–46, 195, 200
journalism
    change in, 21, 84, 144, 146, 148,
        196
    ethics of, 74
    feel-good, 6 146, 147, 181, 185,
        195, 198, 202n
    function of, 88n, 180
    Ghanaian, 137–38
    ideal of, 75, 118, 126, 145, 153,
        185
    Indian, 4, 22
    politics and, 86, 92, 95, 117, 145
    practice of, 14, 69, 118, 137
    pressure on, 150, 176
    as profession, 94
    sociology of, 10

study of, 3–4, 8, 11, 55, 85,
128–35, 200
training in, 28, 31
see also politics, reporting
journalists, as professionals, 2, 11–12,
15, 17, 28–29, 44n, 72, 81–83,
92–95, 101, 106–109, 111, 115–29,
134–37, 143, 149, 151–53, 163,
171, 180, 182, 194, 199

K
Kalyan Singh, 95, 101, 105, 110–12,
121–24, 139n,140n, 141n, 153,
155, 158, 164, 169
Kant, Emanuel, 84,
Khatik cast, 60–65, 78, 87n

L
leader
gain status as, 16–17, 45, 53, 55,
96, 193
image of 137–39, 144, 151, 163,
170, 171–74, 182, 186, 195
and journalists, 6, 8, 49, 78, 91,
96, 97, 98–139, 143, 161, 166,
170, 176, 180, 182, 188, 194–95
mockery of, 143, 164–75, 189
and the press, 201
in the press, 48, 50, 55–57, 65, 76,
78, 84, 85, 89n, 97, 121–24,
135, 143, 153, 163, 174, 186
and the public, 71, 141n,
'worship' of, 144, 175, 186
leader-centeredness, 17, 53, 55–56,
72, 86, 97, 116, 138–39, 143–44,
163, 166, 173, 188, 194, 196
leadership
competition, 48–49, 56, 59–65, 84
in corporations, 181, 195
display of, 54, 56, 80
and Indian politics, 4, 53–54, 64,
78, 85, 138–39, 143, 175, 193
in the newspaper, 24–28, 30–39,
130

in politics, 52, 85, 89n, 95, 118,
140n, 164–65, 168–69, 177–80,
190n
of *Times of India*, 146, 197
Luhmann, Niklas, 11, 16, 92, 127–32,
134, 136, 141n

M
management, 33, 44n, 46, 59–60, 63,
70, 103, 130, 145–46, 150–51, 160,
168, 182, 195
Mankekar, Purnima, 4, 9, 202n
market ideology, 144, 198, 201
marketing
of newspapers, 5, 7, 146, 150
Marx, Karl, 93, 129, 184, 190n
Mauss, Marcel, 93
Mayawati, 105–106, 109, 113, 126,
166, 174, 190n
Mazzarella, William, 4, 18n, 89n, 146,
182, 188, 190n, 199
media practice 7, 10
media-related activities, 12, 41, 45,
58, 83, 187, 194
Mehta, Deepa, 45, 48–52, 86n, 140n
Mines, Mattison, 53, 55, 87n, 139n
modern, *see* modernity
modernising, *see* modernity
modernity, 1, 5, 10–11, 75, 80, 82, 84,
92, 129, 131, 134, 146, 187, 191n,
193, 198–99
Mulayam Singh Yadav, 58, 100–106,
110, 118–20, 122–26, 140n,
172–73
Murdoch, *see* Murdochisation
Murdochisation, 146, 185–86, 201
Muslim
against, 53, 56, 111, 141n
community, 18n , 53, 69, 103, 111
Hindu-Muslim relation, 56–58, 60,
111, 141n
organisation, 2, 69
rule, 22
vote, 100, 122, 140n, 141n

N

negotiation
  of exchange value of news, 94
  of identities, ideologies and values
      3, 48, 81
  among journalists, 70, 176
  between journalists and sources,
      3, 73, 91, 116, 137–38, 188, 195
  of power relations, 2, 11, 34, 48,
      60, 84, 88n, 92, 96, 136, 160, 200
  of power structures, 17
  of public images, 49
Nehru, Jawaharlal, 5, 145, 175
neo-liberal, 541, 185,198
network/s
  citizen, 196
  communication in, 3, 13,14, 65
  information, 137
  media, 10, 17, 46, 48, 73, 194–95,
      198
  news, 2,12, 16–17, 21, 24, 38–39,
      46–47, 69, 72, 79, 81, 85, 194
  of patronage, 36, 53, 54, 64,
      71–72, 85, 194
  political networks, 123
  power networks, 84, 134
  public as, 45, 72, 80
  of relations, 81, 83, 85
  society, 17, 194–96, 200
networking
  between journalists and
      politicians, 91, 135, 138
news
  agency of, 93–95
  breaking the, 95, 101, 108, 156,
      176, 181, 194
  city, 23–24, 42n, 87n, 147
  as commodity, 2, 10, 93–95
  as constructed, 41, 76, 148–49
  as cultural asset, 3, 17
  as cultural practice, 13, 10, 17, 46,
      193, 200–201
  and empowerment, 45, 47, 95, 200
  exclusive, 96
  as fetish, 3

hard, 98, 148
  as instrument, 2, 47, 65, 92, 93,
      200–201
  as invented, 91
  local, 23–24, 35, 38, 46–48, 54–55,
      71–73, 84–85, 95, 144
  as negotiated, 154
  as object for exchange, 3, 12, 16,
      91, 93–95, 97, 194, 200
  performative power of, 46, 73–81
  personalisation of, 182
  as practice, 92, 200
  and relationships, 13, 14, 16, 45,
      48, 91–94, 99, 118, 138
  routine news, 127, 171–72, 175, 183
  as social force, 3
  social life of, 74
  soft, 144, 148
  state, 23–24, 34, 86
news discourse, 2, 3, 16, 55, 65,
      80–81, 92–93, 107–108, 136,
      138–39, 148,189, 200
news editor, 25–30, 32–33, 35–36, 38,
      117
news ideologies, 5, 188
news models, 176
news network, *see* network
news policies, 11, 143
news relations, 4
news room, 2, 105, 136, 150, 200
news selection, 136
news sources, *see* sources
news values, 10, 95, 97, 99, 105–107,
      109–110, 116, 121, 136. 138, 156,
      172, 176–77, 180
news-worth, *see* news values
newspaper
  cuttings, 1, 78
  local, 6, 24, 40, 72–73, 79, 83–84,
      196, 202n
  market, 21, 42n, 145
  national, 40, 44n, 52,146, 196
  Ninan, Sevanti, 4, 23, 41, 195–97,
      201n, 202n
  revolution, 6, 200

O
OBC (*Other Backward Classes*), 53, 100
Om Prakash Singh, 98, 100–101, 109,
112, 125, 169
open-door policy, 6, 46, 57, 193

P
pack reporting, 49, 96, 139n, 177
patronage
exercise, 39, 72, 92
logic of, 194
and network, 21, 36, 69, 64,
71–72, 85, 194–95
political, 17, 53, 196
politics of, 45, 64
seek, 2
system, 40, 72, 79
Pedelty, Mark, 49, 99, 128, 139n, 177
performative politics, 48, 53, 80–81,
87n
performativity of speech acts, 73
Peterson, Mark Allen, 4–5, 18n, 41,
71, 76, 141n, 146, 186, 197
political class, 139, 143, 149, 182,
189, 193–95
politics
city, 24
coverage of, 6
critique of, 6, 17, 143–44, 163,182
devaluation of, 17, 49 189, 163,
193
image of, 151, 163, 173, 182,
186–87, 188
Indian, 22, 53
liberalisation, 3, 174
practice of, 80, 83–86, 88n, 98,
107, 112, 135, 154–55, 157–58,
164, 178–80, 193
press and, 6, 16–17, 75, 86, 92, 92,
103–105, 110, 116–17, 122,
135–39, 140, 145, 161, 188,
193–94
state, 2, 64, 105, 107, 118
see also BJP; caste; patronage;
performative politics

Postman, Neil, 184
power, 55, 74
of advertisers, 17, 145, 150, 151
constellation, 144, 182–83
of consumer, 5
contestations, 6, 11, 40, 53, 57, 64,
72, 83, 93, 96, 135, 174–75,
194–95, 200
control those in, 73–75, 80, 118,
173
of corporations, 6
hierarchies, 12, 63
mechanisms of, 74
mediation of, 74
negotiation of, 160, 200
networks, 84, 134
of news, 93–94
people in, 16, 43n, 53, 100, 102,
107, 118, 136, 138–39, 152,
160–61, 163, 171–73, 176, 180,
191n, 194, 198
political, 52–4, 74–75, 91, 113,
122, 151, 168, 175
press, as corrupted by, 117
of proprietors, 12
relations, 6, 11, 40, 63–64, 104,
118, 132, 136, 159, 188
structures, 17, 136, 160, 181, 198
subvert, 175
see also news, performative power of
powerful
journalists as, 72, 79, 107–108
political elite, 6, 72, 84–85, 94,
100, 118, 130, 152, 160–61,
174, 195
press as, 3, 5, 16, 47, 63, 68,
75–76, 76, 80, 89n, 93, 138
promotion
of an image, 69, 107, 138–39
of rational debate, 81
scheme for, 31–32, 43n
self-, 2, 6, 85, 93, 99, 120, 135, 153
promotional event, 68, 160
proprietor, 12, 56, 65

public, 77, 81, 89
  announcement, 63, 65, 81
  attention, 80, 85
  changes in, 41
  character of, 2, 17, 43n, 48, 75, 80–86, 89
  image, 17, 49, 53, 92
  institutions, 54
  land, 66
  media-public interface, 45, 48, 72, 80–81
  as network, 16, 45, 80
  notion of, 16, 46
  opinion, 58
  performance, 56, 80, 87n
  press produces, 12, 41
  protest, 53, 80
  reasoning, 40, 74, 85
  split, 7, 40
  statement, 50
  urban, 2
  see also pubic sphere
public arena, 53, 55, 64, 72–73, 80
public domain, 38–39
public sphere, 55, 74–75, 80–86, 88n, 91
publicity, 45, 47, 49–50, 56, 63, 66, 68–69, 72, 78, 80, 86, 87n

R
Rajagopal, Arvind, 6–7, 9, 40, 56, 70, 87n, 88n, 89n, 111, 146, 195
Ram Prakash Gupta, 95, 98, 108, 111–15, 139n, 164–72, 181, 190n
reader
  feedback from, 25
  image of, 107, 148, 193, 196
  of newspapers, 8, 40, 46, 105, 122, 130, 147, 150–51, 159, 181, 197–98
  newspapers' policy regarding, 68–69, 81, 85, 144, 146, 188, 195, 197, 202n
  relation between writer and, 3, 48, 83, 85, 135, 194, 201
  see also audience

reader-friendly language, 17, 149
readership, 23, 42n
reception
  of articles by journalists, 144, 166, 181
  research into, 8, 10, 54, 79, 80, 82, 182, 194
regionalisation, of news-making, 6–7, 21, 38, 41, 46, 143, 193–96
reporting
  advertiser-friendly, 146–47, 197
  critical, 151, 173
  fact-, 144, 148
  on gender, 43n
  on the government, 17, 136
  by Hindi-newspapers, 7
  leader-centred, 86, 107, 173
  local, 46, 56–57, 85
  new areas of, 43n, 147
  of news, 77, 139, 141n, 147, 151, 161, 164, 170, 180
  partisan, 114, 138–39
  political, 6, 17, 43n, 91, 94, 97, 104, 107, 118, 131, 138–39, 170–71, 175, 182, 194–95
  positive, 153, 159
  redundancy in, 51
  routine, 181
  staff, 34
  standards for, 8, 185
  style of, 56
  teams, 25–26, 3334
  see also pack reporting
reporting practices, 139
residential editor, *see* editor
ritual
  of objectivity, 136
  political, 186
  see also festival
ritualised events, 183
ritualised production of status, 54
RKP (Rashtriya Kranti Party), 121, 140n, 141n, 169

S

Sahara Company, 98, 151–63, 174, 176, 179–82, 190n

Sahay, Uday, 75, 94, 146, 194

seniority
in journalism, 27, 30, 32–34, 44n
in politics, 175

social systems (Luhmann), *see* systems theory

sources, 3, 11–12, 16, 24, 91, 94–95, 99, 110, 116–17, 127–28, 135–37, 158, 177

SP (*Samajvadi Party*), 99–104, 106–107, 110, 119, 123,125–26, 140n, 172–74

split public, *see* public

Ståhlberg, Per, XII, 4, 11, 22, 31, 42n, 70, 76, 100, 138, 194

status
in the Hindu family, 31–32, 44n
as journalist, 69, 70, 104, 107, 119
among journalists, 27–28, 35, 38–39, 44n, 123,
as leader, 16, 18n, 52, 54–55, 59, 93, 107, 135, 188, 198
of newspaper, 6, 198
public display of, 53–54, 56, 180, 198, 200
in society, 85, 87n, 88n, 199

status quo, 85, 136, 159, 182

structure
in the political field, 108, 112, 116, 181
power, 17, 136, 160, 181, 198

professional, in journalism, 10, 11, 15–16, 18n, 24–25, 30, 33, 35, 38–39, 40–41, 44n, 136, 150, 176, 200–201
of relations, 2, 109
social theory on, 11, 73–74, 128–39
in society, 3, 38, 59, 73–74, 78, 92, 199

studying up, 1

systems theory, 16, 93, 128–31, 134

T

television, 9, 41, 42n, 100, 112, 134, 146, 153–57, 184–85, 202

Thussu, Daya Krishan, 41, 146,185–86, 194, 198

transformation, 3, 5, 6, 39, 43n, 75–78, 122, 128, 139, 143, 146, 151, 161, 181, 186, 197, 201

tv, *see* television

V

Vajpayee, Atal Bihari, 22, 112, 121, 180

visibility, 3, 11, 27, 51, 54, 56, 76, 80–81, 84, 175

W

Warner, Michael, 82–83

Water controversy, 45, 48–53, 55–58, 64, 77, 86n, 107, 114, 115, 168

Y

Yadav caste, 100, 103, 140n

www.ingramcontent.com/pod-product-compliance
Lightning Source LLC
Chambersburg PA
CBHW060035030426
42334CB00019B/2338